FUNDAMENTALS OF TRAVEL AND TOURISM

Fundamentals of Travel and Tourism

Edited by
Anand Ballabh

AKANSHA PUBLISHING HOUSE
NEW DELHI - 110 059 (INDIA)

AKANSHA PUBLISHING HOUSE
R-37-B, Vani Vihar, Uttam Nagar
New Delhi - 110 059
E-mail: ektabooks@yahoo.com

Showroom
4649/21B, Ansari Road
Daryaganj, New Delhi-110 002
Ph.: 23263193, 9811582579

Fundamentals of Travel and Tourism

First Published, 2005

ISBN 81-8370-009-8

PRINTED IN INDIA

Published by M.P. Misra for Akansha Publishing House,
New Delhi - 110 059 and Printed at Tarun Offset Press, Delhi.

Dedicated

to

The Great Explorers of the Globe

Who paved the way of

modern Travel and Tourism

Contents

Preface

Man has been a traveller from the very beginning i.e. Adam stage. For one reason or another like food, shelter and security he travelled from one place to another.

Gradually with development process causes of travel changed. Thus, evidently man has had the wanderlust from ancient times. As organised activity travel and tourism is a recent development. Whereas in medieval period pilgrimage, exploring new lands, commerce and trade etc. were the prime motive, now travel and tourism is a multidimensional activity—pleasure and holidaying adventure, sports, recreation, health, education and research, ecology, space and business and trade etc., being in its fold. Now tourism has emerged as a flourishing industry and for many nations it is the major contributor to exchequer.

The rapid growth of tourism can be associated with the advancements made in modernising transport and communication systems. The impact of modern transport technology, specially in the aviation field has brought about a completely new meaning to travel and tourism. Travel to far remote destinations has now become a reality. The present book aims at estimating the salient features of travel and tourism. This also reviews the factors responsible for evolution and growth of tourism from earliest days to the present.

This book encompasses a variety of themes pertaining to travel and tourism. The topics include—tourism and travel: history and evolution; tourism and hospitality industries; accommodations infrastructure; principles of tourism planning; tourism planning a global scenario; environmental aspects of tourism; tourism and national development; tourism planning in India; global ecotourism; economic importance of tourism; tourism under WTO regime; and new horizons of tourism, etc.

The material is borrowed from different authoritative sources which makes this an authentic source of information on the theme. Basically entire source of information is secondary i.e., books, journals, travelogues, monographs, reports, personal notes, magazines etc. As such entire credit goes to those on whose works this work is devised and built.

The editor owes a deep sense of gratitude to all those whose works are cited partially or substantially made use of. He also thanks to different libraries and officials therein for making available the requisite material. Family members and near and dears deserve gratefulness for their inspiration, moral support and assistance of one sort or other. Last but not the least, the editor is grateful to Mr. M.P. Misra for undertaking the publication of this book.

—Editor

1

Tourism and Travel: History and Evolution

> "A good traveler is one who does not know where he is going and a perfect traveler does not know where he came from."
>
> —*Lin Yutang*

Since time immemorial man had a thrust for wandering. The ancient Greeks had a remarkable wanderlust. The Roman Empire had the history of pilgrimages. The great navigators of the 15th and 16th centuries expanded the horizon of the world, as compulsive voyagers and adventurers; they were rich people and had the monopoly of travel in Europe.

Prior to the middle of the 18th century, nature and its beautiful but rugged objects had little appeal and mountains in particular were disliked and avoided. Until 1763 Switzerland was avoided. Climbing glaciers and snow peaks had not been introduced. Later on, few daring innovators had taken an interest in mountain climbing and tried to explore the high mountains of Alps. Gradually Chamonix became the target of adventures. This unique change of attitude and taste transformed Switzerland into the first playground of Europe. Goethe declared, "Switzerland at first made so deep impression on me that I was bewildered and restless." The concept towards mountains changed and people began to feel an irresistible urge to travel to the mountains.

In the beginning of the 10th century rich people started

visiting Switzerland for acquiring health and knowledge and gradually that attitude changed and they felt an inner urge to visit and enjoy nature's bounty. In 1811, with the ascent of the Jungfrau, sport of Alpinism began and grew rapidly. Alpine societies were founded in Austria, Germany and Switzerland. Mountain chalets and footpaths encouraged Alpine adventures. The first mountain hut was constructed in 1865 in Kapnm, Salzburg as per the recorded evidence. The end of the 19th century and the early 20th century were the periods of strong growth in mountain tourism. Alps became the center for summer as well as winter tourism. Walking on snow and crossing the glaciers was not unknown to Indians. The 3500 kms long majestic Himalaya on the northern border has always held a strong fascination for men. The Himalaya offers challenges, inspiration, sublimity, relaxation and satisfaction. 'Me Vedas' (written some 5000 years ago), the ancient literary masterpieces are full of praises to Himalaya, which reverentially was and is believed to have proximity to the Gods. The Hindu religious books—Puranas, *Bhagvada Gita* and *Ramayana*—all are full of praises to Himalaya, the "Abode of Gods", where Gods lived and mortals meditated for salvation. According to Hindu mythology the liquid essence of life, Ganga, descended from heaven to earth in Himalaya. Therefore, our holy men took the journey to Himalaya, hence it had become the place of pilgrimage for the devout Hindus, Sikhs and Buddhists since centuries.

Tourism and travel is the inherent trait of man. In recorded history there have been instances whereby one is able to know that man has been travelling throughout the ages. From the very early historical period, travel has had a fascination for man. Much of the travel in the beginning was largely unconscious and rather a simple affair unlike the sophisticated travel in the modern times.

Travel in the distant past, however, was not undertaken for the purposes of pleasure, since the motive was not to seek any holiday from the work situation. The primary motive for which travel was undertaken was related to trade, commerce and the activities associated with it. The traveller in the ancient past was thus a trader and a merchant looking for merchandise and engaging in trade and commerce.

Another form of traveller was there, whose motive was other than trade and commerce. This traveller was a pilgrim, a scholar in search of ancient texts, and a curious way farer looking forward to new and exciting experiences. His primary purpose for undertaking travel was seeking knowledge.

Business was the another prime motive of travel. Throughout history, traders and merchants have travelled to far off lands in order to trade with other nations and tribes. Travellers from distant lands started moving about in large numbers and visited many places for the purposes of commerce. With the gradual opening of the trade routes, travel became easier as well as regulated. At the market-places, travellers made contacts with each other which resulted in increased flow of trade and commerce. Trade relations gradually matured into cultural relations and better understanding of each other's way of life. This was a favourable development towards increase in travel activity during this period.

On the other hand Phoenicians were probably the first real travellers in the modern sense. These were also the people who were credited for the invention of money. The medium of money was being used in various business and commercial dealings. Many traders could now pay for their travel to different centres of trade and commerce and also for the accommodation they required. The invention of money and the development of trade and commerce beginning about 3000 B.C. perhaps can be said to be the most significant development of the time which paved the way for the development and organisation of travel.

Early travel in the orient, particularly in India and in China, was also largely based on trade and commerce. Travel to India in particular was undertaken by travellers from all over the ancient world. Both India and China enjoyed the reputation of being countries of fabulous wealth where trade and commerce flourished. This trend continued and became more marked in course of time with Europeans heading towards Indian shores for the sole purpose of trade and commerce.

The urge to explore new lands and to seek new knowledge in ancient and distant lands was yet another motive of travellers in subsequent periods. Although trade and commerce continued to be the strong force for many travellers to undertake journeys to distant lands, seeking new knowledge and exploring the unexplored lands was becoming a strong urge in ancient times. Homer in *Odyssey* records the wanderlust of the ancient Greeks and Romans. There are innumerable references to great explorers who spent many formidable years of their lives in search of knowledge. These great explorers can, perhaps, be credited with the distinction of being the pioneers who subsequently paved the way for modern-day travel.

Medieval Era

Travel for religious purposes assumed a significant importance during the middle ages. The practice for travelling for religious purposes became a well established custom in many parts of the world. By the end of the Middle Ages, a large number of pilgrims were travelling to the main shrines in Europe and elsewhere. The adoption and spread of Christianity subsequently led to numerous pilgrims making their way to the holy land. So deep and strong was the hold of faith that the ritual of pilgrimage flourished over the centuries. It became a great unifying force and the pilgrimages strengthened religious bonds. The pilgrimages also provided the necessary impetus for a 'stay-at-home' agrarian society to break out of its narrow geographical confines and visit places associated with religion.

In India, pilgrimage assumed a great importance. Emperor Ashoka the Great, travelled a great deal in his eagerness to spread doctrines of Buddha. Ashoka and his entourage first travelled to Nepal starting from Pataliputra and then ventured to Lumbini Gardens, the land of Buddha's birth, on to Kapilavastu, the place where Buddha spent his childhood. Through his travels, Emperor Ashoka had special memorials set up at each spot and also rest houses where travellers could rest. Harsha was another emperor who was greatly influenced by the Buddhist scriptures. He built institutions and Dhramshalas for the travellers. Rest houses were built in towns and villages. Many monasteries and temples were also built for the Pilgrims.

The powerful influences of a crusading religion that slowly penetrated a foreign land, such as Christianity in Europe and later in America and Buddhism, Islam and Hinduism in Asia took place to permit an assimilation and perpetuation of very distinctive languages, literature, art, architecture, philosophy and forms of government. Religion thus played and continues to play a crucial part in travel.

Persian traders were, perhaps the earliest travellers from distant lands to the Indian soil. Evidence of caravans of Persians visiting India lies engraved in the inscriptions dating to the Persian king Darius. During the rule of the Guptas, there was free access to the ports along the Western Coast, seaborne commerce with Europe through Egypt was yet another reason for travel in and around the country.

Great travellers from various far away lands visited India. Probably the greatest traveller remembered from the distant past is Hieun-tsang. A devout Chinese Buddhist, he made the perilous journey to India around A.D. 633. His main mission was to collect and translate ancient Buddhist scriptures. Some other travellers whose names need special mention are Alexander the Great, Marco Polo, Benjamin of Tudela, Ibn Batutah, Francisco Friar, Alfonso D' Albuquerque and Mark Twain.

This period saw the emergence of some sort of communication system and accommodation. Development of trade and commerce necessitated this development. Shulgi, the ruler of ancient Babylonia, claimed to have built roads and rest houses at various places for way farers. With trade and commerce forming a link in development, it was inevitable that some sort of communication system connecting the centres of trade, commerce and learning were found to be in good shape. When Alexander the Great, during his journeys, reached India, he found well maintained roads covered with shady trees. Along one royal highway, 1,920 kilometres long and about 19 metres wide, people travelled in chariots, palanquins, bullock carts, on horses, camels and elephants.

Benjamin of Tudela, a Jewish scholar, the first medieval traveller to reach the orient who left Saragossa in the year A.D. 1160. He wrote a detailed account of his thirteen-year long journey through Europe, Persia and India, giving information on the Jewish communities, and the geography of various places he had visited. Ibn Batutah wrote a detailed diary of his travel experiences. He was born at Tangier in A.D. 1304. In the year A.D. 1325, he left his home and passing through various countries in Africa and West Asia, crossed the Sindhu in A.D. 1333. His travels took him to as far places as Indonesia and China. Marco Polo, spent almost twenty-five years in Asia during the latter part of the 13th century. Young Marco Polo left Venice in the year 1271 with his father and uncle. The three together travelled through Persia and Afghanistan to the "Roof of the World", the then unknown Pamir Plateau. After crossing the Gobi desert, they reached Kublai Khan's palace and remained in China for over twenty years. On his way back home, he stopped in Sumatra, Java, India and Ceylon.

Marco Polo's description of a place Zipangu (the present day Japan) in his memoirs, set the course for Columbus on his historic journey in 1492. Two of Columbus's contemporaries who also became famous and wrote excellent accounts were Vasco da Gama—who opened the sea route from Western Europe to India in 1498—and Ferdinand Magellan whose ship sailed around the world. Francisco Friar, John of Monte Corvino, visited India on his way to and back from China during the last decade of the thirteenth century.

In the 16th and 17th centuries, many more European monks, travellers and adventurers visited India and many other places in search of knowledge. The first great sailor to do a westward circumnavigation of the world was Francis Drake who was knighted by Queen Elizabeth I in the year 1581. From 1768 to 1779 Captain James Cook made three long voyages to the Pacific in search of a non-existent southern continent mentioned by Ptolemy who earlier in the 2nd century A.D. had travelled widely and who wrote an eight-volume work on geography.

Coming to Romans probably were the first pleasure travellers. Travel received a great stimulus from the good communication system and security of the Roman empire. There existed a fine network of roads and new roads were built increasingly wherever the Romans went. Travel literature was published extensively giving routes, the names of the major roads, distances between places and time required in travelling to them. The Romans were able to travel over a hundred or more miles in a day using relays of horses. They journeyed primarily to see famous temples in the Mediterranean areas, particularly the monuments and the famous pyramids of Egypt. The Romans also travelled during holiday occasions, particularly the famous Olympic Games. Spas and seaside resorts which developed during this period may be associated with pleasure travel. Medicinal baths and seaside resorts which later were named as *Spas* were very popular with the Romans. The inland spa had its origin in a belief in the efficacy of its mineral waters for medicinal purposes, either by drinking the water or by immersing in it. The visitors now not only enjoyed the medicinal baths but also various forms of entertainments. Theatrical productions, athletic competitions, festivals and other forms of entertainment and amusement were often provided at the sites where spas were located.

Development of various seaside resorts is also linked with spa. In the latter half of the eighteenth century, people started realising the possible curative effects of sea water. Seabathing also became very popular and many believed that bathing in sea water was more beneficial than inland spas. By the year 1865, there were-major seaside resorts in Britain, France, Italy and a few more countries of Central Europe. Nevertheless, both the spas and the seaside resorts paved the way for the modern pleasure travel all over the world where millions of people visited various seaside resorts.

The Renaissance marked the next important stage in the history of tourism. The reappearance of tourism in Europe follows the Italian Renaissance and the development of a full scale urban system and network of roads. By the end of the fifteenth century Italy itself became the centre of attention.

Subsequently, the development of the Grand tourism followed a shift in the focus of culture and of economic and political power. The wealthy and educated, of states whose position of dominance in the world was comparatively new, visited countries that had passed their peak of prestige but were still venerated for historical and cultural reasons. Thus Romans visited Greece and the eastern Mediterranean, the English, from sixteenth century onwards, visited Italy. The Grand tourist respected the learning, antiquities and social refinements of the world. The eighteenth century is conventionally considered, the golden age of the Grand Tour, especially the thirty years between 1763 and 1793. With the new wealth of the English bourgeoisie the number of tourists had multiplied. The Grand Tour was no longer an aristocratic preserve.

The term holiday derives from holy days associated with religious observances. In the present day parlance it is used generally in a secular sense meaning a respite from the routine of daily workday life and a time for leisure and recreation. It is significant here to note that the introduction of Annual Holiday in Europe was yet another important landmark which enabled many people to undertake travel in large numbers during the eighteenth century. The annual holiday was the forerunner to the 'paid holiday' which later on was responsible for an extraordinary growth of tourism during the 20th century.

In the year 1552 in England an act was passed during the reign of Edward VI "for the keeping of holidays and fasting days". This act still continues to be on the Statute Book. Subsequently, public and semi-official offices in England frequently closed on certain saint's days. There were, however, no general public holidays until the time of the Industrial Revolution.

The 'travel bug' in the modern sense had its seeds in the ancient past. Although the purpose and motives for travels in the subsequent periods underwent a great change, the urge to travel has always been there. The growth and development of travel has been closely linked with the growth and development of society as a whole. The travellers of the ancient past were in fact the explorers in search of knowledge of different lands, of people, their cultures and their traditions. They were also traders interested in development of trade and commerce. In fact, these very developments paved the way for development of travel in the subsequent periods.

Tourism Scenario during 19th Century

The beginning of the nineteenth century witnessed a

great technological development, first in England, and later on in Europe and U.S.A. This development had a great effect on transport which resulted in the growth of travel in general. This great technological development led to the advent of the railway. The introduction of railways in the nineteenth century was a crucial landmark in history. The first rail link between Liverpool and Manchester was started in the year 1830. The newly completed railway track in England featured special provisions for carrying passengers in addition to freight. Later on, an extensive programme of construction of railroads to provide trunklines between major centres of population and commerce and industry was taken up in England. Although the railway network in the beginning was responsible for carrying goods from industrial centres to the centres of trade and commerce, it had, however, initiated the process of carrying the passengers which later on was to become a mass movement. Railways provided the necessary vehicle for the movement of the people from the place of their residence to newly formed and expanding pleasure spots like seaside resorts.

Railway companies in England were slow to take advantage of the various opportunities available to them for the expansion of the pleasure travel and thereby the passenger travel. These companies were concentrating in meeting the demands, of trade and commerce as a result of their expansion. Gradually, the railway companies started to concentrate on carrying more passengers which resulted in the development of short day trips. This trend was later to be followed by railways by way of organising excursions for the Public. These excursions were offered to the public at special fares. The birth of the organised rail travel, however, came in the year 1841. A baptist preacher of Derbyshire on his way to a temperance meeting in Leicester was inspired with the idea of engaging a special train to carry the friends of temperance society from Leicester to Loughborough and back to attend a quarterly delegate meeting. The man behind this idea was none other than Thomas Cook who later on came to be known as one of the greatest travel organisers of the times and, in fact, a pioneer. Thomas Cook broached the idea to his friend and a few weeks later the idea culminated into collecting as many as 570 passengers who made a journey by the Midland Counties Railway at a specially reduced return fare of one shilling per passenger. Encouraged by the success of this venture, Thomas Cook arranged similar such ventures by chartering trains to places which were now becoming popular with the excursionists. In the year 1843, nearly 3,000 school children were taken on a trip from Leicester to Derby. Many more excursion trips were arranged by Thomas Cook on a fully commercial basis. From the year 1848 to 1863, Cook conducted circular tours of Scotland with almost 5,000 travellers a season. By the year 1855, Thomas Cook had extended his field of operations to other countries in the continent.

Thomas Cook's name will always be remembered in the history of modern travel. In fact, he was the pioneer in the area of conducted tours. The concept of 'chartering' the transport for excursion trips can also be associated with Thomas Cook who initially broached this idea to hire a special train to carry the friends of temperance society from Leicester to Loughboroug and back to attend a meeting. Another important development which can also be associated with Thomas Cook is the spurt in, pleasure travel. The large scale movement of people to various pleasure spots like beach resorts and spas was a result of organised conducted excursion trips by Thomas Cook.

Railway tracks were laid in France, Austria and Switzerland. Across the Atlantic the tracks were laid in America which ushered in the spurt of travel to and from places where the tracks were laid. This great revolution in rail transport technology produced an immediate expansion in European travel. With the phenomenal success, the railways were now keen to stimulate travel further and also to improve the system. There was also now an element of competition and the various railway companies tried to make travel as comfortable as possible. In the early 1870s first class railway travel was introduced by an American, named G.M. Pullman, who developed the pullman coaches with their luxury furnishings and having dining facilities.

The longer distances in America necessitated the ensuring greater passenger comfort. Long distance travel could now be undertaken in comfort and with pleasure. The Pullman coaches manufactured in America were being imported by some railway companies in England and other countries in Europe. By the year 1872 the Pullman company had over 700 coaches working over 30,0000 miles of railway track under contract with over 150 different railway companies.

India tookup the construction railways in the same century. Soon after its introduction in England the business community there was pressing the East India Company to introduce railways in the subcontinent of India. After prolonged negotiations with British rail-road companies the GIP Railway Company could be incorporated in an Act of the Parliament in 1849 and a contract signed between East India Company and the GIP Railway Company requesting them to raise the requisite capital required for the construction work. The contract for the actual construction was awarded to an English company, Messrs Faviel and Fowler.

It was on April 16, 1853 that the first train in the east took off from Bori Bunder in Bombay to Thana, covering a distance of 33 kilometres. Four hundred guests selected from various segments were invited to travel by the first train in India. From a small beginning on 16 April 1853, when the first train steamed off from Victoria Terminus for Thane, 33 kilometres away, the Railway System in India has grown into the world's second largest system under one management, second only to the USSR.

Sea Routes

Besides the railways, the shipping made a significant contribution to travel during the nineteenth century. While railways were responsible for inland travel, especially in Europe, the steamship crossed the boundaries and made strides in intercontinental travel. The shipping technology made a number of innovations in the nineteenth century. In America a number of sailing ships were built which were considered to be superior to those built in England or elsewhere. The English felt a great need for improved communications across the Atlantic with America for the purpose of trade and commerce and passenger transportation. As a result of this there were greatstrides in the development of deep-sea shipping. The History of the Cunard Steamship Company in England demonstrates important features in the growth of North Atlantic Shipping. A subsidy in the form of the award of mail contract represented a recurring theme in the development of passenger transportation. With the passage of time toward the last quarter of the nineteenth century, emigrant traffic became an important factor in North Atlantic travel. A great number of people from the continent started going to America in search of fortune. First Great Britain and later Germany along with of countries became the principal generators of emigrants to 'new world'. Many travelled to see the new world. Use of the ships in the cruising fashion for the charter and operation of cruises on a limited scale dates from the nineteenth century. The worldwide growth of shipping companies to was the end of the nineteenth century led to the formation of ship in conferences which developed cartel-like agreements. The agreements were on fare structure applicable to the carria passenger traffic and cargo to various territories to which vessels of these companies operated.

The second half of the nineteenth century, in fact, witnessed growth of travel as a result of development of industrial societies. These societies which developed in Western

Europe and North America greatly felt the urge to travel purely for purpose of rest and relaxation. This trend certainly gave way what came to be known as the tourism phenomenon in the later part of the century and in the twentieth century.

Evidently an accurate analysis of the measurement of tourism can be traced back to only about one and a half century ago, the scatter figures published from 1855 onwards point to the relationship between the development of industrialised societies and the expansion of tourist movements. This has also supplemented by various official statements, observations travel writers, and the various travel guides and other literature on sale from time to time. The emergence of the industrialised societies was a direct result of the industrial revolution in the West, initially beginning in England. In its wake the industrial revolution brought about tremendous changes in the society. The very concept of society under went a change.

The industrial Revolution was responsible for changes both in the economic as well as social systems prevailing at that time. A large number of factory towns, both big and small, sprang up which in turn necessitated large scale migrations from the country side to towns and cities. The Industrial Revolution was responsible for the emergence of the working class which was needed to run factories. In the beginning the working class was burdened with long working hours and poor working and living conditions and lower wages. The sudden concentration of population in towns and cities created unhealthy conditions. For a large number of workers there was little relief from the routine of putting long hours of work in difficult and unhealthy working conditions.

As the industrial momentum gathered and the cities and their populations increased at an enormous rate, the need for some relief was acute. Escape from the routine of work began to be felt in more intensity. The prosperous and well-to-do who could afford the escape proceeded to various resorts for rest and recreation. By this time a large number of such resorts had been developed around the English coast and in near by countries. A number of large scale pleasure zones were developed at some considerable distance from the large cities and towns of central Europe. The French Riviera with Nice Cannes and Monte. Carlo were some of these pleasure zones.

The industrialisation brought in better working conditions and increase in material wealth for a large number of workers. The simultaneous improvements in transport and communication systems during the second half of the nineteenth century enabled a large number of industrial workers not only in England but elsewhere as well to avail of holidays for rest, relaxation and pleasure. The substantial increase in workers' purchasing power and disposable income for travel were two important factors which helped the growth of pleasure zones. By the end of the century the Riviera was unmistakably the most popular pleasure zone. Its development became possible when escape to the South had become a major feature of pleasure travel in Europe. Many resorts were developed to cater to the increasing needs of people who could afford a holiday.

Tourism Industry in 20th Century

By the turn of the twentieth century all the main characteristics of advance tourism were evident in embryo. Changes in mental attitudes towards pleasure seeking, the recognised value of travel for education, increase in material wealth coupled with social prestige, a growing need to find relief from working routine, improvements in passenger transport systems—all these factors produced a fertile ground for the development of excursion traffic on a large scale.

Up to the first quarter of the twentieth century travel including pleasure travel was essentially a luxury commodity within the reach of privileged sections of the society having both free time and considerable purchasing power. The Pleasure tourism had by now assumed a class and a charm of its own associated as it was with elegant luxurious hotels. Pullman coaches, prestigious nostalgic long distance trains, such as the 'Orient Express' and the 'Blue Riband' and trans atlantic liners like the 'Queen Mary'. During this time also there appeared a number of associations, which enrolled members from among the embryonic middle and working classes and organised excursions, holiday camps, family rest and holiday homes for them. This class of people had emerged as a result of increasing prosperity due to industrialisation and urbanisation. Not many people, however, benefited from such activities at that firm.

The unprecedented boom in tourist movements in the twentie especially in Europe and America, can be directly linked to, the introduction of the private motor car. The motorised private and public road transport and the improved road conditions led to tremendous growth of travel. The invention of the private motorcar and coach received its first great impetus in the ten years which preceded World War I. The motor car revolutionised holiday habits of the Europeans and Americans. It became increasingly important in the pursuit of leisure and tourism. The provision of good motor roads and the road services were important factors in the development of both domestic and international tourism. The concept of mass tourism emerged along with the introduction of holiday with pay. It was in the last quarter of the nineteenth century that increasing attention was paid to the desirability of holiday with pay and at least of cheap holidays for working class people. This group had still largely failed to benefit from the new opportunities, offered by travel by rail. During this period a few factories gave paid holidays to their workers in some countries in the West. The introduction of annual paid holidays is very largely of English origin and this had important repercussions on the development of mass tourism. The annual paid holiday was established during the inter-war years as a reality for a considerable part of the working population. By the year 1939, in UK, some eleven million people were covered by the Holidays with Pay Act (1938). Introduction of paid holiday had led to great mobility of the population, created new industries, resulted in the creation and growth of many towns of distinctive function and broadened the horizons of millions of people.

The modern tourism really got under way when, at the instigation of its trade union representatives, the International Labour Organisation (ILO) adopted the first convention that was to support serious movements to promote paid holidays and, in turn, tourism in 1936. That convention on paid holidays was an innovation well ahead of time, when only fourteen countries, mostly European, had enacted general legislation on paid holidays. Soon afterwards tourism experienced an extraordinary growth. Paid holidays are now established all Over the world, and in most countries a minimum duration of one to three weeks is specified either by law or by collective agreements, between the employer and the workers. The trend is to grant longer holiday periods. The employers have realised that the Paid holidays have not adversely affected industrial production. The legal minimum in many countries present is three weeks. Some countries have even gone this and grant four weeks of paid holiday. Today it is recognise that in Western Europe the fifth week, even from the stand of output, may also be regarded as a productive investment. Sweden has recently enacted legislation introducing this additional week of paid holidays. World wide, more than 500 million wage-earners are entitled to paid holidays. Out of this number, roughly half are in Europe, little less than 30 per cent in the Americas, and the rest in Asia and the Pacific. Presently the main potential for tourism markets is made up of wage-earners and their families. This concept of paid holidays which originated with the advent of industrialisation in the West has given modern tourism tremendous boost.

As a result of economic and social changes due to further industrialisation the world over and the rationalisation of the tertiary sector, the number of wage earners in the world bound to grow at a much faster rate than before.

The post-World War-II period brought in a rapid development of tourism. As the world began to settle down after the years of readjustments immediately after the war ended in year 1945, there has been a rapid increase in domestic as well as international tourism. The United Nations reported that in the ten years period between 1955 and 1965, number of tourist arrivals in some sixty-five countries increased three folds around 51 million to over 157 million. This trend in growth of international tourism continued till the mid-1960's. It continued to be determined by the living standards in the developed countries. The widespread introduction of the holiday with pay to a large majority of people during this period was yet another important factor responsible for growth of tourist traffic.

There were nearly 220 million international tourist arrivals in the world in 1976. This was an increase of more than 90 per cent over the year 1965. This period was a period of intensive economic and technological development in most industrialised countries which had earlier suffered a great deal as a result of war. Most of the developing countries during this period were also able to benefit from the growing trend in the developed counties to engage in tourism.

Any domestic or international economic fluctuations or political disturbances result in a temporary set back to the growth of tourism in 1974. As a result of the energy crisis there occurred inflation which was responsible for lower purchasing power which in its wake had brought in a steep fall in tourist movements. Like all other sectors of production and consumption, the economic consequences of that crisis affected tourism too.

Notably, the late twentieth century period can be termed as a period which is, responsible for introducing a phenomenon called 'mass tourism'. Although the enormous expansion of tourism has taken place primarily in the advanced industrialised countries, where tourism has become a part of the lifestyle and consumption pattern. The key role of air transport has been a major factor in the growth of international tourism, especially in respect of long distance and inter-continental travel. Although commercial travel was introduced even before the World War-II, air transport for the masses has essentially been a post-World War-II phenomenon. With the tremendous increase in speed, safety and comfort provided by the new civil aircrafts like Douglas DC-6s and DC-7s and Super-constellations, there was a noticeable increase in the long distance international as well as intra-regional tourism. In the year 1952 the two-class travel introduced was made possible by the larger capacity of new aircrafts. The increase in the aircraft capacity was also responsible for lower air fares. The steady fall in the cost of flying also resulted in the increased traffic across the Atlantic. This period also saw the first attempt to introduce a package holiday around air transport which subsequently became, the model for most of the Present day's global tourism.

Revolution Through Airways

The most dramatic event which introduced an entirely new dimension of speed, comfort and efficiency to air transport and brought mass travel to its present level was the advent of the jet travel in the year 1958. As a result of the entry of advanced jet aircraft in the civil aviation industry, air travel from the year 1960 onwards grew tremendously. Great advances have been made ever since in the aircraft jet technology with the introduction of newer and sophisticated planes having emphasis on comfort, luxury, speed and safety. Added to all this, the technical brilliance of the supersonic aircraft like the Concorde and of the Tupolev 144 have added glamour to the passenger aircraft industry. It will not be out of place to mention here that the international tourism as we know it today, has been largely shaped by air travel.

Introduction of 'inclusive tours' is yet another most decisive development during this period responsible for mass tourism. In all inclusive tours' travellers are carried on charter flights at rates substantially below those of normal scheduled services. The principal causes of the rapid growth of demand for tourism in the highly developed industrialised countries in the course of recent decades can be summed up as economic, social and technological in nature.

Comparatively, a larger proportion of people can now afford an 'annual holiday.' In fact, many can even afford to take a 'second holiday' for a shorter or a longer duration. The economic prosperity has also resulted in many more people owning a private motor car increased mobility as a result of use of motor car for travel, therefore, is yet another important economic factor which is responsible for growth in tourism in Europe and North America.

Traditionally considered a luxury, travel now is considered to be a normal activity and an indispensable part of lifestyles and consumption patterns of a large majority of people enjoying a higher standard of living. The present day tourist is much more informed having a different kind of background than a traveller of the past. His ideas about travel are quite different and he comes from a wider social background. His tastes and desires are much more varied.

The rapid growth of tourism can be associated with the advancements made in modernising transport and communication systems. The impact of the modern transport technology, specially in the aviation field has brought about a completely new meaning to travel and tourism. Travel to even remote destinations has now become a reality. The technological developments have now made it possible for an increasing number of people to travel to far away places which only a few decades ago were regarded as being almost inaccessible. The gradual evolution of the originally homogeneous air travel market into two separate and distinct segments-charters and schedule air travel has greatly increased the demand. Added to this the newer marketing methods like the 'package tour' is a major contributing factor to the growth of tourism. Opening up of new travel destinations, particularly in the developing countries, creation of new facilities to receive a larger flow of tourists and increasing tourism promotion and marketing efforts by the tourist service enterprises have greatly increased the tourist flows.

2

Tourism and Economic Development

> "When you travel, remember that a foreign country is not designed to make you comfortable. It is designed to make its own people comfortable."
>
> —*Clifton Fadiman in Holiday*

Tourism has become an important source of income for most of the countries of the world. Worldwide, international tourist arrivals in 1999 are estimated at approximately 700 million, resulting in over $500 billion in tourist receipts (Edgell, 1999), and tourism generates nearly 250 million jobs worldwide (WTO, 1999). The increasing fascination with tourism has been motivated in large part due to its potential economic benefits for destination areas. Early literature in tourism development emphasized the role of tourism in economic development, particularly for developing countries (Erbes, 1973).

However, in the past two decades increased attention to the negative social, cultural and environmental impacts of tourism has also emerged, calling for more careful planning and management of tourism development (WTO, 1996; Mathieson & Wall, 1982, Wahab, 1997). As discussion of responsible tourism growth is still in its infancy, the dilemma for many countries is devising a way to develop a sustainable tourism industry — one that maintains economic benefits and limits associated negative impacts. In other words, how can countries develop a tourism industry which provides the much needed economic benefits such as foreign exchange, employment and income while protecting the human and natural resources it is built upon?

Tourism: An Attractive Economic Development Tool

The potential economic benefits of tourism are a major attraction for developing countries due to three pro-tourism arguments (Mill & Morrison, 1999). First, the trend in demand for international travel is projected to continue at astonishing rates due to the economic stability and travel preferences of people in the developed regions such as Europe, Asia and North America. Second, the income elasticity of demand for tourism means that as the household incomes of people in the developed world increase, more disposable income will be directed towards travel. And thirdly, developing countries are in need of foreign exchange earnings to support their economic development initiatives and to satisfy the demands of their own residents.

Due to these pro-tourism arguments, many developing countries are choosing, or being encouraged to develop tourism over some of the more traditional industry alternatives such as agriculture and manufacturing. Although between 50-70 per cent of people in developing countries are directly dependent on agriculture, reliance on the industry can result in numerous problems (World Bank, 1979). One of the primary problems with agriculture is that countries can be overly dependent upon a few specific crops or products (Mill & Morrison, 1999). In the competitive global market, where externalities are uncontrollable and price unpredictable, countries dependent on agriculture have an unreliable and inconsistent source of revenue. In these cases, tourism may play a role in diversifying the economy and complementing the income brought in through agriculture. For example, after introducing tourism into the Caribbean island economies, the $9 billion tourism sector brought in six times the revenue of all traditional agricultural exports (Simon, 1995).

Other developing countries have sought manufacturing as an economic development policy option. As with agriculture, there are inherent problems when relying upon manufacturing. In order to manufacture something, a country must have easy access to a source of raw materials for production. Thus, manufacturing is more successful in nations that are richly endowed with natural resources. Many developing countries are also plagued with chronic shortages of skilled labour, one of the necessary inputs for a strong manufacturing base. And, even when these problems are nonexistent, export oriented industries still face full international competition in selling their products (Mill & Morrison, 1999).

Tourism, like manufacturing, requires similar access to land, labour and capital resources. Yet, tourism, in the way that the product is produced and delivered, may be a more viable alternative for developing countries. Most countries have the basic raw materials required to establish a tourism industry. Whether using its heritage, architecture, landscape, water or people, the mix of natural and cultural resources is what makes a destination unique and marketable to visitors. As international policy agreements on trade of services advances, there are fewer restrictions on international travel than trade (Edgell, 1999). Demand for tourism is expected to remain strong into the new millennium and with advances in technology reducing the time required to travel, the distance between the consumer and the tourism product is becoming negligible. Finally, unlike other industries, tourism prices are more under the control of the seller than the buyer. These traits combined, tourism is seen as an attractive economic development option for many countries in the developing world. But, as the OECD cautions, "there are few if any developing countries which could, or perhaps even should, rely principally on tourism for their economic salvation" (Erbes, 1973).

Tourism also allows countries more leverage in

manipulating exchange rates to influence visitor expenditures on site. For example, destination areas can lower exchange rates to attract a greater number of visitors. More than other industry, tourism is multifaceted and either directly or indirectly affects other sectors of the economy. For example, the tourism product relies directly on, and produces economic benefits for, transportation, accommodations, food and beverage and entertainment sectors. Indirectly, other businesses that are involved in servicing the aforementioned sectors receive increased economic benefits as well.

The decision whether or not to enter into the tourism system in not one to be made lightly. The industry differs from agriculture and manufacturing in many ways including the organization, nature of the activity, required human, social, technical and natural capital, and resulting economic, social and environmental impacts. And, although scant evidence exists in the literature, the development of tourism differs from the developing and developed worlds (Liu, 1998). To put it most succinctly, Jenkins (1980: 27) suggests that "tourism in developed countries can be regarded as mainly a social activity with economic consequences; in developing countries it is largely an economic activity with social consequences". Many of the suggestions in this paper reflect the difference that tourism has from other industries, and from the developed world. Partly, the intent of this paper is to bring attention to these differences in order to suggest strategies which will work given the context and unique position of developing countries on the path to sustainable tourism development. International tourism is usually price-elastic and income elastic, meaning that it is sensitive to changes in price or income. Shifts in either can result in significant changes in travel patterns. This can be positive when the household incomes of visiting markets are stable, but can result in problems for destinations dependent on visitors who are experiencing an economic crisis. This effect was recently experienced in the Pacific Asian region where many countries who depended on Asian visitors experienced lower visitation levels due to the 1997 Asian economic crisis (WTO, 1999).

Issues in Retaining Foreign Exchange Earnings

The assertive economic impacts of tourism are commonly listed as increased foreign exchange earnings, increased income, and increased employment in destination areas (WTO, 1996; Mill & Morrison, 1999; Edged, 1999; Lundberg et. al., 1995). All three forms of economic impact are central to economic development. There has been a lot of attention on economic impacts of tourism in the literature (Loomis & Walsh, 1996; WTO, 1999), mostly focused however on methods to estimate income from tourism via economic impact assessments, or claims of direct and indirect employment generated by tourism. This has not been without good reason, as both of these methods produce convincing figures that are used to show the significance of tourism. In fact, public relations literature for tourism destinations are often laced with claims of the economic expenditures and jobs created by tourism.

Economic impacts from tourism typically report the amount of new income being received in a destination area, and then use a multiplier to account for the additional respending that result afterwards. There is a danger, however, of overstating the foreign exchange earnings of tourism when leakage is not taken into consideration. Leakage refers to the amount of money that leaves an economy to import goods and services needed for tourism development. For example, materials imported from another country to build tourism infrastructure, people brought in to fill tourism positions, and supplies purchased elsewhere to cater to specific needs of tourists are all examples of leakage. This leakage must be subtracted from foreign exchange earnings to obtain a true estimate of the economic impacts associated to tourism.

Leakage results from at least six factors (Mill & Morrison, 1999). First, the costs of goods and services purchased to satisfy the needs of visitors. If, for example, visitors to a destination want to eat food that is not grown domestically, the destination must make arrangements and pay to bring in the food from places it can be obtained. If the destination is marketing itself on being able to deliver this aspect of the tourism experience, it must then satisfy the desires of the visitors it has attracted. A second form of leakage occurs when destinations must purchase materials and equipment from other countries to supply the needed infrastructure for tourism. Many developing countries do not produce for example, the materials or expertise required to build hotels, transportation and sewage facilities that are essential to support tourism. A third form of leakage is for payments to foreign factors of production. Here, any commissions, interest payments, rent or profits that are paid outside the country for tourism related products should be considered as leakage. Many foreign owned hotel chains and entertainment corporations for example, import everything from building materials, furnishings and labour to construct and operate in developing countries (Pleumarom, 1999). A fourth form of leakage to consider is the expenditure for promoting a destination abroad. For example, most countries operate a National Tourism Organization either inside or outside the destination. Costs involved in promoting the destination and attracting tourists must be deducted as leakage, which is not a common practice among countries economic impact assessments (Mill & Morrison, 1999). Transfer pricing is a fifth form of leakage. Here, profits and taxes accruing to a destination area are reduced when payments are made in the country of visitor origin rather than the destination. For example, many visitors purchase packages from tour operators who use foreign owned hotels, attractions and services in the destination area. These visitors, particularly when purchasing all-inclusive packages, leave very little new money in the destination area. Local banks can also miss out on the opportunity to generate income when visitors rely on the use of credit cards and traveller's checks for purchases. Finally, a sixth form of leakage occurs when destination areas exempt foreign owned companies from paying duties or taxes as an incentive to attract investment.

Getting an estimate on the amount of and forms of leakage from tourism is a critical issue for developing countries. Unfortunately, many countries are under pressure to bring in foreign exchange earnings quickly to offset the initial costs involved in developing tourism infrastructure. As well, many do not have access to the materials or human resources needed to establish tourism, and therefore depend heavily on imported content. Some small island nations such as in the Caribbean have import content levels of over 50 per cent for tourism (Mill & Morrison, 1999; Archer et. al., 1995). Hastily, many of these developing countries see no other way to establish tourism than to import capital and labour, and attract foreign investment. The critical issue for developing countries then, is to devise strategies to minimize leakage.

In short, the way that developing countries can maximize the economic benefits from tourism is to bring in more money from visitors and organize tourism to minimize leakage of both money and jobs. Although this sounds rather simple, the number and agenda's of various stakeholders involved in tourism development make it complex. This section will discuss some strategies to enhance the economic benefits to host countries.

Tourism in the developing world differs in the role that government and the private sector play in establishing policy and encouraging development. National policies on tourism in developing countries are usually the domain of the state, whereas in more developed countries, private entrepreneurs often dominate policy formation and enactment (Liu, 1998). In most developing countries, owing to the small size of the private sector and the shortage of funds, the government necessarily takes on the role of entrepreneur (Shurland, 1998). This is usually in response to proposed private foreign investment. The aims of the private sector often oppose those of the public sector, with the former hinging upon profitability. The state, on the other hand, must take into account non-economic ramifications as well — for without governmental involvement, short-term developments can foster long-term problems. Governments in the developing world generally have the responsibility of formulating and enforcing tourism policy, and for many, sustainable tourism goals are central to their tourism plan. This should include, as already stated, increasing the economic impact of tourism to the local economy by reducing the leakage of foreign exchange earnings.

One of the ways to increase economic impacts of tourism is to bring in tourists who spend money in the developing country. As mass tourism markets have been criticized for the negative environmental and social impacts they cause, there is growing attention on targeting fewer visitors, and those with higher household incomes expecting that they will spend more during their visit. Although this sounds logical, the strategy has its critics (Mill & Morrison, 1999). There is little known about the net foreign exchange earnings that result from different types of visitors and types of tourism purchases. Although it has not been clearly shown, visitors with high household incomes may spend more, but they may also require substantial investment in infrastructure and facilities with high import content. The question for many destinations to consider carefully is: "is it better for the destination to mass market visitors who arrive in greater numbers and spend less but require fewer imported goods and services?" Clearly, as this strategy is being chosen by many destination areas, further research into the nature of nature of tourism expenditures by different visitors is needed, especially in comparison to the amount and types of infrastructure needed to attract high spending tourists.

Another strategy to maximize economic benefits is to encourage import substitution within developing countries. If quality products and services are available within the host country at a reasonable price, then the amount of imports [and therefore leakage] does not have to be so high. Unfortunately, many developing countries do not have these products and services readily available, but governments who are keen to establish tourism as a form of economic development could become involved by offering subsidies, grants or loans to local businesses. As well, to encourage use of local goods and services, quotas or tariffs on the use of imported goods could be implemented. The last strategy may be viewed as aggressive by other countries, however it may be necessary in developing countries where loyalties to brand images on foreign products has already been established.

Governments of developing countries may want to consider implementing incentive programmes to local and foreign investors to encourage the use of local architecture, design and materials. Through a range of fiscal and other incentives (see Table 1), governments can stimulate and influence the amount of local content used in tourism development. Many of the incentives listed in table one are to attract capital investment, however for many developing countries the issue is a shortage of local labour. In this case, efforts to train and educate the local workforce may be necessary to ensure that leakage from employing outside labour is kept to a minimum.

Perhaps one of the more complicated but necessary strategies for developing countries to consider is finding a way to work with transnational tourism corporations (TNC's). The demand for travel in the past few decades, coupled with the globalization of trade and services sectors has resulted in the rise of numerous TNC's in the tourism sector. Hotels, airlines, restaurants, travel agencies and tour operators have become more sophisticated in marketing and serving millions of travellers. With their success, has come a wave of criticism from smaller companies who view TNC's as operating for their own profitability at the expense of destination areas. For example, Pleumarom (1999) writes that many overseas chain hotel and resort properties are operated without any foreign equity involvement with headquarters in the developed world. Others, with their own agenda, can engage in policies that run counter to the national tourism plans. TNC's generate lower foreign exchange receipts than do smaller local owned operations, an important realization for many developing countries.

Many international hotel chains employ a core of expatriate managerial staff. Thus, another criticism of multinationals is that they do little to provide meaningful employment opportunities for local populations. To maximize the employment benefits for local populations, the governments of developing countries should ensure that when attracting TNC's, that there is direct financial involvement in developing the human capital in the destination's tourism mix. The World Tourism Organization has been working with many countries such as China, Russia, North Korea and Mongolia to identify ways to address manpower scarcity in tourism (WTO, 1999).

One remarkable portion of international tourism expenditures are made on transportation to and from the destination. Although most developing countries own and operate a centrally owned airline, people from developing countries tend to use airlines from their country or origin. This may be due to the aggressive marketing of airlines to develop customer loyalty through rewards programmes, or the fact that safety standards on airlines in the developing world are substandard. Regardless of the cause, the economic benefits involved in transportation are not reaching many developing countries. Again, to survive in the competitive airline industry and to reap more of the profits, airlines in developing countries may want to partner with the larger airlines and focus on providing safe, reliable domestic air transportation. Once destination areas have made substantial investments into the infrastructure necessary to cater to their chosen tourism markets, they can often become dependent upon large foreign tour operators to supply them with visitors.

This important intermediary role can make it difficult for small local tour operators to survive. The large tour operators can bring in more people and often deal directly with local hotel chains and transportation services. Without the smaller local operator, these sectors can become dependent upon foreign tour operators to supply them with visitors. Due to the differing interests of foreign vs. local tour operators, developing countries can find themselves in a precarious position when foreign tour operators follow trends and pull out of the destination and provide packages in other locations. It is therefore in the long-term interest of developing countries to invest in, and encourage support of local tour operators who establish and secure their role in providing packages with local flavor.

Another obvious way to maximize foreign exchange earnings is for developing countries to ensure that foreign currency is spent as much as possible. Some countries such as Cuba, have limited the amount of foreign currency that visitors can bring into and take out to ensure that foreign currency is used. Other countries like Belize, require that visitors show that they have $50.00 U.S. for every day of their visit.

Research in this area should explore the types of, and extent of leakage incurred in tourism in the developing world. A thorough description of foreign exchange leakage may help to identify where experimental research could be done to "plug the holes" and measure the resulting benefits to destination areas. With increasing attention being paid to alternative forms of tourism such as ecotourism, researchers should attempt to measure the economic impacts and compare them to those brought about by mass tourism. Indeed, these forms of tourism are being considered due to their ability to limit the negative social and environmental impacts of tourism, but if they are found to contribute to the positive economic benefits as well, they may be an even more attractive alternative for areas to consider.

Summary

Differing from the traditional industries of agriculture and manufacturing, the service industry of tourism is a viable alternative for developing the economies of many third world countries. In need of foreign exchange earnings, income and employment opportunities, developing countries often make the decision to become involved in tourism hastily. Due to the initial costs required to establish tourism infrastructure and attract visitors, developing countries can enter into tourism by importing a significant amount of materials and labour, and by attracting heavy foreign investment. With these systems left unchecked, however, the potential for leakage of money from the destination is high.

REFERENCES

Archer, B.H. & Fletcher, J.E. (1990), Tourism: Its economic significance. In M. Quest (ed.), Horwath Book of Tourism (pp. 10-25). London: The MacMillan Press.

Britton, S.G. (1982), "The political economy of tourism in the Third World", *Annals of Tourism Research*, 9(3): 331-358.

Cater, E. (1993), *Ecotourism in the Third World: Problems for sustainable tourism development*. Tourism Management, 14, 85-90.

Edgell, D.L. (1999), *Tourism Policy: The Next Millennium*. Advances in Tourism Applications Series, Sagamore Publishing.

Erbes, R. (1973), International tourism and the economy of developing countries. Paris: Organization for Economic Cooperation and Development.

Harrison, L.C.; and Husbands, W. (1996), *Practicing Responsible Tourism: International Case Studies in Tourism. Planning. Policy and Development*. John Wiley & Sons, Inc.

Loomis, J.B.; and Walsh, R.G. (1996), *Recreation Economic Decisions: Comparing Benefits and Costs* (2nd Edition) Venture Publishing, Inc. State College Pennsylvania.

Lundberg, D.E., Stavenga, M.H. & Krishnamoorthy, M. (1995), *Tourism Economics*. New York: John Wiley & Sons, Inc.

Mathieson, A., & Wall, G. (1982), *Tourism: Economic, physical and social impacts*. New York: Longman Scientific and Technical.

Mill, R.C.; Morrison, A.M. (1999), *The Tourism System: An Introductory Text* (3rd Edition) Kendall/ Hunt Publishing Company, Dubuque, Iowa.

Pleumarom, A. (1999), "Tourism, globalization and sustainable development" in Third World Network Dossier for CSD 7, Third World Network, Malaysia.

Potter, R.B.; Lloyd-Evans, S. (Winter/Spring 1997/98), "Sun, fun & a rum deal: perspectives on development in the Commonwealth Caribbean" *Focus,* v. 44, no. 4, pp. 19-26.

Shurland, G. and Clark, A.F. (1998), "Tourism educational and training policies in developing countries: a case study of the Cayman Islands (Caribbean). *Journal of Third World Studies.,* v. 15 (1) p. 205-20.

3

Geography of Tourism

> "Traveling in the company of those we love is home in motion."
>
> —*Leigh Hunt*

'Geography of tourism' concentrates on the physical features, climate and landscape of different regions of the world—tourism generators and tourist destinations—both.

Here in this chapter, we have divided the global tourism continentwise followed by geography of tourism of important nations. Besides giving the vivid account of these, the information will be of importace for guidelines which will help the readers locating ideal tourist destinations.

Tourist-Generating Regions and Tourist Destinations

Geographers study the spatial expression of tourism as a human activity, focusing on tourist-generating and tourist-receiving areas, and the link between the two. The study can be taken at a variety of scales, ranging from the distribution of climate-zones in the world, through the regional assessment of tourist resources to local landscapes, resorts, etc.

From the geographical point of view, tourism has three main components:

(i) Tourist generating areas which are the countries of origin of tourists.

(ii) The destination areas which are tourist-receiving countries,

(iii) The route area being travelled between the above

The tourist-generating-areas comprise the home of the tourists where they start their journeys and where they end it.

While tourist destinations-countries or regions—have features and climate which the generating areas may not have. For instance, the sunny beaches of Spain, Sri Lanka India and Thailand have a great attraction for the residents of Germany and Scandinavian countries where winters are harsh and bitter.

Tourist routes, which link the two areas, constitute a key element in the system. The efficiency shapes the flow and direction of the traffic, i.e., air, sea and land transportation, etc. The frequency of scheduled or charter air services shapes the traffic pattern. The inexpensive charter air services have made it possible for Europeans to travel- all the way to Sri Lanka or India on a price less than that of their trips to nearby crowded Mediterranean resorts despite longer distances. The frequency and efficiency of air services have turned the Atlantic almost into a ditch to be crossed in a matter of a few hours. Every few minutes, a plane takes off from either side of the Atlantic carrying thousands of people at an affordable price.

Tourism flows as a result of interaction between the two areas. The destination areas have a surplus of a commodity i.e., tourist attractions. The generating areas have a paucity of similar attractions. Tourism organisers convert those needs into demand by organising-packages.

The tourist flow does not occur randomly- There is a regular pattern in the movement and is influenced by a variety of 'Pull' and 'Push factors. Push factors depend on the stage of economic development in the generating markets - general level of affluence, prosperity and availability of disposable income. It also depends upon the number of holidays available to the people in the generating areas. The affluence provides them the means to induige in a holiday but the pressure of living in crowded urban areas 'pushes' them to take a holiday. Availability of frequent charter air services-to beach resorts of Asia have enabled coal miners and laborers in factories of Europe to take a two-week vacation on the sunny beaches of India and Sri Lanka.

On the other hand, 'Pull factor' includes accessibility of a destination and the relative costs. The Japanese, for instance, find it cheaper to-have a holiday in the American Island, Guam and Hawaii in, the Pacific than a, domestic holiday in their own country because of rising local costs. Appreciation of yen in relation to US dollar has helped the Japanese travel overseas. Half the foreign visitors to Hawaii are the Japanese.

Besides the above, marketing and advertising done by a tourist destination in a tourism-generating area also helps 'pull" visitors to that destination. Extensive promotion done by Mexico and Canada in the USA has pulled millions of Americans to these two countries. Americans aw-'bombarded' with television commercials telling, them how nice it is to travel to these two countries and how affordable.

Efforts have been made to explain the factors which govern the tourist flows, for instance- distance between the countries. On long distance the volume of traffic is smalL The shorter the distance the, larger the traffic. An example, USA and India-volume is small due to long distance. USA-Mexico volume is very large. Hong Kong-China—the volume is very, very, large. Shared cultural, ethnic and business ties make a difference in the volume of tourism. For instance, Great Britain is the tourist Mecca for Australians. So is UK for New Zealanders despite the long distance. A majority of immigrants to Australia and New Zealand have been from the United Kingdom and, they want to discover their roots.

The tourist flow can be better explained is offered by the Gravity, Model, based on Newton's Law of Gravity which implies.

(i) The larger the mass of 'pushing' and 'pulling' region, the greater is the flow between two regions. Examples: USA Europe/ USA-Canada. There are very close cultural and economic ties, which lead to massive flow of tourists between the two regions.

(ii) There is a restraining factor too, based on the distance between the two. Distance, time and cost will determine the volume of traffic. Examples: Despite New Zealanders' keenness to visit UK, the number may not be very large due to distance and cost. The other example is Fiji and India. Although Fiji Indians would love to visit India, not many can afford that because of distance. Half the population of Fiji is of Indian origin.

ASIA

Asia has been home to major civilisations and religions in the world—the civilisations of Mesopotamia, India and China. Each contributed a great deal to the uplift of mankind. The four major religions of the world—Hinduism, Buddhism, Christianity and Islam—took roots in Asia and spread to other parts of the world. The continent of Asia is vast and most complex. Almost one out of every two human beings on earth lives in Asia. It extends from the Holy Land-Israel-Jordan region in the west to Indonesia and the Philippines in the east. Both China and Japan are part of the Asian continent.

Asia can be broadly divided into four regions. Middle East from Israel to the Gulf States; South Asia—from Iran to India and Bangladesh; North East Asia-China, Japan, the two Koreas; and South-East Asia from Myanmar to Thailand, Indonesia and the Philippines.

From the angle of tourism Asia is the most exciting region in the world with varied climate, rich culture, fauna and flora, and diversity of its tourist attractions.

Beharain

The small Island State of Bahrain (area 669 sq kms) is also an oil producing state. It is an important stopover for inter-continental flights between Europe and the Far East. It has also become an entrepot and banking center for the region. The completion of Saudi-financed $ 1.2 billion 10-mile causeway linking the island of Bahrain with Saudi Arabia has created a weekend tourism industry.

Bahrain's main tourist attraction is ample supply of nightclubs, hotels, and liquor.

Egypt

The ancient land of Egypt is a famous tourist destination in the world. Tourist arrivals in 1995 were about 3.5 million, with tourist earnings exceeding US $ 3 billion. The arrivals have declined subsequently as Muslim fundamentalists targeted foreign visitors to hurt Egypt tourist industry. Egypt has twin tourist attractions—it has some of the most ancient archaeological sites like the Pyramids as well as a balmy climate which makes beach tourism a year-round business. During winter months, the Europeans come to Egypt in planeloads of charter aircrafts, and during summer the Arabs come to its coast around Alexandria in their cars, escaping the desert heat.

A major part of Egypt is a desert and a vast majority of the population lives in the narrow ribbon of cultivated land along the river Nile. Most tourists arrive by air into Cairo international airport. The country has over 60,000 hotel rooms, most of them in Cairo (capital) and tourist centers of Alexandria and Luxor. European visitors are being attracted to a number of new resorts areas appearing on the Red Sea coast, where private investors have opened seven tourist villages.

Iran (Persia)

To the north-east of the Arabian Peninsula lie the ancient countries of Iran (Persia) and Iraq. Iran is a larger country of 1.6 million sq. kms. It has one of the largest reserves of oil in the world, which earns the country US $ 10 billion annually. Iranians are not Arabs. They are of Aryan stock and speak Persian, which is one of the very advanced Aryan languages. Arabs and Iranians have often differed on religious and political matters. A majority of Arabs are Sunni Muslims while a majority of Iranians are Shias.

Before the Revolution, Iran (ancient Persia) attracted a very large number of tourists. But, the present fundamentalist approach of Iran to religion and politics has severely restricted tourism. It is opening up a little after the victory (in 1992) of political pragmatists who won a majority in the Parliament. Iran has enormous tourist potential with a long Persian Gulf coastline as well as its northern coast on the Caspian Sea. Inland, the historical cities of Isphan, Shiraz and capital Tehran are of great interest to visitors. Isphan, a former capital of Persia, is considered to be one of the most beautiful cities in the Middle East.

Israel

Israel, the homeland of the persecuted Jews from all over the world, attracts, visitors for several reasons. The most important reason is its culture. People come here to see not only the remains of an ancient civilisation but also to observe at close range a nation in the making. Israel is a small country-only 21,000 sq kms but a major political, military and economic power. India and Israel have come closer politically and economically.

Israel has varied tourist destinations. It includes the Dead Sea as well as some high mountains in the Galilee region. Along the Mediterranean coast, the Israelis have constructed a number of resorts, north of Tel Aviv. Eliot, Israel's outlet to the Red Sea has become a famous center for winter holidays. Facilities include skin-diving, water skiing and under-water photography.

Jerusalem, the new capital of Israel, is the most important tourist center of the country because of its ancient history while Tel Aviv, the former capital city, is now the commercial center. Haifa, an attractive city at the foot of Mount Carmel, is a port of call for cruise ships from USA and Europe, touching Israel.

Despite the Gulf War in, 1990, there were 2 million foreign visitors to Israel in 1995,57% of them came from Europe. A major source of tourism is the American Jews who visit their Holy Land frequently and in large numbers. Earnings from tourism exceed US $ 4.2 billion.

Jordan

The kingdom of Jordan is a much larger territory than Israel 100,000 sq kms compared to 21,000 sq. kms. The people are poor. Tourism is, therefore, important for Jordan.

Jordan's most important tourist attraction is Patra, the hidden city. It attracts 150,000 visitors annually. In good years Jordan has been receiving over one million tourists annually. Jordan is promoting the development of a new beach resort, Aquaba, on the Gulf of Aquaba. Interestingly, Jordan has only 24 kms of coastline.

Lebanon

Lebanon is a small mountainous country with a population of about 3 million. In the sixties, Beirut was the financial center of the Arab world with a thriving economy.

In the sixties, Lebanon was the entertainment center of the Arab world, attracting thousands of visitors. The civil war between the Muslim and the Christian half of the population spurred by their Arab neighbors has ruined the country economically and politically. It has been under frequent raids from Israel, as their government believes that Palestinian and other fundamentalist Muslim terrorist organisations are sheltered here. But, things are looking up and a US $ 5 billion redevelopment programme for the devastated capital, Beirut, is progressing.

Saudi Arabia

The Arabian Peninsula stretches between the Red Sea and the Persian Gulf (2,000 kms) south of Syria and Iraq. It is dominated by Saudi Arabia, a. large country, with an area of 2 million sq kms—over half the size of the entire Europe. Most of the region is hot, and is dry desert. But, the entire peninsula is blessed with tremendous resources of oil. It is an absolute monarchy with no formal constitution. Its capital is Riyadh. The region was inhabited by nomadic tribes till oil was discovered and these countries became economically and strategically important to the world. Modern cities have appeared where none existed. Some 35,000 kms of modern highways link major towns and cities. A modern telephone system provides over one million telephones. Electricity and fresh water have been brought to the remotest hamlets of the kingdom.

Conventionally, Saudi Arabia does not encourage tourism, and tourist visas are seldom issued for fear of the Western culture influencing Islam. But, business traffic is welcome. A very large number of foreign expatriate workers live and work in the Saudi kingdom to keep things moving.

Around 2 million Muslim pilgrims come each year to sacred Mecca for Haj, half of them foreigners. Jeddah is the principal airport where pilgrims land.

Syria

Syria, another Arab nation, has an area of 185,000 sq. kms. The country has great tourist potential but conflicts of the Arab world have not allowed the country to achieve much success in the field of tourism. The capital, Damascus, claims to be the oldest inhabited city in the world with heritage going back to 7,000 years.

Dominating the old city is the Ummayad mosque, which was once a Christian cathedral and the place where the famous saint John, the Baptist, was buried. Outside Damascus are hundreds of historical sites from the Classical Hellenistic and Roman periods. The western part of Syria is littered with castles and watch-towers guarding the passes through the mountains.

Syria has a good network of roads making it easy for travellers to reach these historical sites. Syria offers beach resorts on the Mediterranean, north of Lattakia. It has mountain resorts at Kasab and archaeological sites in the Euphrates valley. Syria has good hotels and other accommodation facilities. The bulk of its visitors come from neighboring Arab countries. In 1995, international arrivals were 1.6 million. The future of tourism in Syria will depend on the political environments in the Middle East.

United Arab Emirates

The country known as the United Arab Republic (UAR) consists of seven autonomous Emirates in the Persian Gulf: Abu Dhabi, Dubai, Sharjah, Umm-al-Qaiwain, Ajman, Fujairah and Ras-al-Khairnah. Of the seven Emirates, only two—Abu Dabhi and Dubai are active in tourism promotion. Both have splendid hotels and excellent facilities for duty-free shopping. Many of the world's leading airlines serve the Emirates, bringing business travellers and tourists. Chartered aircrafts visit Dubai to take advantage of its duty-free shopping facilities. No tax is levied in the Emirates. Oil is adequate to take care of the government expenditure.

Islamic restrictions on serving alcohol have been liberalised for tourists staying in hotels. Both men and women can use the same beach and women are also allowed to drive, which is not allowed in Saudi Arabia. The tourist season is from October to April and a majority of the visitors are from Europe.

INDIAN SUBCONTINENT AND SOUTH ASIA

The Indian subcontinent is separated from the rest of Asia by high mountain barriers—the Himalayas-in the North. On the other three sides, it is protected by the Indian Ocean, the Arabian Sea and the Bay of Bengal. Till August 15,1947, the entire 'subcontinent, except Afghanistan, was under British occupation.

Afghanistan

Afghanistan, a landlocked country north of Pakistan, is at present involved in a bloody civil war. In last 15-20 years, Kabul, the capital of Afghanistan, was a favourite stopover for Europeans traveling to India via the Asian Highway. Tourism does not have much chance in Afghanistan in the near future.

Bhutan

The tiny kingdom of Bhutan in the Himalayas (area 44,600 sq kms) is a peaceful and quiet destination. Although the kingdom has reasonably good accommodation, it limits its tourism by pricing group tours very high-US $ 150 to 200 per day. The Bhutanese government would not like its peopje to change their lifestyle, imitating the foreigners. So, it limits tourism—not more than 5,000 in a year. Dragon Air is their national airline which links the capital, Thimpu, with India and some neighboring countries like Thailand; Indians can visit Bhutan without a visa.

India

With a switchover to market economy, Indian economy

has undergone dynamic changes. With a population over the billion people and an area of 3,287,263 sq kms, India had not experienced global competition due to its regulated market economy. The Domestic tourism is booming in India. Inbound tourism, though not very impressive considering the size of the country was in excess of 2.3 million in 1996. Foreign exchange earnings were estimated to be US $ 2.7 billion.

Maldives

To the south-west of Sri Lanka, lie hundreds of tiny coral islands to make up the Maldives. Some 50-resort hotels have been built on different islands. It is an interesting country with its airport on one island and its capital Male on the other. Visitors are transferred from airport to hotel by boats. Male is nowhere wider than one kilometer. Germans, Italians and Scandinavians patronise this country because of its superb under-water wildlife and the easy lifestyle of the local inhabitants.

Nepal

The Himalayan kingdom of Nepal remained closed to foreign visitors till 1950 when it was opened to tourism. It contains eight of the world's highest peaks including Mount Everest and Annapurna. The number of arrivals in 1995 was 3,50,000, one third of whom were Europeans, followed by one-fourth Indians. The Japanese and Americans also had a fair representation. Leading airlines like Lufthansa, British Airways, Thai International and Indian Airlines connect Nepal with the rest of the world. Mountaineering and trekking are the prime attractions. Some gambling casinos in capital Kathmandu provide a diversion. Kathmandu Valley has a problem of acute pollution—a capital built for 40,000 people now hosts 700,000. In, the sub-tropical foothills lies the Tiger Tops Wildlife Reserve. Cultural attractions are in the Kathmandu Valley. Tourism is Nepal's number one export, earning US $ 175 million in 1996.

Pakistan

Pakistan is relatively a poor country. Literary rate is only 35%—females less than 15%. Its economy depends to a great extent on remittances sent home by Pakistanis employed in the Middle East. Ancient cities, forts and gardens are the principal tourist attractions of Pakistan, besides the northern mountains in the Pakistan-held part of the State of Jammu and Kashmir. Not many tourists come to Pakistan—(approximately 500,000 in 1995-out of which 30% are from India who corne to see their relatives. Foreign exchange earnings exceeded US $ 125 million. Pakistan does not appear to make any serious efforts to promote tourism; it has no tourist office overseas. There are Islamic restrictions on serving of alcoholic drinks in hotels.

Sri Lanka

Sri Lanka, the golden island nation, is a famous destination for a beach holiday. Plane-loads of tourists from European countries arrive at the Colombo International airport almost daily during European winter. Apart from beach resorts, the country is rich in cultural resources. It has ancient Buddhist temples and monuments. It has abundant wildlife and a warm sea. Sri Lanka was receiving over 400,000 visitors annually in the early nineties.

SOUTH-EAST ASIA

The region beyond India, from Burma in- the east and the Philippines and Indonesia in th6 west, is called South-East Asia. But the region to the north-east of India, which includes China, Hong Kong, Japan and the two Koreas, is often termed as Northeast Asia. Looking from India, we will call them North Asia and East Asia. The culture of the entire region is a good mix of China and India. Indian culture influenced China when Buddhists traveled through Tibet and Indian scholars went to China to propagates the religion.

The Indian cultural influence is particularly visible in Myanmar, Laos, Vietnam, Cambodia and Indonesia where it has influenced religion, art and architecture of these nations. The Indonesian island of Bali is still inhabited by majority Hindu population who chant the ancient Sanskrit hymns better than the Hindus of India. In this region, rising incomes have produced the fastest growing travel market in the world for the airlines; The Pacific routes have not only become the fastest growing but also the most profitable.

International and domestic both tourism are booming. Young people are especially important to this area's travel industry. In the labor markets of Japan, South Korea, and Taiwan, wages of the workers have soared. Young people live with their parents and they have enough disposable income to travel.

NORTH-EAST ASIA

North-East Asia includes many different and contrasting areas. There is the high energy and dynamic Hong Kong, still a British colony till 1997 when it returns to Chinese control. Also, Macau, the tiny Portuguese colony on the mainland of China; returns to China in 1999, 2 years after Hong Kong. Taiwan, another dynamic nation, is one of the new Asian tigers because of its booming economy and exports.

China

China People's Republic (PR) was not open to tourists till 1981. Visitors could come to China only by invitation. Now visas are generously granted and the government is making serious efforts to boost tourism and attract foreign investment for hotel construction. China, a country of over 1.2 billion people and an area of 9,600,000 sq kms. Is a great tourist draw, especially as it remained closed to tourism for several decades. It is the third largest country in the world after Russia and Canada. China has doubled its standard of living in a few years. The lifespan of an average Chinese has reached 70 years, compared to 60 in India.

In order to, improve the tourism industry, the government has relaxed control of its tourism by the state-owned company The National Airlines has been split into several regional airlines to give competition a chance. A venture has been set up with McDonnell Douglas Aircraft Company to produce jetliners in China-estimated cost -US $ 12 billion. China has about 2,000 tourist hotels with a capacity -of over 300,000 rooms. Beijing has 25,000 Western-style rooms and Shanghai another 25,000. China, being a vast country, has a tremendous variety of climate. North China is cold with barren landscape. The China capital Beijing contains the, former Imperial Palace. The Great Lake of China and the ancient capital Xian are only 50 kms from Bejing and connected by rail.

In South China, the scenery is luxuriant and the climate warm and humid. The gorges of the Yangtze River near Ichong and the Karst mountains, around Guilin are particularly impressive. The great ports of Shanghai and Gwangdzhou (Canton) are important centers of business and trade. Western China is also now open to visitors. Lhasa, the capital of Tibet, is famous with Western visitors. It is linked by Royal Nepal Airlines from Kathandu by air. China has now become a major tourist destination, attracting about 35 million foreign visitors in 2001.

Hongkong

Hong Kong because a small city is not only a major tourist destination in its own rights but is also one of the principal entry points for visitors to China'. It has an area of 1,034 sq kms has topped the 11 million arrivals mark in 1996. Its receipts, from tourism exceed US $ 6 billion. Many visitors to South-East Asia start their journey from the many visitors region of Hong Kong, which is one of the most highly developed cities in Asia in business, commerce and communications. It is also one of the busiest airports of the entire region. A new airport is now under construction. Hong Kong has no unemployment at all.

With a booming economy, Hong Kong has also become an important source of outbound tourism. Its citizens take about three million overseas trips annually.

Japan

Japan is a leading industrial nation in the world. With an economy largely based on foreign trade, during the many many decades, it has transformed itself into an economic superpower. US and Japan together produce 40% of the GNP of the whole world. Japan's 120 million hard-working people live in a relatively small area of only 370,000 sq kms with a density of 327 per sq kms compared to 250 in Great Britain. The situation becomes more acute when we realise that 80% of land in Japan is mountainous and geologically unstable. Japan consists of four main islands: Honshu, Hokkaido, Kyushu and Shikoku. There is one more island, Okinawa, 2,000 kms to the south enjoying the sub-tropical climate. The west coast of Honshu, has continental climate, becoming even more severe in winter from blasts of cold Siberian air. A warm current influences the east coast. Hokkaido in the north also has a severe climate. More than three-quarter of the population of Japan live on Honshu Island with 15% of them living in urban centers like Tokyo, Yokohama, Nagoya and Osaka.

Japan kept a close watch on its economy till the mid-sixties, not allowing its people to travel overseas. When it found that it was piling up large reserves, it gradually allowed its people to travel. The Japanese have since become major travellers in the world, third after USA and Germany in terms of spending.

Japan's largest travel agency is Japan Travel Bureau (JTB)

with 300 offices in the country and an annual turnover of US$ 10 billion followed by Kinki Nippon with a sale of US $ 8.6 billion. Japan Airlines has been privatised and now shares its foreign routes with other private companies like All Nippon Airways (ANA) and Japan Air Services (JAS). Japanese tourism has benefited from the opening of the new US $ 10 billion Kansai Airport in Osaka. At Tokyo's Narita Airport, a second terminal has been opened. In addition, six new airports are under construction at various locations in Japan. Japan is now leading the world in developing tourist attractions that move outdoor recreation indoors. To relieve the public from spending long hours on crowded highways to reach beaches or ski resorts, the "Japanese have found "ways to mimic nature in huge warehouses. Indoor beach going or skiing are now available, rain or shine, day and night, 365 days a year.

The world's largest indoor ski center, which opened in July 1993 in a suburb of Tokyo, is cooled like a refrigerator.

The Japanese government is recommending, to its people that they spend more on foreign travel as a way of helping to overcome the embarrassment of running such large balance-of payments surpluses.

However, compared with the island nation of Great Britain, the Japanese are only modest travellers.

Japan's tourist resources are a unique mixture of traditional and modern. Despite problems of pollution due to industrialisation, Japan has done much to preserve its landscape and offers 26 national parks in the most scenic areas. The most important tourist centers attracting foreign visitors are Tokyo, Osaka, Nagasaki and Kyoto, the ancient capital of the country. The most scenic region is Kyoto, the inland sea between Honshu and Shikoku, studded with beautiful islands and many Buddhist temples. Sapporo in Hokkaido was the venue of Winter Olympics in 1992. Inbound traffic to Japan in 1994 was about 4 million.

Macau

The small Portuguese Colony of Macau (area 175 sq kms), can be reached from Hong Kong by hydrofoils in one hour. Its attractions are casinos for gambling and Portuguese ambience of cobbled streets and leafy boulevards peaceful contrast to the hectic life in Hong Kong.

North Korea

Communist North Korea (area 120,538 sq kms) has not yet come out of the shock of the collapse of the USSR. In recent years the country tried to break ice with its other half, South Korea, and countries like Japan, for foreign investments. But the problems of North Korea's nuclear control came in the way. In recent years. North Korea has been offering adventure tours to foreigners for rock-climbing, sunbathing, bird-watching and martial arts. At present, it receives over 100,000 visitors annually. North Koreans are building a 105-storey pyramidal Ryugyohg hotel in capital Pyongyang, the tallest hotel in the world.

South Korea

During the last 30 years of amazing growth, South Korea (area 98,868 sq kms) has changed from a nation of destitute peasants to a country of urban dwellers addicted to cars, electronic appliances and overseas travel. It is a case history of remarkable economic growth-another Asian tiger like Taiwan. Authoritarian government has since been replaced by a democratic regime. Its capital, Seoul, looks like Tokyo.

Outbound travel now exceeds 3 million. Average annual income in South Korea was US $ 12,000 in 1990. The number of inbound visitors in 1995 was 3.8 million. With growing traffic, a new international airlines, Asiana, has started operating from Korea giving competition to the national carrier, Korean Airlines.

Taiwan

Taiwan, an island nation, off the coast of China, regards itself as the legitimate successor to the Chinese government. But, mainland China considers it as its province, which should revert back. The hard-working Chinese of Taiwan have transformed their country into an Asian tiger through industrialisation and free trade, piling up huge trade surpluses. It is hard to believe that the poor Chinese of Taiwan spent US $ 8 billion on outbound travel in 1994, ranking ninth among the biggest spenders in the world. Its foreign exchange reserves now stand at US $ 88 billion-the biggest in the world, more than that of Japan.

EAST ASIA

Except for Thailand, all of the East Asian countries were under colonial rule till the World War-II—the British-ruled Singapore, Malaysia, Brunei and Myanmar, the French-ruled Indo-China which comprised Vietnam, Cambodia and Laos; the Dutch Indonesia and the Spanish-ruled Philippines, till the Americans replaced them in 1898. From the tourism angle, this region is one of the richest in the world but some parts of it have -not yet fully explored and exploited as tourist destinations.

The five countries of this region i.e., Singapore, Indonesia, the Philippines, Thailand and Malaysia—have joined hands to form ASEAN (Association of South East Asian Nations) which promotes economic cooperation among these countries. Tourism is part of their Agenda and they work together oprornote the entire region.

Indonesia

Indonesia is the fifth most populous nation in the world. The country consists of 13,667 islands. Some of its islands are better known than the country itself, like Bali, Java, Borneo and Sumatra. Indonesia extends over a distance of 5,000 kms from Sumatra in the West to Timor in the East.

In recent years, due to the discovery of oil and gas, Indonesia is doing very well economically. Export of oil contributes half of the country's export revenue. Foreign investors have been attracted to Indonesia due to its large manpower resources and low wages. Indonesia has been actively promoting tourism for several years and has received considerable success after the celebration of 'Visit Indonesia Year' in 1991. Encouraged by the success, the country has declared a 'Visit Indonesia' decade.

The main international gateway in Jakarta, the capital, and the national carrier, Garuda, link this vast fragmented nation. The country has a great variety of scenery, much of it volcanic, and is rich in cultural and historical monuments. On Java, the ancient temple of Barabudur is the largest Buddhist edifice in the world. Bali, the most famous holiday resort of Indonesia, is linked by air from Jakarta and from many other cities of Asia. Foreign airlines have been allowed to fly there direct. Sumatra offers interesting lakes and mountain scenery. Over 65% of visitors to Indonesia are from the Asian region.

Myanmar

Myanmar (Burma) is perhaps the most Buddhist country in East Asia. Surrounded by its two giant neighbors, India and China, and having common borders with Bangladesh, Laos and Thailand, this country has an area of 676,553 sq kms. Rangoon, the capital, has a new name: Yangon. Literally translated, its means End of Strife. This was also its old name two centuries ago just outside the capital a few kilometers from Sule Pagoda, in small villages shaded by tamarind and mango trees, life goes on as it did 200 years ago. There is a perennial rhythm dictated only by planting, growing and harvesting paddy. Othertourist cities of Myanmar are Pagan, once the city of "four million pagodas", even today having the remains of over 2,200 pagodas; Mandalay on the banks of Irrawadi River is the commercial and cultural capital of Myanmar. The Burmese government, presently under military rule, has not been encouraging tourism. But, since 1993, it has started issuing visas liberally.

Malaysia

Called 'true Asia' and situated in the middle of South East Asia, Malaysia has a total land area of 212,000 sq kms. Kuala Lumpur is the country's capital, and business and commercial center. Peninsular Malaysia accounts for 40% of land area and 86% of the population. The East Malaysian States of Sabah and Sarawak are separated from the peninsula by 640 kms of China Sea. The Malay and the indigenous tribes make over half the population while Chinese and Indians are less than half.

Malaysia is a major supplier of tin, palm oil and rubber. In recent years, if has been taking a lot of interest in promoting tourism to offset the problems caused by fluctuations in the commodity prices in the world markets. The year 1990 was celebrated as 'Visit Malaysia' year, which helped put the country on the tourist map of the world. Malaysia welcomed 7.2 million visitors in 1994-up from 3.5 million in 1992. Visitors' receipts were over a billion US dollars.

Malaysia is now encouraging charters to its resort areas like Penang, which has been called the Pearl of the Orient. A 1-km-long Penang Bridge now links Penang Island to the peninsula.

Philippines

It is the only predominantly Catholic country in South-East Asia. English has remained the primary language of instructions since American rule. It is, therefore, easier for English-speaking visitors to enjoy their travel in this country.

It is a beautiful country with Latin charm. Manila, its capital, has excellent hotels and one of the best convention centers in Asia. Tourism development is in the hands of the Philippines Tourism Authority.

Singapore

This small city state of 7 million visitors in1996 has remarkably transformed itself from a swampy island, 130 kms from the equator, to the most modern, the cleanest and the most prosperous city of Asia. The average annual income of its citizens (US $ 10,000) is higher than that of several countries of Europe.

Total visitor-spending in Singapore in 1993 was US $ 5.2 billion-12th among the countries of the world, which earned most from tourism. Shopping accounted for 64% of the spending. Government has taken a lot of interest in promoting tourism through its highly efficient National Tourist Administrations called Singapore Tourist Promotion Board (STPB). It is financed mainly through taxes on hotels and restaurants, which are subsequently allocated to STPB as its budget for tourism promotion and development. Thailand

Thailand

Thailand is East Asia's success story in tourism as well as fast economic development. Many observers believe that Thailand will soon become the fifth economic tiger, of Asia following the footsteps of Hong Kong, Singapore, South Korea and Taiwan.

Thailand, a country of 58 million people, is described as a Land of Smiles where most citizens are cheerful and polite. Among its many attractions is the thai capital, Bangkok. It is the most visited city in the kingdom with some 50 international airlines bringing hordes of tourists every day about 7 million in 1996. Thailand earned over US $ 5 billion from tourism making it the top foreign exchange earner for the country. The city is described as the 'Venice of the East' because of its many canals. Thai culture-dance, music, cuisine and uninhibited night life attracts visitors who come from many parts of the world.

A two-hour drive from Bangkok leads to its most well developed beach resort, Pattaya, with excellent hotels and interesting night-life. Another beach resort has been developed at Phuket in recent years. Chlangmai is the famous mountain resort of Thailand, well linked with Bangkok by rail, road and air. Bangkok now suffers from problems of property. The capital roads are so crowded that it takes hours to travel from one place to another. The city is considered to be one of the most polluted in the world. Bangkok has an excellent airport capable of handling 16 million air travellers in a year.

Vietnam and Cambodia

Vietnam (capital Hanoi) is still recovering from the trauma of the Vietnamese War. Although the country welcomes foreign visitors, tourism is still limited due to inadequate infrastructure. Arrivals touched 750,000 mark in 1993. Demand far exceeds the supply because of the novelty of the country, which was able to withstand the might of America and its allies. In 1994, Vietnam announced its arrival targets for the year 2000—3 million.

Cambodia (capital Phnom Penh), has great tourist potential.

It is a country of about 10 million people. The Hindu influence is discernible everywhere. Cambodia's Buddhist temple Angkor Vat near the capital Phnom-Penh ranks among the world's greatest historical monuments. When peace returns to Cambodia, it will draw much larger number of visitors.

EUROPE

The continent of Europe is the world's principal destination for international tourism with its rich supply of natural resources and its wealth of cultural heritage. Western Europe alone currently accounts for well over half of all international tourist arrivals. The majority of these trips, at present, comprise visits made by Europeans themselves to countries other than their own. But, an economically significant segment consists of visitors from other continents. The visitors from outside Europe often consider Europe as a single destination and visit 2 to 5 countries in one trip. By 1994, some 300 million international tourist trips were made to or within Europe of a total of over more than 575 million worldwide.

Outbound travel from entire Europe in 1994 has been estimated at 340 million trips, despite recession. Out of this West Europeans took 201 million trips. A significant new trend from the point of view of Asian destinations is that Europeans are taking more long-haul holidays. It ranges from 25% in UK, 22% in Germany, 13% in France to 9% in Italy.

Charter airlines have played an important role in Europe's long-haul holiday market. The important charter destinations from Europe are Thailand, Sri Lanka, Malaysia and the Maldives, though India's Goa is also emerging as a significant destination.

Although Europe had tremendous edge in tourism in the recent past, it is facing competition from several other emerging destinations-many of them claiming unspoiled environments. Europe's share in world tourism has declined by 8% during the recent past from over 60% to 52%.

Two major trading blocks dominate economic activity in Europe. EEC-the European Economic Community-consists of the following countries: Belgium, Luxembourg, Denmark, France, Germany, Greece, Ireland, Italy, the Netherlands, Portugal, Spain and the United Kingdom - the "Europe of 12".

The economic and political destiny of these countries is firmly linked, though they are experiencing problems relating to currency, national pride and egos.

The second trading block is the European Free Trade Association (EFTA). It is EC's major trading partner and comprises Austria, Norway, Iceland, Finland, Switzerland and Sweden.

In October 1991, the EFTA countries joined hands with the ECC to create the European Economic Area, a common market of 380 million people.

Since World War-II, the Iron Curtain had divided Europe into two ideologically competing blocks: East and West.

The curtain fell with the unification of Germany in 1989. As the new free nations emerged in Eastern Europe, the mighty erstwhile USSR transformed itself into the Commonwealth of Independent Nations (CIS) with an uncertain future. Europe's political map was redraw with the common currency 'Euro'. Europe possess great cultural heritage and some of its monuments attract millions of people every year from all other the world. The following is a list of some cultural. heritages, which attract more than one million visitors annually:

	Cultural Heritages	*Million*
1.	The Eiffel Tower, Paris	3.6
2.	The British Museum, London	3.0
3.	The Pompido Heritages Centre, Paris	7.9
4.	The Louvre, Paris	4.0
5.	The Chateau of Versailles, Paris	2.6
6.	The Prado, Madrid	1.2
7.	Charlottenbury Museums, Berlin	2.2
8.	The Tower of London	2.2
9.	The Rembrandt Museum, Amsterdam	1.1
10.	The Uffizi, Florence	1.2
11.	The Science Museum, London	2.4

12.	The Tale Gate, London	1.1
13.	The National Gallery, London	2.8
14.	Les Invalides, Paris	1.4

Source: Le Tourisme Dans La Communaute Europeanne, 2002.

Now coming tourist geography of each country in Europe, hre we are giving brief note thereon.

Denmark

Denmark, with an area of 93,069 sq kms, is the smallest but one of the most famous tourist destination of the area. Its capital, Copenhagen, has a strategic location between the North- Sea and the Baltic. It is also a major entrepot handling a large volume of international cargo. Its airport, Kastrup, is the busiest in Scandinavia. Greenland, the world's largest island, forms part of the kingdom of Denmark.

Finland

The Republic of Finland, a Baltic state, is a vast country 377,000 sq kms. Its more than 20,000 lakes and rivers are major tourist attractions. Lakes, and rivers take 10% of their country's surface area. Sixty% of Finland is under forest cover. The country, once formed part of the Russian Empire, became independent on December 6,1917. Finland is Europe's last wilderness area and has-capitalised on its emergence as a new eco-tourism destination. Other holiday opportunities include cross-country skiing, hiking, climbing, sailing and spa-tourism.

Finns are not great travellers to foreign lands. No wonder, Finland is the only country in Scandinavia with a favourable balance in its tourism account. Its capital, Helsinki, is air-linked to all parts of Europe.

Great Britain

The British can certainly lay claim to 'inventing' modern

holidays, with Thomas Cook being the father of modern tourism who are pioneers in the field of organised travel.

Great Britain, a nation of over 58 million, area 244,066 kms, is both a tourist-generating country as well as a famous tourist destination. Ninety-two per cent of its population lives in urban areas. Its outbound tourism far exceeds the inbound, virtually double—35 million against 19 million in 1993. The Britons love inclusive tours. In 1993, some 10 million Britons took inclusive overseas tours.

Holiday propensity is very high in the United Kingdom-60% of the British population take a holiday at least once in a year, domestic or international.

Among visitors to Great Britain, 60% arrived by air and 40% by sea. Within the British Isles, the distribution of overseas tourists is concentrated in England, especially in London. Half of them visit UK during the third quarter of the year.

British economy is suffering from deep recession, unemployment is high. In economic terms, it is only ahead of Portugal and Greece whil Germany, France and Italy are ahead of it. More recently the entire Europe has emerged as one entity while Britain is marginalised in many respects.

Iceland

Despite its vast area of 103,000 sq kms, Iceland has a small population. Less than 1% of the surface area is cultivable. Iceland's active volcanic activity causes hot springs and geysers. The abundant geothermal energy is harnessed to heat swimming pools, buildings and greenhouses. There are over 200 volcanoes in the country with periodic eruptions. Iceland is an island close to the Arctic Circle in North Atlantic. The warm Gulf Stream makes its winter mild. During short cool summers, there is perpetual daylight for several weeks, making it an Island of the Midnight Sun. Although Iceland has been trying to promote inbound tourism, annual arrivals in 1994 were recirded less than 75,000.

The national carrier, Iceland Air, and Scandinavian Airlines System (SAS) connect Iceland's international airport, Keflavik, with the rest of Europe. Its airport, built on rolling hills surrounded by mountains, is often used as a stopover on the Atlantic flights. The 9,000 kms of road network provides easy movement within the country.

Ireland

The small Republic of Ireland, or Ire for short-population with area 70,280 kms is a famous tourist destination for the neighboring Britons who comprise 70% of its visitors. Total number of overseas visitors in 1994 was about 4 million, more than the population of Ireland. Its capital Dublin contains one-third of the total population of the country.

The British-ruled Northern Ireland (Ulster), with its capital Balfast, offers attractive scenery, fishing and water sports.

On the political field, when Ireland became independent of Britain in 1932, Northern Ireland (Ulster) opted to remain with the United Kingdom. Since then Irish Catholics have been fighting against the Protestants who form a majority in North Ireland.

Norway

A remarkably elongated country, Norway extends 2,000 km from Kristians and to the North Cape. It has an area of 324,000 sq kms. Although the population is small, 75% of them take one holiday in a year and about 50% of them to foreign countries.

Norway contains some of the most spectacular sceneries in Scandinavia and is, therefore, an important tourist destination. Oslo, the capital, is served by two airports which provide connections to all parts of Europe. Tourists can also use the country's excellent coastal shipping services to the,"Land of the Midnight Sun" beyond the Arctic Circle as far as the Russian border. It is called the "Land of the Midnight Sun" because the sun does not set from the middle of May until the end of July nor does it rise above the horizon from the end of November to the end of January.

Scandinavia

Scandinavia is a peninsula comprising Norway and Sweden. Further can be included Denmark, Finland and Iceland. The region has similar cultural heritage. Scandinavian countries have achieved tremendous economic prosperity during the current century.

The Scandinavia accounts for most important tourist resources due to: uncrowned, unpolluted countryside, the spectacular scenery of mountain and coastal regions, islands and holiday villages, and typical Scandinavian culture.

Barring Denmark and the Atlantic coastlands of Norway, the region experiences severe cold winters with long hours of darkness, icy winds and frozen seas. In summer, the region, warms up a little with nearly 2,100 sunshine hours in a year. Together, these countries mainly concentrated in the southern region.

They received over ten million visitors in 1993—half of them to Denmark alone. Germany is the most important tourist generating market for Scandinavia.

Sweden

Sweden is the largest Scandinavian country with an area of 450,000 sq kms. In terms of area, it is the fourth largest country in Europe. Most Swedes live in urban areas. Its economy is good. Swedes have the highest propensity in holiday making-90% of those between 16 and 65 take a holiday. Thirty per cent of Swedish holidays are to other Scandinavian countries, 4% to other European destinations. Some 7,000 Swedes travel annually to India.

Stockholm, the capital city, is a well planned, beautiful, and picturesque modern city. Swedish tourist resources include its large, unspoiled forests and lakes, beautiful countryside setting, varied coastline, their folk customs and dances. The central lake region contains many lakes; the two largest ones, Venner and Veter, are linked by a 190-km-long Gota Canal the southern Baltic coast of Sweden enjoys exceptionally long sunshine hours.

Facing the North Sea is the 'golden coast'-1,400 kms of white midnight sun coast along the Gulf of Bothnia. It is also the gateway to Lapland-the largest unspoiled wilderness in Europe. Sweden is a constitutional monarchy.

CENTRAL EUROPE

Apart from the short German coast, Austria, Switzerland and Germany are three landlocked countries. Physically the region can be divided into three parts: the coastal lowlands, the central uplands and the Alps. The combined population of the three countries is 95 million with highly developed economies and high standards of living. The demand for tourism and recreation is equally high. Germany is the second largest generator of international tourism after U.S.A. While Austria and Switzerland are the major international tourist destinations. All the three countries have a federal structure with considerable devolution of power to the states in Germany, provinces in Austria and the cantons in Switzerland.

Austria

Tourism has emerged as Austria's major industry. Foreign tourists contribute about 20% to the country's gross national product. The Republic of Austria's tourist resources are immense. It contains 35% of the Alpine area compared to only 15% in Switzerland. About 15-16 million visitors arrive in Austria every year. The seasonally element is not so significant-forty% of the visitors come to Austria during winter to enjoy skiing and other winter sports. Two-thirds of visitors to Austria come from the neighboring Germany, followed by the Netherlands and U.K. The country has over one million beds to accommodate the visitors. Most visitors come to Austria by car using its excellent 18,000 kms highway network.

Recently, Austria has developed convention facilities in its major towns like the capital Vienna, Linz, Salzburg, Innsbruck, etc., attracting business travellers. Vienna, the former capital of the great Hapsburg Europe and a port on the Danube, attracts over 5 million visitors annually. Salzburg is known for its castles, cathedrals, baroque architecture and an International Music Festival.

Deutschland

Despite its teething troubles due to its merger with the erstwhile East Germany, the unified State of Federal Republic of Germany is the largest and the richest State in Europe. It maintains a high profile of being the biggest producer of international tourism—62 million trips in 1994. The Germans spent 37 billion US dollars on foreign, travels in the same year. Foreign visitors to Germany spent only 11 billion US dollars.

Unlike most European countries, Germany is not dominated by one capital city, though Berlin, the new political capital, undoubtedly is of great historical interest. Among other German towns, Bonn, the erstwhile federal capital, is relatively small. In the north, Hamburg is Germany's major port, also famous for its uninhibited night-life. Hanover is known for its Trade Fairs, Dusseldorf is the center of Ruhr industrial region while Frankfurt is the commercial and banking capital. Of the former East Germany, major attractions are East Berlin, Dresden and a cruise on the Elbe River.

Switzerland

Switzerland is a very famous tourist destination -10 million visitors annually spending over seven billion US dollars. Tourist earnings make 8% of the gross national product of the country. Tourism provides jobs to 3,60,000 people.

The Swiss are one of the world's great holiday lovers - 75% of the population take a holiday for at least 4 nights in a year. The favoured destinations of Swiss outbound travellers are Italy and France. Over 15,000 Swiss visit India annually despite its small population of about 7 million.

Switzerland is a confederation with an area of 41,293 sq kms. Its capital is Berne. The Alps Mountains cover over 60% of, the land area. Private cars dominate the 66,000 kms of its road network. The Swiss government collects enormous sums of money from toll taxes on roads. Swiss National Railways operate 1,400 kms long excellent railway network and their punctuality can be checked with the tick of this clock. During the past one century, Switzerland has transformed itself from a poor country subsisting on agriculture and handicrafts into one of the wealthiest countries of Western Europe. Much of the Swiss success can be attributed to tourism and the country's ability to offer to the world a paradise from political and, financial storms that engulf the world from time to time. Geneva and Zurich are two major financial and business centers where dictators, prime ministers and smugglers keep their money. In 1993, it offered another tourist attraction-by legalising casinos.

THE BENELUX COUNTRIES

The Benelux countries comprise the Netherlands, Belgium and Luxembourg. The region can be divided into 3 parts—the low-lands of the coast, the intermediate plateau zone and the uplands. The climate is not very favourable to tourism.

The Benelux countries were joined by a customs union in 1947 and they are now closely integrated. Demand for tourism and recreation is high. With a combined population about 25 million and a total area of 74,000 sq kms the Benelux countries are not only some of the smallest in Europe but also the most densely populated.

Belgium

Area: 30,573 sq kms. Belgium is an important generator of holidays to foreign countries; over 60% of holidays are taken abroad primarily within Europe. Belgium is culturally divided between the Dutch-speaking Flemings and the French-speaking Walloos of the south.

Belgium's appeal to tourists is derived from its astonishingly diverse cultural scene. For centuries, this region of Europe has been gathering the cultures left by the invaders—Romans, French, Spanish, Austrians, Dutch and Germans. Brussels, the capital of Belgium, is the home-base of the European Economic Community (EEC). On the crossroad of the common market, this nation of ten million has attracted wealth and investment out of all proportions to its modest size. With over 10,000 hotel rooms, Brussels receives 3 million foreign visitors annually—90% on business trips. Other, important areas of Belgium are the art city of Flanders, Bruges-a well preserved medieval city with canals, picturesque bridges, museums and churches, and Antwerp which is the business travel center.

Cyprus

Cyprus is divided between the Republic of Cyprus in the south and the Turkish Republic of Northern Cyprus. The latter is not yet internationally recognised. Greek Cypriots have successfully developed tourism in their part of the country - foreign arrivals in 1995 were 2.5 million.

France

Area: 547,026 sq. kms. France by far is one of the most famous tourist destinations in the world with over 60 million visitor arrivals in 1995—15 million more than USA which ranked third. Tourist earnings amounted to US $ 27 billion. France is also a major tourist-generating country. The French took 16.6 million international trips in 1995 spending US $ 14 billion in foreign countries.

The government, therefore, is taking steps to promote tourism more aggressively. The cabinet has a minister responsible exclusively for tourism. He is called the Secretary of State for Tourism and his ministry is called the Ministry of Free Time. France has about 2,200 travel agents and tour operators. Of these 18% specialise in inbound travel.

The fact that France is one of the world's most famous tourist destinations is not surprising. Within its half million sq km area-, a vast diversity of tourist resources are scattered. These range from historical and cultural attractions of Paris or the Loire Chateaux, to Mediterranean resorts of Nice, Cannes and St. Tropez or winter sports centers of the Alps and the Pyrenees. Of course, the famous French cuisine is another attraction. France has climatic advantages. Here, summer sunshine hours are at their highest and continue through autumn and winter to provide a prolonged tourist season.

The renowned beautiful city, Paris, the French capital, receives over 10 million visitors annually. Apart from its own attractions, it offers excursions to nearby Versailles and Fontainebleau, or the historic towns of Orleans, Chartres, of Beauvais.. Paris has another man-made attraction-US $ 4 billion Euro Disney extending over an area of 4,800 acres on the lines of the American Disneyland.

Gibraltar

The British crown colony, the Rock of Gibraltar, commands the entrance to the Mediterranean. It towers 400 meters over the harbour with the town on its western side. It is only 6.5 sq kms in area and has a population about 25,000. It has a strategic location. Spain claims the Rock and had, therefore, closed its border. The border was re-opened recently. It has enabled people to go to Spain from Gibraltar and vice versa. Excursions to Morocco are possible from the Rock of Gibraltar using ferry links.

Greece

Greece, a nation of 2,000 islands, is the birthplace of ancient Western civilisations. Travellers through all ages have been fascinated by its philosophy, art, literature and legends. Greece is on the Mediterranean sea and occupies the southern end of the Balkan peninsula.

Most holiday visitors fly into Athens, the capital, Thessaloniki in the north or into the airports of the islands of Corfu, Rhodes, Crete, Mykonos, Zakynthos, Kafalonia and Kos. Greeks have excellent shipping services linking coastal towns. Their national carrier, Olympic, has frequent domestic and international flights.

Holland

Area: 41,181 sq kms. It was once a major colonial power with its empire extending to Indonesia. It is a constitutional monarchy. The Dutch, the people of the Netherlands, have one of the highest holiday propensities in Europe. Most international tourism is confined, to the neighboring countries. The Dutch like to travel to India. In 1994, there were 31,000 Dutch visitors to India. The Netherlands received some 5 million foreign visitors in 1993, though their stay was only for one or two days. Foreign exchange earnings exceed US$ 4 billion.

Tourists can enter the Netherlands through Schiphol, Amsterdam's international airport. KLM, the country's national airline, has been promoting Amsterdam as a gateway to Europe by offering a free overnight stay to all those who travel to Europe via Amsterdam and with KLM. It ranks high among the world's top tourist cities. It is famous for its canals, art galleries and uninhibited night-life. Other important tourist centers are the Hague, the political capital, and Rotterdam, Netherlands's major port to the mouth of the Rhine.

Much of the Netherlands and the north-west of Belgium comprise flat plains and polder lands reclaimed from the sea. The average height is 10 meters above sea level. The story of reclamation and constant battle against the sea is proudly told to visitors in exhibitions and museums of the country. The Dutch coast is well protected against inundation by sea but dunes are vulnerable to tourist pressure.

Italy

Italy has been a focal point for international tourism since the Victorian age and has a well-established tourist industry. In 1995, it attracted 30 million foreign visitors and the receipts from tourism exceeded US $ 27 billion-as much as that of Spain.

The 300,000 sq. km. peninsula of Italy is separated from Northern Europe by the high mountain barriers of the Alps. It has a long coastline facing both the Adriatic and Western Mediterranean.

Italy was a tourist country even in the Roman times. With Renaissance, Italy again became the center of European civilisation. At that time, the country was politically divided into several states. Venice, Florence and Genoa had grown rich on the profits of banking and trade. Their rulers used this enormous wealth to decorate churches, palaces and public buildings with art treasures, which have become the mainstay of Italian tourism.

Even today a lot of people are drawn to Italy because of its rich culture and religious appeal as the home of the Pope. Till the sixties of the last century, Italy was the most visited tourist destination in Europe before France, Spain and even USA overtook it. The Italians themselves are great travellers. Their economy has done well and today it is next only to Germany in Europe. They spent US $ 13 billion on foreign travel in 1993, ranking fifth in the world. The Italians have a soft comer for India. In 1994, their arrivals in India exceeded 55,000. The Italians were pioneers in building highways (Autostradas) in Europe—the first one was built in as early as 1925. There are 6,000 kms of autostradas in Italy and users pay toll. The Italian State Railways run an efficient railway system. The country is served by hotels, inns of all grades. Major luxury hotels have been built in principal tourist cities of Rome, Venice and Florence. The Italian Alps are becoming increasingly famous for winter sports and adventure tourism. In southern Italy, the best-known holiday region is around the Gulf of Naples, including Sorrento and Islands of Capri and Ischia. The island of Sicily has a great deal to offer with good beaches and cultural attractions.

Lexumbourg

Area: 2580 sq. kms. The tiny Grand Dutchy of Luxembourg is Belgium's partner in a monetary and commercial union. They use the same currency. It is home to hordes of Eurocrats working for the European Economic Community (EEC) and foreign banks. Over 27% of the resident population of the country is foreign—the highest in the world. About 30,000 Belgians, French and Germans cross the border every day to work in the Grand Dutchy of Luxembourg. This tiny State of Europe has one of the highest standards of living in the world with one of the lowest crime rates. Tourists who stay fora couple of days in Luxembourg are in a position to have breakfast in France, lunch in Belgium and dinner in Germany before coming back to their hotel in Luxembourg. It's really exciting experience to everyone.

Malta

A group of islands (area 184 sq kms), Malta is an independent country with a very small population. Strategically located in central Mediterranean, it has a good coastline. A former British colony, it became free in 1964. Its capital, Valletta, is a fine national harbour. Despite its low profile as a tourist country, about half a million international annually travellers visit Malta.

Portugal

Portugal with an area of 91,985 sq. kms., has long Atlantic coastline, Portugal's climate is milder and more humid. The landscape is greener than Spain. The Portuguese, a seafaring nation, built a vast empire in the 16th century. That is why Portuguese is spoken in Brazil, in some African countries and in small pockets of Asia. Goa in India was a Portuguese colony. Portugal has shown remarkable economic recovery since joining the European Economic Community (EEC). The new prosperity has caused imports to soar. Portugal imports half of its food, four-fifths of its energy, and most of its capital goods. Booming inbound tourist business receipts of US$ 16 billion in 1995 and massive foreign investments have kept the economy moving within manageable limits. The main tourist destinations for foreign visitors are Algrave, a region in the south; Lisbon, the capital; Oporto, and Madeira Island, located 700 kms west of Morocco. Madeira offers 15,000 beds. Lisbon has been called Europe's San Francisco. Its steep streets leading down to the waterfront are lined with ancient pastel-coloured homes with extensive tilework.

Spain

Spain with an area of 505,000 sq. kms. is contained in

the Iberian Peninsula, stretching 800 kms from north to south. Outside the Peninsula are the Balearic and Canary Islands as well as Ceuta and Melilla on the North African coast near Morocco. Spain has a distinct culture due to its relative isolation from the mainland of Europe. From the north, one can cross into Spain from France by rail and by road through the Pyrenees. In the south, Spain is separated only by a narrow stretch of water from North Africa and its Islamic culture.

Very few countries of the world have undergone more profound change in a single generation than Spain. Until the mid 1960s, Spain was one of the poorest countries in Western Europe, ruled by a dictator. Tourism and Spain's entry into the European Economic Community in 1986 have spurred economic growth, which has created its own social problems. Streets of the capital Madrid are crowded with new cars, and apartments are selling at very high prices. Imports have soared to an extent where tourism receipts can no longer make up for the trade deficit. The Spaniards are buying a million car every year crowding their roads. In 1992, Spain celebrated its 500th anniversary of discovery of America by Columbus.

Geographically, most tourist development is concentrated into a few coastal areas and on the outlying islands. The only other areas besides the coast where development has taken place are the capital Madrid and in the Pyrenees. The Spanish islands fall into two groups: the Balearics in Western Mediterranean, and the Canaries in the Atlantic. The Balearic Islands of Majorda, Canaries, Minorca and Ibiz are formed by limestone. Water, therefore, has to be obtained from wells and windmills—a characteristic feature of the landscape. Palma, the capital of Balearics, is one of the main seaports of the Mediterranean. Its airport handles the maximum holiday traffic to Spain. Uncontrolled resort development in Spain has caused environmental damages, exacerbated regional imbalance and affected Spanish lifestyle.

Turkey

Turkey has an area of 779,452 sq kms. On the crossroads of Asia and Europe, Turkey's tourism climbed to record 6 million visitors in 2002, with receipts at US $ 4.5 billion. Turkey is increasingly becoming famous tourist destination. The rapid increase of tourism in the eighties of the last century ignited a hotel boom, which has produced an over-supply of rooms in the Aegean and Mediterranean coastal resorts. Istanbul, the old Turkish capital, attracts one-third of the visitors from abroad.

EASTERN EUROPE

Before the demolition of the Berlin wall in 1989, Eastern Europe consisted of USSR, East Germany, Poland, Czechoslovakia (now two independent nations called Czech and Slovak), Hungary, Romania, Bulgaria and Albania. Together, they constituted what was called the Eastern Bloc. Yugoslavia, a non-aligned country, was not exactly in the Eastern Bloc' but was considered part of Eastern Europe.

After about 5 years of economic adjustments, there are signs of economic revival in some of the Eastern Bloc countries. Many new small businesses have come up in the private sector and some people now have money to travel and buy new cars. Poland, Czech, Slovak and Hungary have better prospects of-recovery than Bulgaria, Romania and Russia.

Following the break-up of the Soviet Empire, there are now 15 new Republics including the Russian Federation, three Baltic States and Georgia.

Albania

Albania, undoubtedly, is the poorest and least developed of the Eastern Bloc countries. It is a small country with an area 29,748 sq. kms., separated from the rest of Eastern Europe by Yugoslavia. Access is through infrequent air services to its capital Tirana as the land frontiers are closed. It became Europe's first Muslim state in December 1992.

Bulgaria

This tiny country of little over 9 million people and an area of 110,000 sq kms has transformed itself from a predominantly agricultural country to an industrial society in past decades. To boost tourism, legislation has been enacted to lower taxes and to give incentives to entrepreneurs building hotels.

Much of the country's tourist business is concentrated in a series of resorts along the western coast of Black Sea. The capital, Sophia, has excellent hotels-two in the Sheraton Group.

Czech & Slovak (Czecholovakia)

In 1993, Czech Republic and Slovak became two independent countries. The Czech capital is Prague and the capital of Slovak is Bratislava in the Eastern Bloc. Foreign investments are pouring in. Czech Republic attracted over 7 million visitors in 1995. Physically, Czech and Slovak Federal Republics are an elongated country and, like Hungary, it has' no coastline.

Hungary

Hungary (area 93,033 sq kms.) is perhaps the most Western-looking country in Eastern Europe with fine restaurants, theatres and, active nightlife in its capital, Budapest. Some of the leading hotel chains are represented in Budapest

In 1988, Hungary was the first country in Eastern Europe to host the annual convention of American Society of Travel Agents (ASTA) which brought 6,000 travel industry leaders from all parts of the world.

Hungary's prime tourist attraction is Budapest, formed from the twin cities of Buda (the old royal city on the hilly side) and Pest (the commercial center of the left bank of Danube). The second attraction is Lake Balaton, 27 kms in length. Beaches, modern hotels, campsites and. nature reserves fringe the lake. The third most important attraction is Hungary's 545 spas and health resorts, some of them in Budapest itself.

Poland

Poland's geography neatly delimits its tourist region. The coast is, by far, the most famous, followed by mountains and lakes. Poland has an extensive coastline, along the Baltic with good sandy beaches. Famous resorts are Miedzydroje and Sopot. The northern two-thirds of, Poland is a plain of glacial drift—a landscape of low hills and lakes which form an important tourist attraction.

Domestic tourism is supported by the state. International tourism appears to be booming with around 19 million people arriving in 2000, mostly from the neighboring countries to buy and sell goods. The old towns of Poland have rich architectural heritage, though many of them were destroyed during World War II. Some of them have been meticulously resorted, especially in Warsaw, the capital of the country. Warsaw has always been a great center of music and culture.

Romania

Of all the countries of Eastern Europe, Romania is finding it most difficult to adjust to the market economy. Under dictator Ceaucescu, the people of Romania were subjected to an austerity programme, which gave them the lowest standard of living in Eastern Europe. There was a severe shortage of heat, light and water during the winter months. But, Ceaucescu spent over US$ 1 billion to build a marble palace for himself which is three times as large as the Versailles Palace in France. It stands on a man-made hill, which opens on to a grand boulevard that is wider than the Champs Elysees in Paris. To make room for this boulevard, one-fourth of Bucharest, the capital, had to be razed. Black Sea resorts are the most famous tourist attractions of Romania, accounting for 75% of the bed capacity in the country.

Russia (USSR)

The new Russian Republic has a population of over 750 million and is still the largest state in the world in terms of area 7,075,000 sq. kms. It stretches across the continents of Europe and Asia. It has 75% of the total area of the former Soviet Union and 50% of its population. It has been promoting tourism even before the break-up of the USSR to earn hard currency. Russians love to travel, primarily domestically. In the former USSR, outbound travel was encouraged to friendly countries. India was one of the beneficiaries and annually received some 50 thousand Russian visitors. Now, again Russians are coming to India on special charter flights.

Russia has tremendous diversity of landscape, climate, ethnic cultures and the people. The foreign visitors travel to five main areas of the country. The most famous is the central part of European Russia which includes Kiev, Moscow and Leningrad. All three cities have historically served the national capital of Russia. Leningrad has since reverted to its old name of St. Petersburg, Moscow is the showpiece of Russia containing the Kremlin, the ancient inner city as well as many impressive modern buildings. The tourist circuit from Moscow includes the Byzantine churches of Suzdal and Yorosiall and cruises over river Volga to Ulyanovsk, the birthplace of Lenin. Moscow's nearest rival is St. Petersburg, the former capital of Peter the Great with its classical palaces and boulevards. The fine beaches of Estonia and Latvia on the Baltic can be visited from St. Petersburg. The second most important area for both domestic and international tourism is the Black Sea coast, especially of Grimea, which enjoys the Mediterranean sunshine. The main resorts are

Yalta and Sochi. To the east of Black Sea are the snowcapped Caucasus Mountains, which contain many spas and ski resorts. Siberia has been opened to foreign tourists in recent years.

Russia's Aeroflot, the world's largest airline, has over 3,000 planes and before its break-up, it carried some 1,000 million passengefs in a year. Now, it has split up into a number of, smaller national airlines.

THE AMERICAS

The United States and Canada together constitute what is geographically termed as North America, one of the world's most exciting tourism markets. Both the countries are nations of immigrants with common bonds of English language and similar European ways of life. The area of the two countries is so large that it accommodates six time zones and a rich diversity of climate, natural scenery and people from almost all stocks and all parts of the world. High Mountain chains, including the spectacular scenery of the Rockies and Sierra Nevada, dominate the western part of North America. Near the eastern seaboard are the thickly forested Appalachians, lower in altitude than the Rockies. Between the two mountain-systems are the vast plains drained by great rivers like Mississippi and its tributaries in the south and St. Lawrence, Athabasca and Mackenzie in the north.

Bahamas & Bermuda

The Bahamas, a group of 700 islands off the Coast of Miami, is a small state. The island provides a good example of how tourism can help a country. The per capita income is US $ 7,300 which is higher than any country in Latin America except Bermuda. The majority of the people are involved in providing tourist services. Beside the beaches, casinos are the main attraction. The capital of the Bahamas is Nassau.

Bermuda has a population of about 60,000 and per capita income of US$ 22,000. Its capital is Hamilton.

In these oldest of, the British colonies, there is no personal income-tax and no tax on capital gains.

Canada

Canada is the world's second biggest country in area after Russia (area 9,976,000 sq kms) and has the-seventh largest economy. The distance from north to south is 4,800 kms. further than the distance between New York and Los Angeles. Most of its population lives along an east-west band about 250 kms from the US border. Canada is a federation comprising four provinces and two territories.

Canada's main tourist resources lie in its mountains, forests and lakes. The severity of the winter season is a major constraint on tourism. The sparse population means that tourist infrastructure is not available in 90% of Canada. Ski resorts have developed near the major population centers to meet the demand from domestic travellers. Summer offers a complete contrast and is very suitable for a wide range of outdoor activities: boating, canoeing, fishing and hunting.

In the early nineties of 20th century, Canada welcomed 16 million foreign visitors annually while the number of Canadians traveling abroad was 22 million-19 million of them going, to USA. Almost every Canadian travels internationally every year. There are no visa barriers between US and Canada.

The Trans-Canada Highway from St. Johns in New Found land to Vancouver links most of the major cities of Canada. Just across the Great Lakes from the US sits the province of Ontario-the country's financial and industrial nerve center, as well as the home of the national capital, Ottawa. This province is larger than the combined area of France, Germany and Italy. Ontario is by far the most visited province, due to its excellent road links with New York to the South and Michigan to the West. The province earns 65% of Canada's earnings from international tourism. Toronto (population

3.3 million) is Ontario's major commercial and business metropolitan city. Montreal is its largest city; it is also the headquarters of International Civil Aviation Organisation (ICAO) as well as International Air Transport Association UATA).

The Maritime Provinces along the Atlantic seaboard are relatively poor and traditional. This is particularly true of Newfoundland where hundreds of fishing villages cling to rugged, deeply indented coastline. The other three provinces of this region are Nova Scotia, New Brunswick and Prince Edward Island.

In the west, the economy of the province of British Columbia has been strengthened by massive investments. The province of Saskatchewan, between Alberta and Manitoba, is the bread-basket of Canada. Manitoba is Canada's central province with its capital at Winnipeg, about 180 kms north of US border.

The North-West territories of Canada are an outdoor adventure destination, which has as its promotional slogan "Within Reach Yet Beyond Belief".

Caribbean Islands

The Caribbean islands extend from Florida to the northern coast of South America. The Caribbean has been the playground of the Americans for decades. Now, the Europeans and the Canadians have also discovered it. This region of some 30 democratic island States is the place where the first Europeans came and settled down. They began to produce wealth, which was used for building many of the stately homes in Spain, England, France and Holland.

The Caribbean celebrated the 500th anniversary of the arrival of Columbus in the Bahamas in 1992. Columbus's eldest son was an early Governor of the Santa-Domingo in the Dominican Republic.

The Caribbean Sea is often called the "American Mediterranean". But, it is warmer and is less polluted than its European counterpart. It has a shoreline, which is greener and has better beaches than the Mediterranean. Politically, the region is highly fragmented, consisting of 30 island states of which two-thirds are the members of the British Commonwealth of Nations while the remaining also are members of CARRICOM —the Caribbean Economic Community. Some retain links with France and the Netherlands. The rest Cuba and Dominican Republic-have more in common with the Latin American mainland.

Tourism is the main source of income for some of the Caribbean islands. In the Bahamas, 80% of its GNP comes from tourism expenditure.

Cuba

Cuba with its capital Havana, is more than half the total land of the islands of the Caribbean. It has an area of 110,860 sq. kms. It is a beautiful country with 5,000 kms of prime beach-front property. Because of its proximity to Florida, Cuba, until 1950, was the leading holiday destination of the Caribbean. After the Communist takeover, USA blockaded the country and tourism collapsed. The Government of Cuba is now taking more interest in promoting the European and Canadian traffic to Cuba.

Greenland

Geographically part of North America and sparsely populated, the huge island of Greenland is a self-governing Danish territory. The Eskimo Inuit population mostly inhabits it. Its capital is Godthaab.

Jamaica and the Cayman Island

The largest of the English-speaking islands, Jamaica has a well-established tourism industry with frequent air services to its capital. Kingston. Its area is 11,425 sq. kms. Columbus visited Jamaica in 1494. The country is known for its excellent beaches backed by forested mountains. The Cayman Island to the west of Jamaica is, known for its diving holidays. The offshore banking is the main source of income for this British colony-it is a haven for those hiding their ill-gotten incomes. George Town is its capital.

Latin America

Latin America is a cultural identity of all the countries of the Western Hemisphere, south of USA-Mexico border. The mainland here was colonised by the Europeans who came from the Iberian Peninsula i.e. Spanish and Portuguese. Their rule was stern and they strictly imposed their language, religion and culture on the native 'Indians'. The natives came to be described as 'Indians' because Columbus believed that he had discovered 'India' and not a new continent.

Mexico

Mexico, with an area of 1,973,000 sq kms, is one of the major travel destinations of the world. And, with rising incomes the Mexicans, too, are traveling overseas in large numbers. Mexico contributes the second largest number of visitors to the United States after Canada. In 1995, Mexico was one of the top 15 tourism spenders in the world. Although Mexico has developed a reputation of being a great country for sea beaches, it has tremendous cultural assets.

To the north of Mexico City (capital) are the impressive pre-Columbian sites of Teotihuacan and Tula. There are numerous reminders of Mexico's Spanish past and legacy all over the country. Mexico City has suffered in terms of arrivals due to an intolerable level of pollution. Among its most well-known beach resorts are Acapulco and the newly developed Cancun.

Trinidad and Tobago

The two Island nations with a population of about1.1 million lies just a few kilometers off the South American mainland. People of Indian ethnic origin constitute half of the population. Tourism is a recent phenomenon. The petroleum sector of the economy accounted, for 70% of the country's economy. The capital is Port of Spain.

United States of America (USA)

USA, one of the largest countries in the world, has an area of 9,372,614 sq. kms. Over 75% of the population lives in urban areas-thirty-five of these urban areas now have a population in excess of one million. Mega cities create a lot of domestic and international tourism in USA. In the early nineties, USA was receiving 45 million international tourists annually and outbound travel was also of similar magnitude. Half of the international tourism arrivals in USA are from the neighboring Canada and Mexico. Domestic tourist spending of the Americans estimated by US Travel Center in 1995 was US $ 700 billion-not matched by any other country in the world. USA is a vast country with 52 States of the American Union.

The entire Latin America is part of the developing world but there are areas of affluence where income is better than the developing countries of Asia and Africa.

CENTRAL AMERICA

Central America is a mountainous neck of land linking the continents of North and South America. The countries included in this belt are Guatemala, Costa Rica, Honduras, Nicaragua and Panama.

Costa Rica

Costa Rica (area 57,000 sq. kms.) has the most dynamic tourist industry in Central America. Its success is derived from the growth of eco-tourism market. The country has protected its national resources very well. The number of. visitors has been steadily rising and is now around half a million a year. The capital, San Jose, is a beautiful city. In an area of the size, of the Punjab State in India, Costa Rica has rain forests, high mountains, cloud forests, coral beaches, and 28 national parks set aside to, protect natural ecology.

Guatemala

Guatemala (area 108,889 sq. kms.) has a large Indian population retaining many of the traditions of their Mayan ancestors. Its capital is Guatemala City.

Honduras

The Honduras with area 112,088 sq. kms.) is one of the poorest countries in the Western Hemisphere, after Haiti. The capital is Tegucigalpa. With similar tourist resources-as Costa Rica, Nicaragua (area 130,000 sq kms) has not been able to develop its tourism due to unstable political conditions. Its capital city is Managua.

SOUTH AMERICA

South America is a large continent with a tremendous variety of scenic beauty and cultural diversity. It is inhabited by fun-loving and friendly people.

Argentina

Argentina has a population of about 28 million of whom one-third live in the capital, Buenos Aires. The almost featureless pampas grasslands form the heartland of this country of 2.8 million sq kms. The areas of touristic interest are the Andes foothills to the west with many historic towns.

Bolivia

Bolivia's development as a tourist destination is held back as it is a landlocked country. La Paz, the capital, has rich art treasures dating back to the colonial era. Bolivia has an area of 1,098,581 sq kms.

Brazil

Brazil has a population of over 156 million, making it the fifth most populous nation in the world and one of the worlds largest in area (8,511,965 sq kms). It is only slightly smaller than LJSA. Like USA, Brazil is the 'melting pot' of immigrants from Europe, Africa and Asia. Unlike most Latin American countries, Brazil has a well-defined tourist image based mainly on its wonderful beaches and Carnival of Rio de Janeiro. Brazil has five tourist regions. Of these, Amazonia holds a fascination for foreign visitors as an ecological resource threatened with destruction. The north-east is Brazil's poorest region where drought is a perennial problem. A major city, Salvador, with colonial architecture and a spectacular carnival, attracts visitors. In the south of Brazil, a major tourist attraction is the Iguassu Falls—three times larger than the Niagara.

Chile

Most of Chile's people live in the fertile central valley, which resembles California in climate and landscape. The capital, Santiago, at the foothills of the snowcapped Andes is one of the most attractive cities of Latin America, and its seaport, Valparaiso, is often compared to San Francisco.

Columbia

Columbia (area 1,139,000 sq. kms.) is South America's fourth largest country in area and the third largest in population. This is a progressive South American state where literacy exceeds 80% and annual per capita income is US $ 1,150. Columbia has had a bad image of tremendous violence related to drug trafficking. Tourism, therefore, gets a back seat. Columbia's capital is Bogota and its national airlines is called Avianca.

Peru

Peru has always had political turbulence during its 470 years of history. Drug mafia is quite powerful. Fujimori, the present President of Japanese origin, has tried to bring about some stability in the nation. Peru's capital Lima is an important gateway to South America. The principal attractions of Peru are the ancient mountain city Cuzco and the nearby lost city—Machu Pacchu.

Uruguay

This small country of Uruguay (area 176,000 sq kms) has a population of only about 3 million and a GNP of US $ 9 billion. Tourism is the third biggest money-spinner after meat and wool.

Venezuela

It is a rich oil producing country with 2,800, kms of Caribbean Atlantic coastline. Of its population about19 million, 4.5 million live in the capital, Caracas. Venezuela has one of the highest per capita income in South America-US $ 3000. Tourism, today, is exceeded only by oil and aluminum in foreign exchange earnings.

The two tiny States of Guyana and Surinam, not far from Venezuela, have much to offer to the wildlife enthusiasts, but tourism is of little importance here. Guyana has a majority population of people of Indian origin.

Surinam, too, though held by the Dutch, has a sizeable Indian population. There is the French Guyana also, famous for its former role as a penal colony called Devil's Island. It is still a French overseas territory.

AUSTRALASIA

Australia, New Zealand and the islands of the Pacific, east of Indonesia and the Philippines, form a separate entity described by geographers as Australasia. Another name for this region is by Oceania.

Australia

Australia is a multi-cultural society. Four out of ten Australians are first or second generation immigrants. One in five of the population is overseas born. Australia is a large country slightly smaller than-the United States, and is as large as Europe without Russia. But, its population is very small. It has a total surface area of 7,687,000 sq kms. Its economy is about the same size as Holland. The core of its wealth is land and its rich mineral resources. It is the world's largest exporter of wool and is a leading exporter of bauxite, alumina and steam coal. It is also the second largest exporter of zinc and the fourth largest producer of gold.

In the past, most immigrants came from Europe. Now they are coming from all over the world. One of the most sparsely populated nations it is one of the most urbanised, with 85% population living in towns and cities.

The states are New South Wales, Victoria, Queens land. South Australia and Western Australia. The state capitals are Sydney, Melbourne, Brisbane, Adelaide, Perth and Hobart, respectively.

Since three-quarters of its exports are primary commodities, the country's economy is subject to violent swings in commodity prices. The government, therefore, has in recent years been serious in promoting international tourism to provide a batter balance to the economy. Tourist arrivals have been on the increase and were 3.8 million in 1996. Australia's earnings from tourism have increased at an average of 20% in recent years-faster than any of the industrialised OECD countries.

Historically, New Zealand has provided the maximum number of tourists to Australia but the pattern has changed recently with the "Japanese tourist invasion." They now exceed New Zealanders—over 600,000 annually compared to a little less from New Zealand. For more than a century, Australia and New Zealand were destinations for a large number of relations of immigrants, especially from the UK, who came as visitors, traveled to meet friends and relatives. But, today, it has all changed. Tourist earnings account for over 7% of all exports of goods and services from Australia. Australia has rich tourist resources. Most of it, with the exception of Tasmania, lies within tropical and sub-tropical latitudes; so the winter is seldom very cold. Snow is almost unknown except in Tasmania or the Australian Alps where skiing is possible from June to September.

Australia has a developed economy with standards of affluence matching that of the USA. The ownership of motor vehicles is similarly high. On per-capita basis, the Australians are great travellers and spenders, both domestically and internationally. Sydney is the most frequented tourist center of Australia with its attractions of the famous Suspension Bridge, Opera House, its beautiful beaches and harbor. Melbourne rivals Sydney in its cultural attractions and is conveniently placed to reach picturesque Victoria Coast as well as the Australian Alps. Tourism has become a major driving force in Queens land's economy, contributing 10% of the gross state product. Japanese investors have taken over 70% of the land earmarked for tourism development on Queens land's Gold Coast-directly investing US $ 17 billion.

New Zealand

The climate of New Zealand favours outdoor holidays with equable temperature and pollution-free environments. The Tourist Board claims ZOW sunshine hours in a year. Much of the New Zealand 270,000 sq km area is hilly and the country's greatest assets are the beauty and variety of its scenery. The two large islands that make the bulk of New Zealand offer different menus. Much of the North Island consists of a volcanic plateau while a range of high mountains-the Southern Alps dominates the South Island. They contain glaciers, snowfields and a fjord coastline.

The New Zealand government was one of the first to recognise the importance of tourism; it set up an official tourist organisation as early as 1901. The tourist organisation has now shaped into a National Tourism Board, a federal corporation headed by a private business executive. New Zealand is almost as large in area as Japan.

Tourism today is a thriving industry. New Zealand reported 1.5 million arrivals and foreign exchange earnings of US$ 1.5 million. There is a boom in the hotel industry and several new hotels, especially small motels, have been opened.

New Zealanders are great international travellers. Neighboring Australia is their favourite holiday destination, which is separated by only 1,900 kms of Tasman Sea. The airfares are quite low and New Zealand and Australia allow each other's citizens to enter without visa. They can also take employment in each other's country.

As part of New Zealand's privatisation programme, Air New Zealand has been sold to a consortium of, investors including Qantas, American Airlines, Japan Airlines, some local investors and the staff. The government has also spun off its state-owned agency, which owned hotels and handled inbound travel reservations. Much to the delight of the travel industry. New Zealand got its first casino in Auckland in 1994.

The Pacific Island

The Pacific region has several gun-drenched beautiful Islands of interest to holiday seekers from principal markets of Europe and North America. But, the long, distance from major markets has prevented the development of a strong market. Despite the constraints, some important Islands like the Fiji, Tahiti and Guam are doing quite well. Most of these island nations have third world developing economies and to them tourism is an important source of income and employment. The islands fall within three culturally distinct regions: Polynesia to the east, Micronesia to the north-west and Melanesia to the south-west Pacific. They all have a tropical, humid climate characterised -by abundant rainfall with temperature around 201 centigrade round the year. Sea breeze mitigates the heat. The larger is lands are of volcanic origin, mountainous and covered with luxurious vegetation. The smaller islands are mostly coral atolls with extensive lagoons.'

No Pacific island destination has captured the imagination, of romantic writers and artists, better than Tahiti, Morrea and Boro Boro, which are part of French Polynesia.

Fiji, a former British colony, has the most, well-developed tourism infrastructure, catering-mainly to Australians, New Zealanders, Americans and the Japanese. Major hotel chains-like the Sheraton, Regent, Travelodge and Shangrila have their properties in Fiji. The country has numerous island resorts. Fiji's capital is Suva. Walking through the streets of the capital one constantly, hears, Hindi music from shops owned mostly by people of Indian origin who were taken to Fiji in shiploads, as indentured laborers 100 years ago to work in sugar plantations. They are now successful businessmen and professionals. Fiji has an area of 18,333 sq. kms.

AFRICA

Africa is the world's second largest continent, rich in both natural and touristic resources. But its touristic resources are very much underutilised due to the absence of adequate infrastructure and generally poor organisational framework. The continent of Africa received a little less than 3.3% of tourist arrivals in 1995. Tourist receipts were only 2% of the world tourism expenditure.

Algeria

Though strategically located close to tourist market's of Northern Europe, Algeria could not play well in the area of not done well in tourism. It has been politically unstable. Algeria is the largest country in North Africa (area 2,382,000 sq kms) and its vastness offers a diversity of scenic and cultural resources. In the north lies the Mediterranean, with 1,200 kms of unspoiled coast. The fertile but narrow coastal plain called Tell contains urban centers including.the capital Algiers. Near the capital, a number of seaside resorts have been created for European visitors. Some of these resorts have been developed as self-sufficient Arabic style towns, complete with Souks. The Atlas Mountains provide respite from heat, and skiing is possible here during December to March.

Ethiopia

East Africa may be extended to include the countries of the Horn of Africa and Sudan. Ethiopia's heartland is an ancient Christian civilisation separated from its Muslim neighbors. It has many tourist attractions like Gama Reserve of Rift Valley, Lake Tana, and the monasteries of Axoum and Lalibela. Ethiopia is a vast country (area 1,222,000 sq kms) with capital at Addis Ababa.

Kenya

Among the East African countries, Kenya, with its capital at Nairobi, is considered to be a leading tourist destination. Tourism, however, suffered a setback in the early nineties due to violence against visitors.

To boost tourism, Kenya opened its borders to white South Africa in 1990. Visas were given at the airports even before the abolition of 'Apartheid'. Wildlife is the basis of East African tourism. Kenya, Tanzania and Uganda have devoted large areas for wildlife conservation either as national parks or as game reserves. Wildlife is protected. The present day tourism in Kenya has changed its complexion from wildlife hunting to wildlife photo-safari. Other options in East Africa include fishing expeditions to Lake Turkane, camel safari in northern Kenya, trekking and mountaineering on Kilimanjaro or in neighboring Tanzania or Mount Kenya.

Morocco

Morocco (area 710,000 sq kms) was, the first to enter the tourism market in the 1950s followed by Algeria and Tunisia. Unlike Algeria or Tunisia, Morocco, has an independent monarchy. It has a number of ancient cities like Fez, Meknes, Marrakesh and Rabat—each one has been the capital at one time or the other. The country is also fortunate in having an extensive coastline on both the Atlantic and the Mediterranean. Winters are warm and sunny while summers do not have excessive heat or dust.

Tanzania

Ironically, the rich wildlife parks of Tanzania are more easily accessible from Nairobi than from their capital Dares-Salaam on the coast. The Tanzanian government is now building art airport and hotel complex at Kilimanjaro. Attempt is also being made to link Dares-Salaam with Lusaka, the capital of Zambia, by rail.

The capital, Dares-Salaam, is isolated because roads are not good. A new capital is under construction in Dodama.

Tanzania has many magnificent natural wonders—a palm fringed coastline, the Serengeti plain with the heaviest concentration of herds of wild animals in the world; the Kilimanjaro—Africa's highest mountain—and Ngorongoro, Crater-home for wild animals and birds.

Tunisia

Tunisia has developed as an important playground for Europeans seeking sun, sea and sand holiday. Tunisia is a destination for mass tourism catering to the needs of Europeans coming by charter flights through its capital Tunis, or Monastir an airport specially built on the coast to handle incoming flights. The inbound visitors were over 4 million in 1994. Tourism in Tunisia is well-managed and the country offers 52,267 rooms of all types. The government is presently financing a new resort in Tabarkaon the coast near the Algerian frontier, providing some 10,000 beds.

Uganda

Uganda (area 22,402,000 sq kms) has many tourist attractions such as Kabagera Falls and Ruwenzori National Park. It can be reached from the airport at Entebbe, or Kampala, the capital of the country. The Ugandan capital is linked by ferry services across Lake Victoria and by road and rail links to Nairobi. Tourism industry has suffered badly due to mismanagement and political instability. The East African coast is also attracting conventional sun, sea and sand seekers from Europe. New resorts are coming up from Lamu in Kenya to Kilwa in Tanzania. On the coast, many of the ports like the Island of Zanzibar and Mombassa are ancient Arab settlements.

Sudan

Its capital is Khartoum. Sudan, a big country (area 2,505,813 sq kms) has problems between the Arabic-speaking north and the African tribal region of its south. The Nile flows through it and there is scope for Nile cruises and diving in the Red Sea. But, tourism has not yet taken off.

SOUTHERN AFRICA

The countries of Central and Southern Africa have now realised the importance of conservation of wildlife for tourism and, therefore, have taken steps to protect it.

Cameroon

The country (area 475,000 sq kms) has been described as

Africa in Miniature. It has rich game reserves, rain forests, the volcanic Mount Cameroon and good beaches on the Gulf of Guinea. Its capital is Yaounde.The Central African region has a bewildering variety of tourist attractions. An advantage is that English and French are widely spoken in this region of Africa.

Republic of South Africa

The most well developed country in tourism in Africa is the Republic of South Africa where history has been made recently.

Over half of the 4.6 million visitors to South Africa in 1995 came from the neighboring countries. Overseas visitors were about 2 millions.

Most overseas visitors to the Republic of South Africa, enter through Johannesburg, the country's largest metropolitan city. Cape Town, another major town and harbor, is situated at the cross-roads of international seaways. The country has excellent road and rail networks. Its, 'Blue Train' runs between Pretoda, the capital city, to Cape Town, a distance of 1,600 kms. It is a good way of seeing the country. The coast of Natal is ideal for sunbathing and surfing throughout the year, Durban is, the largest holiday resort as well as a major seaport.

Zambia

Zambia (area 752,614 sq kms) is rich in wildlife and has a cooler climate than most parts of tropical Africa (altitude up to 1500 meters). National parks make up 8% of the land area of the country and the Ministry of Tourism looks after them. Important tourist centers are Living stone near Victoria Falls and Lusaka, the capital and an international gateway.

4

Tourism and Hospitality Industries

Tourism, Tourist and Travellers

Generally 'tourism' is a nebulous term meanings. In Britain, the word 'tourism' covers all travel for whatever purpose, whereas in the USA it refers to leisure travel only. In India, the British connotation of term is adopted. The tourism covers what is generally referred to as the visitor industry, the hospitality industry, the travel industry or the convention and tourism industry. The World Tourism Organisation (WTO) definition of a tourist is some one who moves away from home on a temporary or short-term basis for at least 24-hours, whether travelling in his or her own country (domestic tourism) or going to another country (international tourism).

Most people in the industry or those who study it find a definition which limits a 'tourist' to a person who spends at least 24-hours away from home, too restrictive. One may argue that day trippers or excursionists should be included. In Britain, these have been defined as people spending at least three hours away from home and involving a round journey of at least 20-miles which they do not regularly make, thus moving outside the area of their normal daily journeys. As travel has become easier, the boundaries of commuting areas have increased. For some cities this may be up to 100-miles, although for most people ten miles might be a more appropriate figure. Excluded from this definition of a tourist are students, and workers migrating temporality. The term Visitors' could cover both the over-night stayer and the day trappers. Definition of who is counted as tourist is important when assessments are made of the impact of tourism.

Many of the firms associated with tourism supply both tourists and residents, and there is no way to recording division of trade. An industry is often defined on the basis of a product, but how is this defined for tourism? Some authors use the term tourism system instead of 'tourist' industry.

These authors use the notion of component which would include the tourist, the transporter, the attraction, the ancillary facilities, and the planners and promoters of a place. In case of a tourist product we may define it as what attracts the tourist to a place, which include historic buildings, urban landscapes, museums and art galleries, theatres, sport and events. These may be called as primary elements. There are other facilities also which are important for the experience of the tourist, but are unlikely to be the cause of the visitor coming to the city. These include hotels, shops, and other services and are described as the secondary elements. Some visitors travel to a place to purchase one product only, while others are attracted by the possibility of consuming several products during their stay. Many of them are unique to a place, and these include historic buildings, museums, and special events. They can only be consumed by traveling to place where they are found. Just because these attractions are unique does not mean that tourist will come. Individual have special interests for which they will travel a long distance. Most people will travel for something that they perceive as really impressive.

Hierarchy of Attractions

(a) Local appeal

(b) Regional appeal

(c) National recognition with specialised appeal

(d) National recognition with wide appeal

(e) International recognition limited for special appeal, such as, Pyramids, Taj Mahal

(f) International recognition: Many elements of appeal and attracting people from all over the world, e.g., Paris, London, etc.

Strategy for Regional Tourism Development

Tourism is on the increase and needs thorough examination to assess whether it could play a role in the economic and physical regeneration of the areas. On the basis that there would be increasing affluence, easier travel and greater leisure time, it is assumed that the tourism industry is bound to grow. It brings income to the areas. Acting as an economic base it is assumed to be able to give support to the regional economy.

Tourism should never be perceived as a panacea for regional development problems but as a part of the solution. It would be wrong to see tourism promotion simply as one component of regional development policy. Investment for tourism involves the development of facilities, activities, physical environments and infrastructure that will have benefits for the local community. It also involves marketing the region and selling an image, which will assist in the attraction of industrial and commercial activities.

Advertising the region engaged in tourism activities will raise the profile and visibility of the region and will also assist in economic promotion. Many activities being expanded, such as culture, and sport will persuade potential residents that the region is a good place in which to live, that it has the right life-style opportunities. With the renewal of villages and the new image, it will be easier to bring resident back to the interior regions. The money which tourists spend on facilities may make tourism activities more economically viable, which will be of benefit to the local community. The tourist industry must be substantially increased in size so as it may play a larger role in the regional economy.

It means attracting hundreds of thousands of extra tourist to bring in extra income that will create jobs. To bring in more tourists the tourism resources must be expanded. Tourism resources comprise — primary elements and secondary elements. Primary elements are those which attract people, and consists of historic buildings and landscapes, museums and art galleries, concerts, spector sports, conferences exhibitions, entertainment and special events. A person may be attracted by one element and use only that element. Tourists come because of mix of attractions. Secondary elements enhance these attractions or assist in the process of attracting tourists, and include shopping, catering, accommodations and transport and tourism agencies. Any expansion of tourism will involve the development of all there components.

Types of Tourists

The main visitor markets for tourism are:

(a) Short-break holiday makers

(b) Business travellers

(c) Conference and exhibition delegates

(d) Day trippers

(e) Long holiday makers on a tour, stopping off for a short visit.

(f) Visitors to friend and relatives, holiday makers using the region as a gateway to the neighbouring region

Tourism is one of the service sector which is growing rapidly. Another criticism of the strategy arise because tourism is often perceived as providing low-paid, low-skilled and seasonal jobs. We will find that many of the activities of the industry such as conferences, do not experience great seasonal variations, and the hotel industry has a different seasonal profile from that of resorts. No doubt, many of the jobs are low skilled, this could be in favour of regional tourism when it is located near the villages with its labour resources of the unskilled. Another strong argument against expanding the tourist industry is that it involves spending money on visitors when the priority should be to spend it on residents. This ambiguous attitude toward tourism has meant that the funding has been denied or limited. An attempt to cut public expenditure have impeded on the funding of tourism administration and project, and this has affected the regions differently. Other critics perceive tourism as having adverse consequences for the region. Bringing more visitors to a region might add to existing congestion. More tourists will add to the wear and tear on facilities and increase the cost of management. Further, local resident, sometimes does not welcome the influx of visitors, and facilities favoured by the tourist may not be those denied or, needed by the community.

The role of tourism can be gauged from statement in economic development strategies and in structure plans. Tourism promotion unit could be within the economic development department provided the later does not concentrate on traditional policies such as those of constructing industrial estates.

Pleasure Travel Market

The tourism growth has been enabled by increasing influence, easier travel, and greater leisure. The basic task of a region is to persuade tourists to come to it. A study of the pleasure market classified trips into following types: (i) Visit to friend and relatives; (ii) Touring; (iii) Close to home trip (mainly out-doors); (iv) Out-door activities in village/rural areas; (v) A resort trip; (vi) A city trip; (vii) Theme park, exhibition or special event; and (vii) Cruise.

Exhibitions and Conferences

Conferences and exhibition activities are one of the staple of tourism. These are the growth industries in which visitor spends an above-average amount, and which operate for most of the year. These can be considered as two separate kind of events but there are increasing links between them. Many conferences include an exhibition. Conferences are convened for a number of different purposes, such as: (a) Policy making; (b) The exchange of ideas and information; (c) Training; (d) Selling; (e) Social purposes; and (f) Recreational purposes—short holiday during or after the conference.

Companies and other organisations to achieve their objectives arrange corporate meetings. The association conference may involve educational, professional, political, religions and social organisations. Apart from achieving the objectives of the association, they are also a means of generating income which is often easier and less painful than raising subscription. Conferences vary from an inter-governmental summit, the convention of a political party, a company strategy meeting, a religions synod, a symposium of scientists, to the annual conference of a trade common or professional or social association.

The basic accommodation requirement for a meeting is large room or hall of sufficient size to take the expected attendance. additional facilities are required in the form of special lighting, microphones, and loudspeakers, projection equipment, the possibility of simultaneous translation, and catering, including banquets.

While 'Exhibition' is mentioned as an organised pubic display of manufactured goods and works of arts. These serve as a very useful purpose for sellers and buyers. Exhibition can be organised by a trade association, by a company associated with the exhibition site, or by a company which specialises in organising exhibitions. These are held in large halls, many exhibition centers may have out-door space. A special type of exhibition center could be an agricultural fair ground, which is mainly out-door display space. Exhibition centers require catering facilities and office spaces, and may provide rooms for meetings. Convention business is also on the increase and may prove fruit full to the area. Some exhibitions may take place in hotels.

Attractions

The region as a part of its economic strategy needs to develop attractions of a large and high quality. There is a hierarchy of attractions and only those attractions, which rank high that will be able to pull in visitors from a distance. Vision wants something that is unique and interesting, is popular, is entertaining and includes attraction and sightseeing.

These attraction generally include museums and art galleries historic building, theatres, and concert, sport, and the sight, the general landscape of buildings.

Cultural Sports, Tournament and Special Events

Initially, theatres, concert halls and sports grounds were all built to meet the need of the resident population. Now, these are perceived to bring prestige to a region and raise its profile in the outside world. As the region is desperate to attract inward investment, having a high profile in the arts and sport is a good starting point. If the events are of a sufficiently high quality then people will be prepared to travel some distance to attend. There is clearly some validity in this idea since many places around the world have traded on arts tourism for many years. The term 'art industry' and 'cultural industry' are sometime used to include the performing arts, museums and art galleries, cultural heritage, special events such as art festival and the producing art. Here let us concentrate on performing art, and in particular to the role of theatres, and concert halls. Mostly, drama, concert, ballet, opera and other art have been concentrating in cities. Patrons living in interior areas have to travel to big cities to experience live performances and in the process become tourists.

(a) Activities

Sport activities may be perceived to project a high status image of the area via media coverage which may help attract economic development, persuade people to live in the city and attract visitors. It increases civic pride, community spirit and collective self-image. The profits from hosting a mega-event could pay for high-quality facilities which could be of permanent value to the region. To keep teams in the region and to attract them from elsewhere, local governments be prepared to offer inducement, including building and retiring ownership of a stadium which can be let to the team, sometimes on an uneconomic basis. Sport programmes can have their greatest economic impact on the region when they are linked with other tourist attractions and they are family leisure activities. As regards to impact of sport on general economic development, this is the only factor, which will affect the growth performance to the region. It may have both positive and negative effects, positive as the prospect of large numbers of people may encourage investment in other activities, (e.g. catering) and negative because crowd and congestion may discourage investment. Much may depend on the characteristics of spectators. The maximum impact of a stadium is likely to be felt when it is close to other tourist attractions and hotel.

It includes the events, which occur infrequently. A football match or a concert could be described as an event. Typical special event are ones that occur only on an annual basis in the same locality. Special event may have almost any theme and take any form. A special event could be as simple as Annual Street parade. Many special events use related to existing attractions. An art gallery may have a special exhibition, perhaps of pictures on loan from elsewhere, the terms mega-event or hall mark even describe large events of world importance and high profile which have a major impact on the image of the host region. This definition is mainly psychological, as it is difficult to specify a quantitative one that would be widely applicable.

Various special events have a long history but new ones are constantly created. Special events could be used as a means of attracting tourists, and raising the profiles and changing the image of places. The large special events, whether it be a festival, a sport competition or a political convention, gains tremendous television coverage which can be more effective publicity than any other method. The main for special events may be:

(a) To attract people outside the main season
(b) To attract people into the area
(c) To attract media attention and raise the profile of the area
(d) To encourage repeat visit
(e) To assist regeneration.
(f) To add animation and life to existing attraction

An assessment can be made of the long-term effects, including the amount of inward investment and the growth of tourism. Because of the wide diversity of special events it is not possible to cover all of them and attention will be concentrated on art festival, sport events, world fairs and garden festival.

(b) Historical Events

Areas may celebrate the anniversary of their foundation or some events of national and international significance. The motives should be pure celebration, promotion and visibility, attraction of tourists. The celebration may take various forms including festival, fine work and other outdoor spectacles, new buildings and infrastructure, including museum, and art venues, and fairs. The event may last for a few weeks or a whole year. In the event of regional celebration the events may take place in the capital or in an area with a historical connection. Historical celebrations have not been as positive as the organisers expected.

(c) Art Festivals

A festival may be defined as a theme public celebration, which extends leisure and cultural opportunities beyond every day experiences and choices. Art festivals may cover several arts or focus on a single art such as classic music, jazz, literature, drama, ilm, etc. Arts festivals attract mainly the middle class and only the largest or most specialised attract a majority of attention from outside the locality. Many cities have attempted to introduce art festivals. To attract attention and to be able to draw people from distance they have to increasingly focus on a particular art form, such as film or jazz. A recent innovation has been the introduction of year long art events which move from one area to another. In this region an area (place) could be given the little of 'Garhwal culture', Kumaon culture' or 'Himalayan culture' and it could be projected across the whole region. Similarly, arts years for an area could be decided and each year could be a specific theme. Each area may bid for the tittle. Festivals have multiple objectives of extending the arts experience of the residents, of raising the profile of the region and attracting visitors.

(d) Games

Games, national, regional or Olympics are the greatest mega-event. Each time events are held, it gets bigger. The competitive national element plus the various spectacles associated with the event ensure interest well beyond the relatively few that follow sports. The transformation of the economics of the games persuaded many regions of the benefits of hosting them. The profit made could be used to pay for the facilities that are required and which will be left behind after the event. Given the regional prestige, host region hope that government will pour money into the facilities and general infrastructure of the area. Ring roads and railways could be build, new airport constructed, and derelict water-front area cleared and redeveloped for as game villages. For the host region, winning the games offers the prospects of worldwide publicity as well as investment in permanent facilities and infrastructure, which could enable it to attract further general investment, future events and more tourists. During the bidding process public money could be provided to build some facilities and infrastructure. Private finance be covered, both for the bid and for facilities. The greatest importance is the element of unity. Politicians of different parties, leaders of private sector and voluntary groups may come together and agree on the proposals as well as on the direction in which the region should be moving. A tourist industry could be developed and the region could be marketed with arts and manufactures, with pavilions being provided for different regions.

(e) Fairs and Expos

There are various and inter-linked objectives for holding a fair, such as, encouraging trade, increasing the visibility of an area, and region, developing tourism, attracting economic development and thus promoting employment, stimulating land redevelopment and infrastructure improvement, the celebration of past event, and the entertainment of the masses, as well as the often unstated one of obtaining extra funds from higher levels of government. The prime motive holding a fair is to boost the area, but as well as selling the area there is also the selling of ideas. The host area should prepare a special site for the event where many buildings and structures hoped for architectural distinction be erected. These will remain a permanent legacy to the area, as will be general infrastructure put in place. The fair itself usually contains exhibitions of both. Subsequently, some costs would be recovered though the sale of land. In case the festival makes a small loss, the local council for the area Development Corporation could meet it. Garden festival could use a tourism event to support a specific piece of rural regeneration. There are short-term benefits in the form of extra income to the region and resultant employment. These benefits can be increased by an associated promotion of local attractions so that the tourists are encouraged to stay longer in the area. After use of the site need to be carefully considered to get the long-term environmental and economic benefits. The region may get high profile and enhance image resulting in more tourists and general economic gains.

(f) Garden Festivals

The aim of the garden festival is to celebrate the reclamation of derelict land, to bring short-term benefit to a locality in the form of tourists, to bring longer-term benefits in the form of image enhancement, and to provide sites for new land uses including the provision of jobs, to replace those lost in the site then the industries close down. There could be *two* model: *one* laying emphasis on the after-used, and *second,* less on the involvement of the horticultural sector and the provision for park land. The government should pay for the costs of reclamation, while the festival would pay for itself. The economic impact studies of sport events—costs and revenues to the organisers and the impact of the event on the area, indicates that the cost of the games involve direct expenditures on sport facilities, indirect expenditures on infrastructure from transport to hotels for the operating costs of the games themselves and the subsequent expenditures of all visitors, including competitors, team appeals and the media. The larger the injection of funds into the area, from whatever source, the greater the impact of the event on the area. There are long-term tangible and intangible benefits such as improved infrastructure, the ability to host further sport events, improved image, and the attraction of economic development, and civic pride.

Visitor could travel a long distance because of good hotel, interesting shops and varied range of activities for the evening and night. On the other hand the visitor might be deterred from visiting an area if there is a shortage of hotel rooms and it is known that it is very expensive place. Easy availability of these elements, and good quality and not too expensive may provide an additional reason for visiting the area. The provision of these secondary elements is essential if we want to make the area a successful tourist center. The nature of their activities helps in determining the type of employment created, they tend to employ a significant proportion of low-skilled and low-paid jobs.

Hotels

Any region, area, city or town, which inspire to be an important tourist center will require a substantial stock of hotel rooms. Although we presume that not all tourists will stay in hotels, some of them may be day visitors, others may stay with friend and relatives and some may choose to stay in bed-and-breakfast or unserviced accommodation. More important an area is as a tourist center, the higher the proportion that will require some type of hotel accommodation. It is the visitor who stays in a hotel who has the greatest economic impact. It is estimated that about 60 per cent of expenditure may be accounted for by the cost of accommodation and meals bought in hotel restaurants, it is, therefore, pertinent to examine the factors behind the growth of hotels in the area, the type of hotels required, where should they be located, and the employment impressions.

Hotels can be classified by sizes tariff, ownership, and location. The quality and price of services provided may be indicated by star system. Other terms used include luxury, first class, upscale and budget. Much business travel is at the upper end of the market, while the leisure traveler is often looking for the cheaper budget-priced hotel. The nature of the market in the area is reflected in the type of the hotel. The region should attempt to offer accommodation of varying quality and price.

The demand for hotel accommodation varies over the week and over the year. Business travel generally concentrates into weekend, leaving the week with low demand. Leisure market is concentrated towards the week-end. A region should fill its hotels during the week with business travellers and the week-end with the short-break leisure market. The business and conference markets decrease the summer holidays, while the short-break market peaks in spring-early summer and autumn periods. At any time of the year there may be peaks and through.

It will be better to build hotel by a developer rather than a hotel company. The demand for hotel services is a derived demand. The demand for hotel services can be broken-down by market type into business, tourist, conferences, and other. The exact composition will vary greatly from one hotel to another and particularly with location hotels, situated in well developed areas, depend much more on business travel and less on the leisure market, whereas for resorts, it would be reverse. The business market consists of executives travelling to visit other establishment to transact business, salesman visiting clients, as well as many other activities such as activities working at theatres and official government business. The size of business market will depend on the nature of activities undertaken in the area and the role of the area in the region. Well-developed areas with high proportion of manual jobs are likely to require less stock than in important financial center. The conference and leisure market will also vary in size from an area to another. Although most areas are attempting to develop these markets, there may be differing degrees of success.

A growing market in the region is the traveler/a tourist where the demand is likely to be either on the edge of an area or between the areas. Hotel may derive business from non-staying clients through providing meals in restaurant and space for receptions.

Profit on rooms are higher than those on meals and other services. On the cost side a significant proportion goes on interest and depreciation. The greater the capital cost of the facility, the higher their overhead will be, and hence there will be a need for high occupancy rates. For this reason the break-even occupancy rate is usually lower for budget-price hotel than for luxury ones. Land and capital costs may be high in prosperous area and this deters the construction of hotels.

The physical requirements for a hotel building are affected by the rising expectations of customers and high safety standard. Most customers may expect an en-suite bathroom even in low-price accommodation. At the luxury end of the market patron expects a very high standard of design both inside and outside the building.

As demand grows for accommodation, occupancy rates and profit increase. This will increase developers and hotel chains to invest in new properties, thus increasing the stock of hotel rooms. However, because the economy is cyclical as this extra capacity comes on stream, there is an economic downturn, and demand for hotel accommodation falls. With more capacity and lower throughout occupancy rates, profits falls. Low occupancy and low profit discourage any further building of hotels. It may take several years of recovery before occupancy rates and profits reach former levels.

Most of the small hotels are independently owned and

often-family run large firms develop because of certain advantages. They are able to use marketing techniques effectively in order to reach potential customers, and can make use of central reservation systems. They can agree special terms with major clients. They know of major firm that needs conference facilities and offer them a wide range of location. They offer the same formula around the world so that customer know what to expect and comes back to them. Their size can extract good terms from suppliers. All these factors give them an advantage over the independent firm. Having established themselves, they seek to have a presence in all the major markets. Areas that are revitalising inner areas and may even be given grants as an incentive to invest may count them.

The location of hotels is also an important factor. Guests will want hotel close to the place they wish to visit and so cut down intermediate transport as much as possible. Developers look for sites, which are proven generators of patronage. The traditional location for the hotel was the city center, near railway station, or on the fringe of the retail and business zones away from the highest land values. In city center hotel may be included the most expensive and luxurious. Cheaper hotels may be located along the main radial routes. Old buildings can be converted and extended. Hotels could also be constructed on the edge of the built up area, either near the main road which connect with other parts of the area or near airports. The budget-priced hotels/ motels may be located on highways.

The size of the hotel stock, as measured by the number of bedrooms together with the range in the price of accommodation, is an important indicator of the area as a tourist destination. It is a critical factor in determining whether the area can function as a conference and exhibition center. Its size will also reflect the importance of business and leisure tourism.

Many areas may attempt to encourage the building of hotels so as to assist the development of the tourist industry. The areas should be designated for hotels. Grants may be given to encourage the building of hotels. Exemption of the payment of property taxes for a number of years to stimulate employment may also be granted to encourage hotel construction near the specific areas. Hotel development may also be encouraged on the areas where land prices are lower and where budget-priced hotels could operate profitably.

Shopping

An analysis of the behaviour of tourists indicates that a significant amount of time and money is spend on shopping. Surveys of tourists, which ask the purpose of the trip rarely, find shopping mentioned, but when asked what they did, visitors list shopping as one of the most important activities. For many people shopping is a pleasure experience and something they like to do when they have time. People like to spend their leisure time in shopping and so they should wish to do so on holidays. There is also a desire to see if different goods will be found in another place. A survey of festival market places indicate that about 60-per cent of the patrons come with no specific purchase to mind. A pleasant environment may make shopping more enjoyable. Many people like to take gifts back for friends and relatives when they return. A day out or a short break or a long holiday or even a business trip, there is always an element of shopping. Most of the retail processes are found within, adjacent to near the principal tourist attractions. These may vary from the simple gift/souvenir shop to outlet selling a wide rang of speciality goods. When there are many shops of this type they become part of attraction of the place.

Development of comparable facility will attract tourists. 'Speciality' retailing attracts tourists. This includes the goods, which are not found every where. They are not mass produced, and in some cases are genuine craft goods. They could be described as luxuries in the sense that they are not goods, which are essential for living. It includes goods such as art and crafts, including pottery, unusual and designer cloths, books, perfumes and annual household articles. Developers should attempt to bring the various elements together to create speciality shopping areas.

The concept of 'festival market place' could also be introduced. It combines speciality shopping, eating and drinking, and entertainment. It may remain open all evening and at the week-ends and may attract office workers, sub-urbanities, and tourists in large numbers. Close attention must be given to the quality of the shops, the tenant mix, their environment, and security.

Restaurants—Food and Beverages

Of late, there has been a great growth in the demand for restaurant. Restaurant is an establishment, which serves food and drink, which can be consumed on the premises. People travel further away from their homes whether for work, to shop or for leisure activities, and while away they need food and drink. Many people eat out as a leisure activity. There is a growing importance of eating out. The market for restaurants is in various ways such as business market, individual, and as a leisure activity. Body food is consumed to keep the body going. It may be simple, taken quickly and relatively cheap. Soul food does satisfy basic needs, it is sought after as an enjoyable experience. The food will be more sophisticated, the cost greater, the surroundings more important, and time taken much longer. It is also a social event, rarely undertaken alone, and often undertaken as part of an important personal relationship, or as a special family or group occasion. As standard of living arise, individuals want to experience life to the full.

There is an enormous range of foods available from the ethnic, such as Chinese, Indian and Italian, to the traditional sea food, the gourmet, to the menu of the fast food chain such as burgers or chicken.

Restaurant can also be classified by price. Snacks can be provided not only in fast food restaurants or in cafes, but also in more up market surroundings. Full meal can be provided at a range of prices, at different levels of quality and indifferent settings.

Restaurants are busy around lunchtime and also in the evening. In the day time the customers perhaps business people are more likely to be shopper, local workers and some will be in the position of searching for good restaurant with the type of meal they want and at price they can afford. Seasonal factors may reflect several influences, such as business fluctuations, tourist flows, and special event such as New Year, Deepawali, Dussehra, etc., when many people eat out. The demand for restaurant meal is bound to increase.

At the international level, large corporations increasingly dominate the restaurant business. These corporation gain economies of scale in purchasing and marketing. Restaurants are also found within hotels, departmental stores and other places. There are many independent businesses also.

Entertainment

Many tourist staying over-night in an area will want some form of entertainment. This could be in the form of visit to a theatre or concert hall for music, opera, ballet or drama, or possibly a visit to a club for music and dancing. Arts and culture are also a source of entertainment. More tourism resource such as 'adult entertainment' quarters could be developed.

Transport

Tourists be attracted from a wide range of distances, from the surrounding region to the inter-continental, and different forms of transport will be required. There is a need for good transport systems. Differences in quality and cost could influence tourist flows. Air, rail and road is important. A station which is modal in the network and which is central to the city is important For those arriving by car, a lack of congestion and ample car parking is an important factor. Every effort should be made to improve transport and advertise its availability.

Tourism and Hospitality

The world have become a global community for travellers, opening up places, unimaginable decade earlier—the secrets of Himalayas, the wonders of Antarctica, the rain forests of the Amazon, the beauty of the Tahiti, the Great Wall of China, the dramatic Victoria Falls, the origin of Nile, and the wilds of Scottish Islands. Tourism has become a global business whose expanding market now leaves no place untouched. Tourism and travel now affect every continent, country, and city. Every one's economy is impacted either by their people travelling elsewhere (import spending in other places) or travel service exports (expenditure by nonresidents in that place). The Himalayan region has to decide how much travel service it want to capture.

Due to location, climate, limited resources, size and cultural heritage, this region have no real choice but to engage in tourism to grow, develop and improve its living standards. The areas in the region differ in their dependence on/or interest in, attracting tourists. Areas engage in tourism with mixed emotions, and at times, ambivalence. There are instances, where places are concerned that tourism is destroying its culture, as farm land becomes resort and new jobs unravel family values. These areas may not formally welcome tourists. Some people and businesses benefit, others may not. The regional economy may be better off from tourism, however, the costs and losses—quality of life, convenience, cultural or social values—are not worth the benefits. Should the region place too much emphasis on tourism and hospitality industries? Are these full of risks?

The decision is quite tough because of conflicting interest of different voting blocks. Not all regions and people are enthusiastic about tourist generated jobs. This region may think of expanding tourism when its thriving business decline. Tourism's primary benefit is jobs through hotel, restaurants, retail establishment and transportation.

Not every tourist is interested in a particular destination. The region will waste its money trying to attract everyone who travels. The region, instead of a short gun approach, should take a rifle approach and sharply define its target market. The region should identify its natural target markets in *two* ways.

One is to collect information about its current tourists:

(a) Where do they come from?
(b) Why do they come to this place?
(c) What are their demographic characteristics?
(d) How satisfied they are?
(e) How many are repeat tourists?
(f) How much do they spend?

The *second* approach is to audit *the* region's attraction and conjecture about the types of tourists who would have an natural interest in them. The aim in this approach is to identify new sources of tourists. Do not assume that the current tourists reflect all the potentially interested groups. Different tourists are attracted by different place features. The local/ area/ district/ municipal authorities must ask questions keyed to segmentation visually, such as, attractions sought, market areas or locations, customers.

After identifying its natural target market, the region

has to see research where these tourists are found. Which areas out side contain a large number of citizen who have the means and motivation to enjoy the particular place.? Badrinath area attracts mainly religious tourists. The best source for these tourists are Gujarat, Maharashtra, Uttar Pradesh, Madhya Pradesh and even foreign markets. This analysis can uncover too many or too few natural target market. If you have identified many, next step is to calculate the potential profit from attracting each segment. The potential profit of a target tourist segment is the difference between the amount that the tourist segment would spend and the cost of attracting and serving this segment. The attraction cost will depend on the master plan. The serving cost depend on the infrastructure requirements.

For example, Haridwar, Rishikesh Badri-Kedar region of Uttaranchal's primary market is religious tourists for sentimental, historical, and religious reasons are drawn to this area. The area should create a deep infrastructure of educational, social, and political groups that are likely to visit this region. Summer work-study vacations for young students, groups for to study artifacts and religions questions, etc., could be arranged. Some religious minded people visit this area as many as ten or fifteen times during their life time. They receive deep experience rather than a superficial one. Depending on their special interest, they meet leaders, study with scholars, with village residents. The region can begun marketing to a broader audience by launching a campaign with these tourist generating market, that feature a combined visit. The task is to build these new markets and not allow erosion of its successful primary market.

The region should better off attract fewer but higher income tourists who stay longer and spend more. Back packers and campers should spend more to enjoy its natural, unspoiled beauty. They should tour not only its mountains, water and ancient building but also its literary treasure and attract high income culture-seeking tourists to visit this area where the speech and wit of old can be experienced today. Hotel and restaurant facilities should be improved as an act of investment marketing. Whatever tourist segment the region aims at, it needs to be very specific. A ski resort like Auli could attract only skiers; swimming and natural reef would attracts snorkels and divers; arts, and crafts would attract the art crowd; gambling would attracts gaming tourists. Tourist must be segmented by additional characteristics such as the Valley of Flowers, Winter Park; snow slopes, lakes, winter resort, river boating, rafting, mountain trails, etc. to elude the tourists.

Regions that fail to maintain the necessary infrastructure run significant risks. The region should be ready to respond to changing demographics and life-styles. The growing percentage of retired people and vacations may expand the tourist business. Hotel and airlines should accommodate these trends with low-cost excursion packages. Business travel should, include mixed business and leisure. To capture the trend towards shorter vacations, with in driving distance of home, will help in the growth of new local and regional tourist attractions. The whole region should determine its best tourism target. Older citizen and retires drive the regional economy. They have high income, high consumption, and low service demand levels. They take their pension, social security checks securities to the region. Thus, older citizens are much more than a tourist marketing, their visits lead to permanent residency.

The environmental movement has compelled the tourist industry to adopt earth-friendly approaches, and the region should seek to develop 'green' images. Developers and architects should accommodate changing tastes in designs hotels — low rise, more green space, nature architecture, and energy efficient. We find the tourist places in this region are more sensitive to zoning, density land use, and the problems of over-building. Now government tourist agencies, airlines, hotel chains and tourist organisations are all talking about green issues, and how best to accommodate growth while respecting environmental values.

Tourism investment ranges from relatively low-cost market entry for festivals or event to multi-million rupee infrastructure, costs of stadiums, transits systems, airport and convention center. To create a strong destination pull, attractions, facilities and services should be in a convenient and accessible location. In a planned economy the government controls, plans and directs tourists development. Tourism is necessary for an area/region to earn currencies for trade and development and serves regional purposes. Tourist development and expansion in this region is totally dependent on public investment. This is inadequate because of lack of private investment and market mechanism to respond to changing consumer need and wants. The region should promote investment through joint ventures, foreign ownership and time sharing for individual investors. The state investment in infrastructure should work with private investment in tourist amenities such as hotels, restaurants, golf courses, shopping areas, etc. Regional tourism could be build on public-private partnerships, joint development in planning, financing and implementation. Public authority should clear, develop, and write down land costs and make infrastructure investment. The region should provide or subsidise tax incentives for private investment in hotels, convention centers, transit, and parkings.

Non-profit Development Corporation from airlines to hotels should carry out restoration. The tourist industry should provide tax revenues, from fuels, leases, bed taxes and sales taxes to support long-term bond for capital construction of tourist-related infrastructure and other public improvements. Such steps will make it possible for this region to increase its tourist attraction. The region could also require much more finance and investment for tourism promotion. The area/

region must expand public services, public safety, traffic and crowd, emergency health, sanitation and street cleaning. It should promote tourism internally to it's own citizens, and businesses—retailers, travel agencies, restaurant, financial institutions, public and private tourist, lodging, police and public servants.

The region should respond to the travel-basics of 'cost', 'convenience' and 'timeliness' in order to attract tourists. Every tourists to this region would weigh the costs against the benefits of the destination — and investment of time, effort, and resource against a reasonable return in education, experience, fun, revolution and prospective memories. Convenience includes time involved in travel airport to lodging, language barriers, cleanliness and sanitary concerns, access to interests, (i.e., valleys, attractions, amenities), and special needs (elderly, disabled, children, dietary, medical care, communication, auto rental, etc. Timeliness embraces those factors that introduce risk to travel; wars, terrorism, civil disturbances and political instability, currency fluctuations and convertibility, airlines and transit safety, and sanitary conditions.

The region should market its specific attractions. The region should provide easy access to its attraction by bus, boats, carriages, and planes. It should distribute brochures, audio-tapes, and video-tapes to travel agent and individual prospects. All major hotels should provide in- home video packages to assist visitors in planning local tours, booking events, including skiing various sites. Bus companies should prepare half-day, full-day and evening tours to highlight the area's attractions. Concentrating attractions, services and facilities on an area will definitely create excitement, adventure, and crowds. A major strategy for regional tourist attraction is concept integration, i.e., try all diverse elements into one center theme. Associating honeymoon with snow hills, and water-falls, the tourist season could be extended. It would appeal to newly married. Hotels could offer honeymooners a choice of heart-shaped both tubs, Jacuzzis, Canopy beds and waterbeds. The entire romantic aura of champagne waiting in the room, mirror on the ceilings, and quiet and discreet quarters, will encourage the honeymoon market. The large number of honeymooners could find a complete package of dramatic beauty and business community, resulting in a satisfying tourist experience.

The region needs to monitor closely, the relative popularity of its various attractions by determining the number and type of tourists attracted to each location. It should seek to deepen its attractions quality which will transcend the specific attraction and become a platform for building a place's appeal, features, and sites alone will not attract visitors. The region should seek to deepen the travel experience by holding greater values and making the experience more significant and rewarding. Such appeals should be couched in history, culture, and people. The region should be made foreign friendly' by creating tours that emphasise nationality interest designing vouchers in a variety of languages, and providing hassle-free currency exchanges. Tour packages should try to deepen cultural bond and ties between the region and the visitors and thus provide value-added dimension and friendship.

Competition extends to restaurants, facilities, sports, cultural amenities, and entertainment. The region/area should have best hotels, best culinary fairs, museums and theatres, athletic teams, best wine and drinks, best chefs, and best natives, cultural or ethical flair. Regional campaign should be carried out in special publication. In addition to specific sites and attractions, critical amenities are also of vital importance to tourism and hospitality business. The whole region-at first glance seems to bad set as a tourist attraction. It suffered from a poor image and a non-existence industrial base. It requires to recognise the problems and allocate one time grant to explore tourist markets. The audit of potential attractions may be promising, which require a crucial decision. The region needs to be reinvented as a short-break holiday market and be promoted as a weekend packages. The message should reach the main stream tourists. The locals will take pride in the new attention. A general confidence could be derived with the cooperation of all. The result could be a sharp pick-up in holiday packages.

Tourist competition involves image-making. The regional image will be heavily influenced by pictorial creation of the area, often in movies, and on television and some times by music, and other cases of by popular entertainers, and celebrities. Decades later, this regional image still persists. The region exploits the pilgrim as a successful image of the Himalayas. The region should take advantages of its news events, sport and entertainment stars, movies, and whatever else it could to stimulate tourist interest and convey a regional image. Television also affects relative regional/area attractiveness.

Changing of an image of an area is quite difficult. In selecting a mix of communication messages and channels will help in determining the regional identify. State's media investment in attracting tourist is bound to grow rapidly in the future. It should produce multi-language travel guides, video tapes, radio segments, and selected segments for hikers, trackers golfers, fishers, bicyclists and adventure enthusiasts.

Partnership could be formed with travel, recreation and communication business on joint marketing efforts. Advertise in national magazines and travel publications and thus help in vertical marketing with business travel promotions to link the growing business leisure segment of the travelling public. Target its own travel agencies and agent. The region should also target tourism to its own resident, regionalising attractions with brochures, maps and calendars of event targeted for sub-regions.

The region should constantly discover hidden assets that have vast tourism potentials, for example, Auli skiing discovered in Uttranchal/Uttarakhand, needs to be advertised as a tourist product to a particular target. Effective regional image requires congruence between advertising and the region. Glossy photographs of sunrise, sunset, valleys, streams, wildlife, fountains, springs, houses, and events need to have some relationship to what tourist actually experience, otherwise there is a great risk of the region loosing tourist-goodwill and generating bad word-of-mouth. Travel agents should be extremely responsive to region/area. Feedback from customers and tourist could provide the best or worst privation of a place depending on their experience.

Organisation and Management of the Regional Tourism

Making an area/region tourist friendly is the task of the central tourist authority, i.e., the Ministry of Tourism. Tourism promotion is the responsibility of the government and promotion hospitality business is entrusted to be travel-tourist business.

Hospitality Business

The key revenue factors are the size of the group, its length of stay and its service demands. The meetings market is growing very fast and there is a need for meeting space requirement. The hospitality business requires attractive exhibition facilities combined with ample meeting space. Convention includes exhibits and displays, and combining exhibitions with meetings. When hotel's occupancy falls below profitability, pressure mounts to expand exhibition and meeting space as a method to increase hotel occupancy rates. Convention and trade show business involves dealing with dedicated specialists such as trade association directors, site selection committees, and convention specialists who make site selection recommendations based on price, facilities, and various amenities. Space at reasonable rate, discounted hotels, restaurants, theatres, airlines, auto rentals, and other amenities are all part of competitive packaging. Facilities should be upgraded to meet aesthetic and convenience needs—restaurants, shops, rest rooms, cleanliness, security, proximity to shopping areas and recreations, etc.

The Himalayan region is not an interesting site for conventioneers. It has outstanding dry weather, and beautiful natural scenery that includes some of the greatest mountain ranges, snow and skiing in the world. The region is not in a position to attract large conventions and trade shows. The space compares unfavourably. Hospitality locations know their target market and respective niches. It travels a growing universe of new and expanding player whose markets may be local villages, cities, statewide, regional, national and international. When time is tough, organisations outback on travel for professional development, trade shows, and even sales contact. Some travel is being replaced by video conferences, teleconferences, and other media methods.

5

Accommodations Infrastructure

> "If you would win a man to your cause, first convince him that you are his sincere friend."
>
> —*Abraham Lincoln*

The recent surge in popularity of ecotourism has much to do with the search for a richer holiday experience by the guest. It also has much to do with the efforts of hospitality business people to differentiate their product in a world market that is awash with choices. By definition, ecotourism is connected directly to the natural and cultural environment of the destination. It enables the traveler to better appreciate a new environment, to experience a sense of adventure, to relax and perhaps to learn. This is life enrichment and sometimes it is escapism.

The activity of creating shelter is one of the most ancient of the human race's activities, it is therefore without any surprise that the built form of any culture reflects its deepest roots as well as its current direction. A tourism product that can sensitively recognise this, work within it or complement it, will guarantee unique product that is attractive to the traveling customer. The resulting facilities will enhance the visitor experience and have the potential to define its success.

The accommodations and facilities of an ecotourist operation set the tone for the guest experience. They are the structure that enables the business to prosper and guests to enjoy themselves. They are an integral part of the backdrop and stage set for the total combined experience. It is essential that the facilities are well considered in all respects and that they inform, and are informed by, the operations of the property, and are harmonious with the culture and natural landscape of their environment.

General Concepts on Ecotourism Accommodations

Ecotourism facilities are in a uniquely advantageous position since they are inherently more diverse than traditional hospitality products. A wide range of options is available when folding cultural activities with contemporary, vernacular or historical building forms (or variations of them) and applying them to the activities that are promoted in each facility. The design and construction of buildings, however, is not and should not be a casual decision. The need to decide how a new structure may be built for practical purposes, or how an existing structure can be renovated, is also an opportunity to communicate a message. This message can then be determined through the design and finish of this structure to support the goals and objectives of the operations and financial plan.

A property that chooses to affix the label of being an ecotourism facility invariably conjures up the image of an alternative, rustic, low density or low impact facility. This is understandable given the beginnings of ecotourism operations as tents, platforms, vernacular huts and similar lower density, less visible and relatively isolated facilities. This is also exciting in that the guest is able to have access, in comfort, to a lifestyle that would normally be unattainable without discomfort, risk or a time commitment they cannot afford. However, the ecotourism property is not necessarily restricted to this type. The 'eco' in ecotourism can be the 'back to nature, 'get away from it all' or 'adventure' style of experience. It can also have a greater affiliation with the local culture and can be tied to the educational aspects of environmentally responsible living. There is no reason why an ecotourism property cannot exist just as easily as a contemporary structure in a suburban or urban environment provided it is carefully located in a site or building of special affiliation to that culture through its vernacular architecture or iconographic status. It would, in addition, need to be accompanied by an operations programme of appropriate educational, cultural or environmentally focused activities.

An exciting and memorable facility also has the option of being sited in renovated or newly built facilities. The former may be more challenging to adapt but could also be more economical. In any event, existing buildings come with a history and a narrative of their past. It enriches a visitor's experience to be aware of and appreciate the events, the people and the modifications that have engaged their destination. It can be argued that the ecotourist is invariably an interested tourist. The facilities have to be presented intelligently, and they need to be available to provide the layers of interest that can enhance the vacation experience. If these can be made available at the guests' choosing then so much the better, for they will be able to relax and be stimulated when they wish.

In all instances it is critical to avoid being casual in the process of choosing spatial allocations, materials and furnishings. These all have the ability to inform the guest on the culture and activities associated with the property. They can set a standard for comfort, or not, that can then be coordinated with the rate structures and expectations of the guest.

A traditional hotel invariably consists of one building with racked rooms above aground floor assemblage of public spaces. A variation on this theme is a central facilities structure with individual accommodation units in the adjacent grounds. Motels and cottage colonies are polar opposites in the quality of this type of accommodation. The ecotourism product comes into its own most readily with this model of development. There is an inherent sense of an individual identity, and a small scale that appeals to the message of a quality vacation experience.

The field is, however, wide open in terms of considering the possible accommodation types. This is particularly applicable when the accommodation is the passport to access new experiences. Mountain huts for adventure tourists are without any central facilities and are way-points in a journey. A vehicle, like a boat or bus, may become the base for high-end luxury or communal living. Each contributes in its own way to providing a completely unique experience. A low impact tent may permit building approvals where a permanent structure would not normally be allowed. A mobile tent may permit a facility to have limited life span and be viable for a limited time measured in weeks or just a few years. This could allow an operation to exist where land ownership or long-term commitments are not available.

A lightly furnished room can set the tone for a sustainable lifestyle. This may be in keeping with a message on the limited nature of resources. Furnishings do not need to be cheap because they can evoke the quality of an austere oriental, simple living or high modern aesthetic but cast in the culture of the place in which the property is sited. Color, as opposed to clutter, can also enrich both the interior and exterior. Architectural and design solutions may also be eschewed in favour of landscape options in which the materials and horticulture can define the atmosphere. In the appropriate climate this has the added benefit of a constantly changing appearance. Small furnishings and fixtures, for example, can be something as simple as a mirror edged in sea glass. In this instance it can evoke childhood memories, can be made by local artisans, or on the property. It can demonstrate the recycling of materials and provides a unique accessory to a room's decor. It can also be made available for sale, thus providing additional revenue.

Development Practicalities

The ideal of an ecotourism development concept is to marry a vision of the experience with environmental sustainability and the constraints of a successful business venture, in such a way that the enterprise can function pragmatically. A traditional hotel must equate the return on investment of an initial development or renovation with the cost of that investment. Land or property acquisition and development costs become the greatest initial expenses against, which future revenue must be equated. Theory holds that the greater the investment then the better the product could be and the big-her the fee that can be charged. This becomes a more marginal proposition in developed markets where competition is greater and costs are higher. The ecotourism product can circumvent this by offering other advantages to the developer and different standards to the guest. Table below lists various development strategies that need to be taken into account to maximise the probability of product success.

Ecotourism Accommodation: Development Strategies

- Siting to maximise natural amenities in lieu of newly built amenities
- Maximum interface with the natural environment
- Downsizing the central facilities offset by operational phasing and efficiencies
- Communal living options
- Services and facilities provided by local development planners
- Use of indigenous building types that capture the local sense of place
- Self-sufficiency of the occupant to minimise operational overheads and central facilities
- Facilities and activities that minimise the emphasis on individual accommodations

- Use of low impact and low cost structures
- Use of prefabricated building types
- Operations to de-emphasize site requirements
- An emphasis on landscaping

A delicate balance between rates and standards can be attained in which costs and, thus, rates can be lowered and the amenities reduced, while taking maximum advantage of the natural environment, providing a wide range of activities and taking the moral high ground of operating a responsible and environmentally sustainable facility.

There are also fundamental infrastructure requirements that face all guest facilities no matter what scale they happen to be. Guests need to eat and drink and they also require, almost always, the consumption of packaged products. Support services include cleaning and maintenance and the management of all human, commercial and, sometimes, livestock waste. Power and potable water demands are quite often difficult demands to meet. The former is often restricted by location, capacity and storage constraints. The latter is similarly affected by environmental collection, storage, purification and, sometimes, distribution constraints. Communications is, interestingly, most easily addressed given recent advances in technology. However, this is paralleled by increased expectations on the part of guests.

The greater the volume of people, the more sensitive and sophisticated management of these issues needs to be. Certain thresholds in the number of guests can require the importation of sophisticated and expensive systems. For example, sewage treatment plants may be required for facilities of over, say, 100 beds. The good news is that there is an array of exciting and alternative methods of addressing infrastructural issues. The bad news is that they are too often not as cost effective as traditional systems, especially at a large scale.

It can be presumed that the majority of guests are likely to come from Westernised culture:. The daily services to which these people are accustomed are currently managed within their own technologically sophisticated cultural/ industrial economies. Interestingly, this level of consumption is not sustainable on a global basis if it were to be applied to the world population. It is equally likely that this level of consumption will not be sustainable in many area; that are candidates for ecotourism at least in the traditional, unspoiled, naturalistic and undeveloped environment. Properties in these, locations therefore have the opportunity to convert this constraint into a genuine marketing tool by demonstrating to their visitors how comfortable they can be and, possibly, how much happier they can be with a well-managed and more sustainable, alternative lifestyle. In contrast to this, there is no inherent reason why an ecotourism operation cannot operate in a highly developed culture where the use of alternative and more sustainable services and utilities is not required. In these instances the property can act as an educational tool for the visiting guest, and also as a prototype for adjacent communities.

Construction means and methods also provide opportunities for utilising environmentally friendly systems, some of which are listed in table below. Quite often, the indigenous building systems have developed out of natural solutions using readily available materials. The benefits of considering building in the same manner as the existing culture are considerable: readily available first construction and maintenance skills, aesthetic consistency with the vernacular and culture, and the support and cooperation of the local community. It is also likely that in the very long term the materials used can be returned to the environment without generating pollution in the event that the facility is reinvented, relocated or abandoned.

Alternative Infrastructure Options For Ecotourism Accommodation

Power	*Water*	*Waste Management*
Passive and active solar, wind, water Geothermal, tidal, building siting to take advantage of prevailing climate benefits	Non-potable flushing, grey water collection, sewage treatment recycling and reduction in consumption.	Composting toilets, biological treatment, Greenhouse filtration, recycling, glass and aluminium crushing, commercial links to waste as raw material (glass, aluminium, paper and cardboard)

If local materials are not used then their factors can come into play. Prefabricated components can offer educational opportunities and technological advances for the local population. If designed properly they can be installed so that they may be removed in the future without damaging the environment, It is also possible that the finishes and furnishings can be procured from locally sustainable sources or from recycled products. These provide very powerful marketing opportunities for the operator. They will be able to demonstrate to their clients, to local authorities and the hospitality industry that its product is an asset to its community in all respects and that it sets an example for its guests to demonstrate a better way to living.

Inception

In 1995 the Government of Bermuda had four military bases returned to the island. These represented almost 10% of the total land area of the 54 kM2 island. The population in this limited area is approximately 70,000 permanent residents. Bermuda also hosts about 550,000 visitors a year and was voted the fourth most favourite tropical island destination in the world in a 1999 Conde Nast traveler poll. The then government of Bermuda applied a rigorous land use analysis and base utilisation committee and assigned the development to a quasi-autonomous non-governmental organisation (QUANGO), a purpose-formed company called The Bermuda Land Development Company (BLDG).

One of the four parcels of land is a peninsula of exceptional beauty known as Daniel's Head. In the early 20th century this property had been part of a farm, as was much of Bermuda. The British Admiralty converted this into an electronic listening station during the Second World War and flattened half the site, a small hill, into a circular promontory at about 5 m above sea level. After the War and when the British Admiralty-reduced its operations significantly, this base was operated by the Canadian military as a Cold War listening post. Additional buildings and barracks were constructed during this tenure.

The site was zoned for tourism use with a small beach segment held out as a national park to address local community concerns. The BLDC sought proposals from interested developers. Approximately six *were* received, all proposing housing, traditional cotta-e colonies and a proposal for a park, They were all found unsatisfactory, and an alternative tourism-related proposal was sought. After some research the BLDC decided to contact Stanley Selengut who had recently received a number of awards for his low impact and environmentally focused properties on the island of St John in the US Virgin Islands: Malio Bay Harmony and Concordia. Selengut teamed up with a development partner, who eventually assumed control over the project and made a proposal. This proposal was accepted, and the project proceeded.

Tent Design

The tents are 5 in x 5 in squares with internal bathrooms alternating on different sides. They have a verandah on one side and a covered entry opposite. They are designed with white roofs in keeping with the Bermuda architectural vernacular. The white roofs also keep the tents cool, and look attractive as a neutral palette against the vibrant colors of the landscape and the water. The walls are a neutral tone to reflect as much heat as possible without being white, which will show dirt easily. The tents over the water are a light blue-color. In the existing trees they are clad in green. The intent has been to gain a maximum cost benefit from a repetitive building form but to still provide variety of experience by varying the finish and the orientation, and through site placement.

The tents are placed on a platform of six or nine piles depending on their height and the ground condition. One important factor was the building code that required the tents structure be able to withstand hurricane force winds at 110 mph while the fabric has to withstand an 80-mph wind loading. Important technical factors like this can have a significant impact on the cost of a project. It is therefore useful to resolve these as early as possible in the design/cost process.

The structure of the tents was originally conceived as a wood frame built from laminated 2 x 4s. This then developed to a 10 cm x.10 cm, wood structure. Faced with budget issues, a prefabricated tubular pipe structure was considered and this ultimately developed to become a prefabricated aluminum frame. A result of the structure change was to add an interior liner of fabric attached with an industrial grade Velcro. This provides a superior finish, assists with cleaning, provides an insulating layer in the wall and conceals all the services. The ceiling is formed in an upside-down tray, which is a traditional Bermuda architecture configuration. This provides an extra sense of height. The flat of the tray is formed out of mesh (which is not a standard detail) and so the roof void is accessible to act as a cooling plenum in the summer via vents in the gables. These are closed in the winter, thereby enabling the roof to act as a passive heat source. In both instances a central ceiling fan can distribute the air in an upward or downward direction as required.

The tents are connected to the mains electrical supply. It was originally hoped to have all the tents off the god, but further research indicated that this would have required a major centralised solar plant. Since there was insufficient space or first cost budget for this configuration, it was decided to limit the number of tents to five for demonstration purposes as a practical compromise. Almost one-third have are more integrated solar hot water heater to reduce electrical costs, which are exceptionally high in Bermuda. These are sited away from current shaded areas.

The interior of the tents is designed to be comfortable in a bright, casual, cottage holiday style. Furnishings are simple with a queen-size bed as standard, a pull out or trundle sofa and various tables and chair options. A hammock is provided as a standard amenity and the verandah is structured so that the hammock can be hung from it. At Daniel's Head it is also intended that this interior acts as the conceptual starting point for the conversion of 16 rooms in an existing barracks. Fifteen of the tents over the water have 'a window in the floor to view the water and shoreline below. The result is advisable amenity in a location where it can be appreciated, where it will not be covered by a carpet and where it is not unsafe for guests to walk over if it becomes slippery. This level of integration, between environment, structure and interior design, results in a seamless product that contributes to the guests' satisfaction.

The Daniel's Head tent is the result of an extended development processes that goes back to an evolving prototype which has been adapted to suit another climate, market, budget and construction method. The result is a tent that is appropriate to its new site yet still retains the original fundamentals of its environmental considerations, size and use. In a different climate and culture it would evolve as a different form. This is occurring in Destination Villages' Hawaii site where, for example, the climate permits the windows to be left as screens only.

Central Facilities

The Central Facilities at Daniel's Head are of a different aesthetic in that they are in a conversion of a single existing structure. The final form and programme is the condensing of various elements that were originally planned to be distributed through four buildings. This was reduced by budget constraints. This demonstrates that an environmentally focused hospitality operation can successfully compromise usuals 1 and ax4.s in the interests of utilising fewer resources and funds. In this instance the compromises would be in a blending of lounge and bar functions, smaller offices and a simplification of the food service amenities.

Environmental Overview

At the initial planning stages the regulatory authorities were sceptical that Daniel's Head would be an ecotourism facility. It is not located in an isolated area of profound environmental value such as a rainforest. This scepticism was reasonable given the classic perceptions about the appropriate location of ecotourist properties. Similarly, the accommodations were different from the rustic structure, lodge or hut that might be envisaged. This scepticism extended to the activities which would interest the guests, since there were no wide-open tracts of land to appreciate. The ultimate realisation of the government of Bermuda, and hence the approval, was that Daniel's Head had the potential to be a leadership project in environmental restoration. It could also act as an incubator for environmental education as well as adding another dimension to the traditional tourism product that was available.

The accommodations and facilities of Daniel's Head enable a damage site to be restored in a business environment. Its open spaces are the incredible views over the water even though its land plan is quite dense. Its accommodations are comfortable enough to provide a reasonable alternative to the traditional product, that is available, yet simple enough to appeal to the luxury camper. Its design adheres to the culture of its location and this can be enhanced through the direct integration of the local population in the facilities activities. Finally, and perhaps most importantly, the alternative energy, composting, sustainable design and sustainable operations programmes can provide an example to the local community. Table below provides a synopsis of the environmentally appropriate practices that characterize this facility.

6

Principles of Tourism Planning

> "A man who does not think and plan long ahead will find trouble right at this door."
>
> —*Confucius*

Planning may be defined as a proposed method of action or procedure to achieve a pre-determined target or an objective. Certain basic factors are there which are to be taken into consideration in the planning process. First, there must bean objective and that objective must be clearly understood and accepted by all those who are to be involved. Second, there must be a programme leading to the objective. Finally there must be a measurement of progress towards the objective set. The key factors, therefore, for a successful planning are the objectives, programme and the measurement of the objective. The need for planning arises whenever some rational thinking is required to arrive at a choice among a set of limited means so that certain ends are satisfied, especially when the means are substitutable among themselves. In brief, Planning essentially attempts to allocate scarce resources between different competing uses with a view to maximising output, income and employment and to ensure the balanced growth of different sectors. Out of two economic systems (i.e., Planned economy and Market economy), Planned economy is one in which each production unit (or a firm) uses only the resources of men, material and equipment allocated to it by quota and disposes of its products to persons or firms indicated to it by simple order. On the other hand a market economy is controlled by the forces of market, like demand, supply, prices, transport, etc.

Tourism Planning

The need for planned development is of paramount importance in the field of tourism. Many countries in the world, especially the developing countries, have lately realised the importance of tourism and the benefits which it brings out. The use of microeconomic planning techniques for tourism sector is however relatively new. The planning methods for national economic development which have been largely utilised since the end of World War II did not always cover tourism development as a particular field. The increasing significance of tourism as a source of income, employment generation, regional development and as a major factor in the balance of payments for many countries has been attracting increasing attention on the part of many governments as well as others with an interest in economic development. Thus, tourism development became more and more a particular field of research in the economic planning undertaken by many countries.

IT is appropriate here to quote Sigismund von Radecki, the German social scientist from his 'book *Was Ich Sagen Wollte* (1952), inconnection to the expanding growth of tourism:

"Travel today is the most popular form of happiness. Perhaps this has something to do with the fact that a large part of humanity these days is incarcerated in prisons of one sort or another. Or perhaps it might be more correct to say that travel is one of the focal points of happiness. For, if you ask the man in the street, what would you do if you won a big sweepstake? You generally receive one of the two replies: Either "Oh, I would travel see the world", or "I would build myself a house." These two replies, apparently contradictory, are unanimous in expressing two fundamental human longings for faraway places and home, sweet home. And in this, they bear the same relationship to each other as breathing in and out.

"Holiday travel has become the most conspicuous phenomenon of our time. Neither mass migration nor the world wars have succeeded in putting so many million people on the road as the desire for a holiday does year after year. People voluntarily leave their homes to enjoy their vacation in distant places. For more and more people in the industrial countries of the world, an annual holiday trip is an accepted way of life."

"In Germany, for instance, holiday tours took the top spot in 'consumer hit parade', leaving behind savings and household purchases. In other words, holiday tours are the first item on the shopping list of a German household the erstwhile luxury has become a regular feature of life and a necessity. In Great Britain, seventy-five per cent of the British population took a holiday for four nights or more away from home in 1990. In the same year, fifty million short holidays of one to three nights away from home were taken. The, percentage in West Germany and Scandinavia is even higher. A holiday is the 'year's sugar allowance' in the bitterness of the industrial work-a-day world."

Tourism has grown during the last fifty years in most areas of the world as an unplanned activity. The result has been haphazard and a sudden boost in tourism facilities like hotels, rail, air and road transport in places that become popular holiday resorts or to meet the demand to satisfy the profit instinct of the promoters. *Examples:* Hawaii, Miami or Spain. The patterns have been repeated in some Asian countries, especially in Japan, Thailand and Singapore. In Thailand, large hotels were built at a beach resort called Pattaya—about 150 kilometers, from Bangkok. Now, the occupancy of the hotels does not even average 50 per cent a year. Anyone, who has visited a few of these popular holiday resorts in the world, cannot but be aware of the depressing circumstances under which commercialisation has taken precedence over the care or protection of the landscape and environment. A large number of people are going to the same spot at the same time. Holidays are concentrated in certain specific months of the year. The results are crowded beaches, mountains, and lakes, ever-widening roads, increasingly bigger parking lots, and queues of cars on border crossing and bumper-to bumper crawling of vehicles.

Need for Planned Development

Tourism development planning, is of recent origin. It was specially taken note of during the last seventy years after public voices were heard against the unplanned invasion of tourism. In 1950, Gerhard Noble called mass tourism "one of the great western plagues hardly less evil in effects than the epidemics of the middle ages." In a conference held in Limuru, Kenya, the tourist inflow was referred to "as a dangerous invasion." These remarks, however, may be exaggerated apprehensions of the environmentalists. But one can admit the unanimous fact that where modern industrial life makes inroads into ancient societies, traditional values begin to totter. Tourism is a form of social industrialisation with all its advantages and demerits. Its advantages have to be grasped and utilised with care so that the impact of the disadvantages is minimized. Planning is of greater benefit to developing societies where tourism is a new phenomenon and has had little or no adverse effect so far.

The World Bank's warning as early as 1972 is worth remembering:

"In many areas of the world, tourism development, has produced, great disparities in the standards of amenities provided for the visitors and for the local population. This cannot be entirely avoided, but in the long run, the improvement of standards for the local population is probably a condition of successful tourism development. The development of a new resort by the provision of infrastructure costing perhaps millions of dollars has a great impact on land values in the area affected. Were these benefits to accrue largely to a few private landowners, the Bank would have difficulty in financing such a project. The acquisition of land by government or a public agency prior to development... eases the problems of planning on an integrated basis, and of enforcing proper zoning and building regulations. It also helps to ensure that windfall gains do not accrue solely to private landowners and provides the opportunity for the public, agency to offer serviced sites to hotel developers at prices which can include, if necessary, an incentive element. There is a very close relationship between land prices and building densities, and by appropriate land pricing the development authority can help to ensure that acceptable physical planning and density standards are maintained."

Two significant points emerge out of the above statement:

— Planning should be integrated to avoid as far as possible, disparities in the standards of amenities for the visitors and local population.

— Tourism planning should not be left totally to private enterprise in search of profit. Government must actively participate in it.

In the past, tourism Planning simply implied that new hotel construction should be encouraged, more airlines should start operation, promotional campaigns may be launched within the country and abroad and border crossing must be eased. Although it worked to some extent, it was at best an erratic method of planning tourism. That is how most developing countries started their own tourism planning, resulting in multiple drawback.

Currenlty, tourism has become a major industry in many countries of the world and has thus a pervasive effect on the economy of the nations as well as their social structure. Unplanned tourism can hamper, a nation in getting maximum benefits from its development. The development of the tourism sector is one of the several options before a government, making claims on its resources which, in most cases, are limited. It is, therefore, necessary for tourism planners to place their case before the government in justifiable terms listing anticipated contribution to the economic development of the country through tourism development.

The two economic arguments in favour of developing tourism are:

- — the contribution in terms of foreign exchange; and
- — multiple employment potential of the tourism industry.

National Goals

Decision at the national level has to be taken by the government, preferably in consultation with various interests involved. A national policy is called for incorporating the directions in which tourism development should take place.

National objectives could be as under:

- — Preservation of cultural resources and the heritage.
- — Generation of new employment.
- — To develop infra- and super-structure to provide recreation facilities for visitors and the resident population.
- — To maximise economic benefits in terms of improvements of standards of living of the people.
- — Stimulation-of development at regional levels.
- — Maximising visitors' satisfactions.
- — Ensuring development at tourist centers and resorts consistent with the needs of each urea.

Demand and Supply in Tourism

Tourism development is a complex phenomenon requiring in-depth study of resource and demand pattern in each country. The local visitors have their own preferences regarding what they want to do during their holidays. A 1990 study in UK revealed that 60 per cent of domestic visitors go to the sea for their holiday which is accessible in a few hours from any part of the country. Fortunately, for Britain, most overseas visitors are not interested in sea holidays. For them, London is a tourist 'Mecca'. Some 10 million foreign visitors add to the congestion of London, annually, along with another 15 million domestic visitors. The French also prefer the sea. In the case of France, the sea is also the focus of attention of the foreign visitors adding to the congestion on its beaches. The Italians prefer the lakes, while the visitors opt for the history and culture of Rome and many other cities of Italy spreading millions of visitors thinly over the entire country.

The pattern of traffic has to be kept in mind while planning the development of tourism in a destination, especially at the supply side as it is not flexible. Hotels are not built in a day nor are the airports. For successful tourism planning, current and future supply has to be correlated to current and future demand.

Factors for Tourism Development

Some of the major factors which influence tourism development in a destination area can be summarised as follows:

- Diversity and vitality of already existing tourist activity.
- Whether the facilities were planned and planted in the area or grew spontaneously because of some man-made or national attraction.
- Size of the existing population.

- — Availability of land and finance.
- — State of the local economy-options of alternate development.
- — Impact on the local community-benefits and social costs.
- — Whether the area is extensive for future expansion or only limited expansion is possible.
- — Attitude of the local people towards the tourism projects.
- — Magnitude and speed of development.
- — Availability of local manpower a dynamic population.

Opposition by local population against tourism projects, however beneficial to the community, can create problems, as it happened in Australia. Yeppon is a small town on the coast of central Queens land Australia's sunshine state described by its 6,000 inhabitants as 'Paradise. It has beautiful views and miles of glorious beaches. A Japanese businessman saw the area and fell in love with it, deciding to develop it into a resort. The beach here is 10 times longer and wider than Waikiki in. Honolulu. He bought 20,000 acres to develop it into an international resort, building a number of hotels, guest houses, wildlife parks and several other attractive features.

Though the scheme was approved by the Australian Government but the local residents did not like it. They could not tolerate the idea of thousands of tourists crowding their beaches all the year-round. The investor tried to woo the local population, offering them millions of dollars to build a retirement home and other facilities. In November 1981, a bomb exploded under a motel under construction destroying property. This is an example of the type of problems a developer can face-if local cooperation is not sought.

Constituents Tourist Attractions

Planners must know what makes a tourist destination click. The following are some of the factors which would create tourist attraction:

Scenic

- — Natural scenic beauty.
- — Wildlife, flora and fauna.
- — Wildlife safari parks.
- — Attractive coastline/long beaches.
- — Mountain location, rivers and lakes.

Climate

- — Mild temperature
- — Hours of sunshine.
- — Salubriaus clionate.

Cultural

- — Ancient buildings, monuments, archaeological sites, history and culture.
- — Customs and traditions
- — Religion.

Local Way of Life

- — Handicrafts
- — Folk arts
- — Traditional music
- — Classical and folk dances
- — Festivals/Fairs
- — Art

Amusement

- — Night life

— Theatre, cinemas
— Local leisure, good food
— Recreational/ Amusement parks,
— Health resort, spa, springs
— Sporting activities, adventure sports
— Zoo and ocean marinas.

Any or several of these attracts visitors to a destination as per their choice.

Research and Exploration

Surprisingly in the tourism field, an insignificant amount of money is spent on research compared to total turnover of tourism earnings though research is necessary for tourism planning.

The unprecedented tourism development in certain areas like Majorda in Spain or Hawaii in America was due to the fact that these were some of the first areas developed for a particular type of holiday. Today, they are no longer alone in the field. The sun, sea, sands and reasonable prices are available at other places too. Fast jets have made inexpensive travel possible to distant lands—like Sri Lanka, India, the Maldives. Thailand and Malaysia—where prices are comparatively much lower. As such, for any new resort development, planning, both physical as well as economic considerations, are essential. A country which decides to develop tourism should take a hard look at places offering similar attraction, study their economics and call for specialists to prepare a tourism development plan. Technical assistance from foreign experts has proved useful in many cases as they can provide an objective assessment of the tourist resources of country. Among the aspects to be studied are:

— Speed of construction to attract public investment.
— Characteristics of the land available for development, and the price structure.

— Composition of the facilities to be provided—hotels, non-hotels and other services, industries like restaurants, stores and beach services.

— Infrastructure includes all forms of construction on and below the ground, that is, roads and parking areas, railway lines, airports, water supply, power houses and sewage disposal. Superstructure consists of hotels, motels, restaurants, entertainment, and shopping facilities. Total cost of infrastructure and superstructure in the area proposed to be developed.

— Feasibility of direct and indirect taxes from tourism-related activities to justify public investment.

Planning Levels

Generally Planning may be done on two levels—national and local. At the national level the central government will be involved developing selected areas on the basis of research and study. The guiding principles in the selection of the areas are their marketability as tourist spots to international and domestic travelers, anticipated receipts from the tourism sector, and projections of future demand. The national plan shall also lay down the broad framework for development at local and regional levels.

The detailed planning of the local needs has to be done at the local level with financial assistance or subsidies from the central government to some of the activities. This arrangement is prevalent in countries where tourism is not highly developed and the state has to play a pivotal role. In India, although the government is involved in tourism planning, the private sector plays a significant role in developing tourist facilities. Some of the facilities are planned, developed and managed solely by the state. Now, most countries including China have opened their tourism sector for private participation.

A government cannot afford to do everything at once. They have to select priority areas for development where some infrastructure may exist and whose tourist attractions are relatively better known. The development of completely virgin areas, though a worthwhile proposition in time, has to take its turn depending upon the resources of the country and the political will to develop tourism on the part of the government.

The World Tourism Organisation published an inventory of tourism development plans of various countries in 1977. Out of the forty-three member-countries, which replied to the WTO questionnaire, thirty-seven had an integrated planning system at the national level. But in majority of the cases, the plans remained on paper and when these were acted upon, action was half-hearted or partial implementation. Some countries, like the USA, and Canada, have, strictly speaking, no national tourism plans. In the USA, a study for making federal policy and programme involvement in tourism more coherent and responsive to national interest was undertaken only in 1976. After six years of intensive efforts by the travel industry, the then President Ronald Reagan signed into law a National Tourism Policy Act on October 16, 1981.

Under this Act, the US Congress created the US Travel and Tourism Administration to 'optimize' the contribution of tourism and recreation industries to economic prosperity, full employment and international balance of payments to the US. Resultantly in 1996 USTTA has been axed in an economy drive by Clinton Administration. In Canada, each of the ten provinces and two territories are involved in tourism development planning. In USA, states are more actively involved in the promotion of tourism even more than the federal government. France has a full-fledged Ministry of Free Time which deals with tourism.

Integrated Planning

The tourism planners, had two different tasks : one of physical planning in new areas with potential but with little or no existing touristic activity, and the other of re-shaping the areas where tourism already existed. Two, re-planning of existing high density tourist areas.

There has been little coordination and regulation in physical planning for tourism development. Resorts have developed in attractive settings while ancillary facilities like transportation were created belatedly to meet the demand. Industrial and commercial cities found themselves receiving more visitors. The new, substantial facilities created were shared by foreign visitors and the local people. Existing infrastructure designed for the requirements of a relatively static age came under the strain of anew and mobile society.

Where should the planners begin? The first thing is to analyse different types of national or other tourist resources of which each country has many-that could attract tourists. These maybe of scenic beauty, history, a mystique, and so on. An inventory of all these resources of the country has to be made. Then, there are cities like London and Paris which have their own natural draw for visitors. London, the biggest tourist attraction in the world, is visited by over 10 million tourists and Paris by about 20 million foreign visitors annually.

After preparing the inventory, areas have to be selected for tourism development keeping in view the availability of economic resources. While taking up the areas for development in a city, it is necessary to define the minimum urban planning parameters which, if taken note of, may prevent the degradation of the environment through unregulated building activity.

The basic parameters in planning a sea resort should indicate

(a) the space between buildings,

(b) the distance of the road from the beach; and the capacity of tourist accommodation on the beach or off the beach.

It is most desirable that the guidelines should also give building specifications, length, suggested dimensions, and characteristics of the road network providing access to the sea. The creation and development of a green belt should be clearly marked. Non regulated or unplanned structures should be allowed in the area proposed to be developed. Similarly, the tourism development plan of an area with historical monuments as a major attraction requires that the view of the monuments should not be concealed by any haphazard construction in the area surrounding the monument.

To conclude the following must be considered in any area planning:

- Determination of broad parameters of urban planning and architectural specifications.
- Preparation of overall inventory of national tourist resources.
- Exploration of possibilities of investment in private and public sectors.
- Cost benefit studies of the proposed projects.

Tourism Development and Investment and Income

'When a tourism project is taken up for implementation, the time relation between investment requirements-and revenue expectation has to be kept in mind. The following 8-point project structure for tourism planning and development may be more guiding.

- Establishment of goals after a feasibility study.
- Market and resources analysis.
- Conceptual planning.

— Approval of the plan.
— Master planning.
— Phased implementation programme.
— Evaluation and direction.
— Monitoring operations for ensuring services quality and operational success.

Systems must be devised to provide continuing feedback on volume of tourism and levels of satisfication provided.

Role of Govt. in Tourism Planning

To make a tourism plan work/Governments have to create a favourable climate for investment through regulations and fiscal measures. Since most private investors would expect a reasonable return on investment, special financial incentives are *necessary* to make tourism investment attractive. A tourism project needs to be assisted at two stages: first at the time of making investment, and subsequently at the operational stage. Participation in the development of a tourism plan by government may be more attractive to investors, if the government offers ' direct financial subsidy. Another form of help is special credit facilities for tourism projects as in countries like UK, France, Spain and India. A common form of credit is long-term loans for hotels at less than the market rates of interest. Since tourism financing is different from other industries, some countries have created special institutions to disburse such loans. France has Caisse *Centrale* de Credit *Hotelier,* Portugal has its Tourist Fund, Israel its Tourist Industry Development Corporation. In India, hotels are financed, on the recommendation of the Department of Tourism, by Industrial Finance Corporation of India (IFCI) at central level and State Financial Corporation at state level.

In India, in the late eightiesof the last century, an India Tourism Finance Corporation (TFCI) was created to finance tourism projects and it is doing a good job.

Tourism related industries could have a preferential rate of interest. Other alternate measures could be grant of interest rebate on tourism investment by making up the difference between the commercial rate and the rate proposed for the hotel industry. This is one of the several incentives given to hotels in recent years in India. Special facilities for the purchase of land at concessional rates for tourism superstructure can be a powerful incentive-especially in the backward regions of the country. Some governments recognise tourism as an export industry, as in India lately and offer same fiscal benefits and incentives as are available to other export industries. These include duty free import of equipment required for tourist services or reduction in customs duty or their waiver. The government can also make tourism investment attractive by giving tax relief at the operational stage to improve profitability.

The Government can help tourism planning through manpower development by running hotel and tourism training schools/courses. Finally, the extent of government concessions to tourism is basically linked with the importance a state attaches to the tourism sector compared to other sectors of economy. The involvement of the government in tourism planning, development and promotion varies from country to country.

Tourism, Environment and Government

The control of planning of physical environment in tourism is imperative. The following points must be taken into consideration:

— What facilities should be erected and when?
— Alternative uses of land
— Pollution
— Serenity of atmosphere
— Integrity of landscape

— Cost of land and its ratio to building and development costs
— Traffic circulation
— Zoning and density
— Services-water, electricity, gas, sewerage, etc.

Architectural style, building regulations, site-layout density, and preservation of the natural features of the land are part of the environmental control. Protecting lakes, hills, beaches, rivers and historical monument from the onslaught of large masses of visitors are also the responsibility of the government. A couplet in the Atharvaveda says: "Whatever I take from the Earth may that have quick growth again. O Purifier, may we not injure the vitals of Thy heart."

The Atharvaveda *pronounced* these words of wisdom more than five thousand years ago when Indian cult-are was being formed in the magnificent forests teeming with wildlife. It is remarkable that people in that age realised that the resources of the earth were not something which could be damaged at will. But we must also rember the warning of Krishna Chaitanya.

> "If we do not realise that the beauty and variety of the earth are autonomous values in their own right, if we believe that we have life and health on earth and not with the earth, we will exploit it greedily and come to ruin speedily. If we treat the earth without reverence and ruin its beauty and order, the end will be the failure of the earth to produce any food for us. Demands for tourism are as diverse as the resources. It is not easy to match the supply with the demand, for tourism can create pressure on local facilities; can affect the landscape and the lifestyle of the people."

The problems of conservation were taken note of in the early stages of tourism development. America established the Yellowstone Park within an area of 3,350 square miles in 1872. The British founded a national trust for places of historic interest and national beauty in 1895. A separate Ministry of Town and Country Planning was created in 1943 in Great Britain. National Physical Planning began in the United Kingdom as early as in 1947 with the passing of Town and Planning Act. The National Park Access to the Countryside Act in 1949 established a National Park Commission with the objective of natural beauty and provision of opportunities for open-air recreation. The ten national parks created in England covered nine per cent of the land area. In 1971, a Department of Environment was set up in England. In India, too, a Ministry of Environment and Forests was set up when Rajiv Gandhi took over as Prime Minister in 1985. The concern for preservation of ecological balance was not confined to the USA and the UK; it has its worldwide impact. In 1968, the Council of Europe launched the Air Pollution and Water Charter and Water Conservation Campaign. The African convention for conservation of nature took place in the same year. In the USA, the Council of Environmental Quality was established in 1970 and President Nixon promulgated, a 37-point programme of preservation of environmental quality.

India is already facing problems relating to environmental pollution mainly due to pressure of population and only partly due to tourism. The case of Dal Lake in Srinagar (Kashmir) is evidence of this.

Not doubt, Tourism can be a boon to any country, especially to a developing country like India. But tourism planning has to ensure that India preserves be Himalayas in their original glory, and the wide variety of wildlife, which is a great asset for tourism. The government took a wise aecision in banning the hunting of tiger, panther and other species which were in danger of becoming extinct due to wanton killing. The Tourist Development Council, an advisory body of the Government of India, in a resolution passed as early as 1972 at Goa, requested the Government of India to take steps to ensure that:

— Any new construction in the vicinity of monuments should meet aesthetic requirements.

— Any unnecessary interference from electric lines, power plants, petrol stations, and advertisement hoardings is avoided.

— Special care should be taken to prevent pollution of water and air, working of mines and quarries, dumping of domestic, commercial and industrial waste in the vicinity of monuments.

— Deforestation of the area around monuments is avoided.

— Financial assistance be given by the state governments, local, bodies to improve and beautify roads and environment of monuments and other places of tourist interest.

— To avoid haphazard peripheral growth, the location of facilities like canteens, book shops, curio shops, etc., in the vicinity of important monuments may be done only after clearance from the Archaeological Survey of India and the Department of Tourism.

As a follow-up on this resolution, the Department of Tourism selected ten archaeological complexes of tourist importance comprising thirty archaeological centers. Master plans for these have already been prepared.

Tourist Destinations in Danger

To a question whether tourists were concerned about the environmental quality of the destination they visit, 63 per cent of the tour-operators surveyed answered yes. In reply to another question whether they offered any products that might be classed 'environmental friendly' or 'Green', 61 said yes. Seventy-nine per cent of the group said that they offered green products in Europe, 16 per cent in Asia Pacific, 13 per cent in Americas and 37 per cent in Africa. It seems that tour-operators were taking their business to alternate destinations from areas where environmental degradation was accentuating.

7

Tourism Planning: A Global Scenario

> "There is greatness in tradition—when it is kept alive and not worshipped in its tomb."
>
> —*Lord Wakefield*

The United Nations Conference on International Travel and Tourism held in Rome in 1963 emphasised the need for planning in tourism and made several recommendations. Some of the important recommendations that the United Nations Conferences made in the area of need for development plan in tourism were as follows:

(i) that the governments of developing countries should give high priority to projects concerning the development of tourism in their respective countries

(ii) that the governments of developing countries should consider the possibility of seeking the assistance of the United Nations Special Fund for Regional and Sub regional Surveys of existing and potential tourist traffic estimates and forecasts, with a view to the establishment of short term and long-term plans for the development of tourist facilities and plant.

The conference endorsed the relevant comments of the Groups of Experts who had pointed out that tourism was expanding swiftly as world economy improved and more and more travelers sought new places to visit. It further stated, that, to the extent permitted by its economic resources, a country should see a steady growth in the number of new tourist resorts developed. Existing possibilities of attracting tourists for mountaineerings, winter sports, fishing, hunting, beaches, spas, national parks, game sanctuaries, national monument sites and shrines, folk traditions and customs, pilgrimages, festivals and sporting events, should likewise be developed and protected.

The conference also agreed that a developing country which proposed to set up a national tourist organisation should consider obtaining a preliminary survey in order to assess clearly what positive tourist attractions the country already had, what Potential tourist attractions existed, and how they would most effectively be developed within the limits of the funds available. The recommendations had far-reaching implications as far as planned development of tourism was concerned. All member states and the specialised agencies of the United Nations were called upon to consider and implement as appropriate the recommendation Contained in the report of the conference. The recommendations of the conference were of particular interest to those countries which were just beginning to develop tourism until quite recently tourism was principally a feature of, and was largely confined to, the developed countries. Many of the developing countries saw the possibilities in tourism development. Encouraged by the conference recommendations many developing countries introduced tourism development programmes.

As far back as in 1965 United Nations Conference on Trade and Development (UNCTAD) put stress the promise which tourism held out for the developing countries. For some countries, tourism offers a major opportunity since it provides employment for many, it stimulates investment and is an important source of foreign exchange. The third International Union of Official Travel Organisations (IUOTO) Travel Research Seminar held in Prague, Czechoslovakia, in 1964, examined in great detail the many problems involved in the development of tourist industry and concluded that planning, whether at national, regional or local level, was indispensable. It concluded that all tourist planning should be based on two types of preliminary surveys: (1) detailed survey of the characteristics of the area being considered for development and, in particular, of its tourist resources; (2) studies of future customers based on surveys and forecasts.

Concerted planning is a prerequisite for complete success of any programme. The haphazard development in many countries had made the planners aware of the need for planning of tourism development based on scientific research. Any country, whether it already has an active flourishing tourist industry or is thinking of developing a tourist industry has to decide on many crucial issues before launching tourism development. The official government agencies, especially in the developing countries, have to be extra cautious as they cannot afford to waste scarce resources on development plans which do not bring benefits.

As per Report of the Organisation for Economic Cooperation and Development (OECD) seminar held at Estpril, "much of the discussion turned on the fact that tourism is by its nature somewhat different from other sectors of the economy, since it is an industry based on movement of people rather than goods. For this reasons it is particularly susceptible to subjective considerations quite apart from the play of the economic forces. Political and social pressures, psychological attitudes, changes of fashion, may all influence the course of tourism development markedly and unpredictably. It is essential therefore that tourism industry should be as flexible as possible to be able to adapt to changing conditions and requirements." The discussions at the OECD seminar also drew attention to the fact that tourism involves several considerations which are essentially of noneconomic nature. The report of the seminar stated: "Tourism often has significant cultural implications (for example, the restoration of ancient monuments); and political (the improvement of international understanding). The fact that tourism is by its nature somewhat different from other sectors of the economy makes it more necessary that there should be careful planning. This is much more important for the developing countries which cannot afford to waste scarce resources. The various issues involved in the planning and development of tourism especially in the developing countries show how necessary it is for these countries to adopt a monetary policy, a policy of agriculture, of public works, of health, of transport, etc.; as different elements of its national economic plan, and it should on the same grounds, adopt a specific policy of tourism development.

Coordinated Planning

Tourism, as an integral part or specific sector of the general plan of economic development, can only prosper within the context of the country's overall progress even though it calls for its own particular policy. Tourism like other economic activities flourishes best when it fits into a context of general economic policies and programmes designed to lead to the optimum growth of the economy of a country as a whole. This calls for coordination. Coordination between tourism planning and the general plan must, therefore, be based on coordination of effort in all the sectors concerned. Tourism policy must therefore be a global policy of development, taking into account the important implications, affecting the progress of this activity. Besides this the overall tourism development plan must take into account the social and cultural components of the phenomenon, as these also acquire prominence in the development process.

The planning of tourism, whether at the national or the regional level, must be regarded as an integral, and, therefore, coordinated part of the country's general economic and social planning. This coordinated approach has a direct bearing on the success of the tourism industry, more so in a developing country it is also to be remembered that tourism is not one business but involves many industries and a whole range of complex processes. A plan for tourism can only survive and serve its stated purposes, if there is coordination among all the processes A first requisite is the need to ensure that the government organs specifically responsible for the tourist sector play their important role, which is that of cooperating with all those governmental departments responsible for other branches concerned with the expansion of tourism.

Tourism Planning Process

There are several processes or analysis of a plan. For tourism development, it is very important that these processes are properly adhered to. The description of these planning processes as given here can only be briefly indicative and limited to mere suggestions of the topics or steps without entering into detailed analysis. Any plan must take into account these processes if it is to attain objectives in a given period of time.

The following are the main steps or phases in the planning process of tourism:

(a) assessment of tourist demand and supply;
(b) establishing objectives;
(c) financial planning;
(d) basic infrastructure;
(e) territorial planning;
(f) time factor;
(g) monitoring progress; and
(h) administrative structure;
(i) human resource planning.

Tourist Demand and Supply

The formost of early steps in planning is gathering

information on the things the way they are and on the potential available for desirable growth. Recording of information and the development of statistics is, therefore, of utmost importance. The important initial steps evaluating a potential for tourism development lies in determining present status. An analysis of the present structure of demand and supply in tourism is a precondition of any other estimate. This information base is a prerequisite for initial tourism planning programme. In the first place there must be a survey of the tourists attractions of various types which the country has to offer. Without the full study of the attractions a country possess, it is not possible to plan the for future expansion. It is therefore, of fundamental importance that a very careful assessment be made of all attractions—physical, cultural historical—that a country possesses.

First, it is highly desirable that the attraction should be developed progressively throughout the entire country so that tourism is spread as widely as possible. In this way the benefits which accrue from the industry are also widely spread and most parts of the country benefit. Secondly, areas and attractions which are singled out for special development should appeal to the widest possible cross section of tourists over the longest possible season. By adhering to this principle, over dependence upon a particular season of the year, will be avoided. Thirdly, priority should be given to those attractions which can be most easily and most successfully developed. Those attractions which can be based upon the existing infrastructural services should be given priority as these would require 'less finance. Fourthly, since it is very difficult, rather impossible to develop all the potential attractions at the same time, it is important that similar or competing attractions should not be embarked upon until the volume of visitors can justify them. Finally, it is important to know that the tourist is usually looking for something new, he desires new experiences, different environments, new thrills, etc. Any country possessing attractions which are unique or out of the ordinary should attempt to capitalise on these for they are likely to have a great drawing power.

Then on must estimate the Demand, for both national and foreign tourists. Both internal and external data on tourism activities affecting the area under consideration should be assembled. This task should use published statistics on travel and tourism which are readily available from international and regional organisations. In addition travel and accommodation statistics, can be assembled from the region under study. Next the tourist supply must include all the different types of facilities additional to various types of accommodation establishments. Special attention must be given to the seasonal factor.

Objective Setting

The initial data or the information thus gathered should develop a composite picture of what tourism can do for and to a particular area. In order to relate these projected results to a decision on whether to proceed with tourism development, there must be a basis for comparison. This basis is the cumulative set of objectives which should be developed concurrently. Basically, objectives for tourism should be a sub-set of the overall objectives for nation, the economy, and the people and the social structure with an area. There are, however, no hard or set rules as to what the objectives should be. In general, however, tourism objectives should deal with growth leading to increased standard of living, employment levels, opportunities for intellectual growth, and enhancement of the investment potential in an area or country. Cumulatively, tourism objective should describe the set of conditions under which a favourable decision should be made.

As a first step towards preparation of conceptual plan for tourism development, a market study begins with a determination of the type of tourism business which exists and can be expected. Market study provides the basis for conceptual planning. The conceptual plan provides a general view of the future tourism development programme and the steps necessary to achieve targeted results. The various steps involved in conceptual planning, once the market survey has been performed, include:

- Statement of objectives
- Selection of site
- Requirements of various facilities
- Supplementary attractions
- Land use allocation and control
- Budgets, and
- Legislative requirements

Another important step in planning is preparation of master plan. Master planning is a process for completing detailing additional work on the portions of the conceptual which is approved for further development. The difference between conceptual and master planning lie largely in the level of details involved. Where conceptual planning for example, indicates the need to expand airport runways and terminal facilities master planning would go into specifics on land and construction.

Basic Infrastructure

Infrastructure elements comprise the system of services and utilities which are necessary to the operation of a tourism destination. The estimation of the basic infrastructure required for tourist expansion accordingly becomes a key economic factor in proceeding to the active phase of implementation. This infrastructure will be either specifically tourist in nature, e.g., transport, or more general such as energy producing units, and will in any case relate with the type of tourism envisaged. The requirements for infrastructure will vary for different areas. The requirements, for example, will be different for a mountain resort and for a tourist pole adjacent to some cultural attraction. The requirements will be for both tourists and local residents. As various agencies are responsible for the development of infrastructural services, coordination is very essential. Without coordination, different elements of infrastructure may infringe upon other resulting in wasteful expenditure. Specific areas of infrastructure are power, water, communication, sewage and drainage, roads and highways, parks, recreation and health care facilities.

Financial Planning

Financial planning is very essential for a successful tourism development plan. Before any major attraction facility of destination gets into full swing & considerable expenses are involved. There follows the study of a vital element in tourist development, that is, the financing of both infrastructure and superstructure. Assessing the cost of the project is relatively easy when compared to assessing benefits. There may be a choice of locations or a choice of techniques. Estimates must be made for each choice within a feasible range. Each proposal must be assessed separately to establish its feasibility, cost benefit and degree of priority in making a plan. Agencies concerned with the development of an optional national investment programme should compare investments in tourism facilities and related infrastructure with alternative investment opportunities other sectors. In World Bank Group Operations, this comparison is attempted on the basis of economic rates of return for well defined investment proposals.. In evaluating tourism investments the World Bank Group pays very close attention to the projected financial results. In general, tourism projects financed by the World Bank Group are justified in terms of both their economic impact and their financial viability.

Except in centrally planned economies, such as in countries like USSR, Poland, Yugoslavia, public investment will be supported by private investment as happens in the mixed, economies like France, Italy and India. The government may take the initiative in project development, but it will expect private investment support. If the government is anxious to develop and promote an active tourist industry it will help the private investor to the maximum extent. This can be done first, by creating favourable climate for investment and, second, by assisting private, investor to consider tourism development as an attractive investment proposition. This could be done by way of offering special financial incentives such as subsidies, tax concessions, preferential rates of interests, credits, special facilities for purchase of land, etc.

Besides the public and private finance, foreign capital also plays an important role in tourism development programmes. Attention will have to be given to financial means and facilities designed to attract foreign capital. A basic obligation at this stage will be the calculation of the output capital ratio, which will depend for the most part in the external economies which can be achieved. Foreign investment is usually welcomed by many developing countries, largely because of their own acute shortage of capital resources.

Human Resource Planning

Tourism basically being a service business, a developing destination must take the necessary steps to build a pool of efficiently trained manpower to man various jobs which will be created subsequently. A variety of jobs will have to be created to look after and manage various tourist services. Special attention, will have to be given to needs in manpower and personnel to be trained and rendered qualified for the various tourism professions. Special care has to be taken to ensure that there will be no shortage of trained manpower in case there expansion of facilities and services. In the case of a developing country, it will also be appropriate to study at this stage the volume of manpower required for activities complementary to accommodation industry, in particular in the commercial sector.

For human resources development, programmes should be made to screen and tram prospective employees that they could acquire both attitudinal as well as technical skills. Attitudinal characteristics contribute to an employee's success in tourism position and include pride, flexibility, adaptability and judgment. Technical skills required include facility and equipment operation and maintenance, financial management, food and beverage production and service, personnel management and administration and system analysis and design. In order to determine the need for various personnel required, a staff planning exercise may be done.

This involves a series of measures including job analysis, preparing job descriptions, job specifications and preparing staff forecasts. This sequence of activities leads to a detailed forecast of exactly what types of persons, with which specific qualifications and, skills will be required at all major facilities within the tourist destination. All this helps in determining the development of requisite education and training programmes within the country for local residents.

Administrative Structure

It is to be noted that if a tourism programme is to succeed, the responsibility of success must be assumed by some entity in the form of an organisation. This organisation should have a charter and resources appropriate to carry out various functions. Many countries have established special departments or agencies to manage and coordinate tourism programme. Depending upon the economic, social and political structure in the country, the tourism organisation may be a governmental department, a semi government agency in the form of corporation supported by government but operating outside its organisational structure. It may also be a private sector organisation with government support and recognition. The Administrative organisation looks after both the legal aspects, viz., the preparation of the legislation required for the installation of the various tourism services, dealing with such matters as the classification of hotels or the control of travel agencies, etc. It has various departments for planning, marketing, research, training, administrative and legal service.

Marketing and Promotion

The main concern of tourists is having an enjoyable and pleasant experience rather than details associated with planning their journeys. Most of the tourists leave these details to travel professionals and intermediaries who look after all the details of the travel plans. Contacts with and support of travel professionals and intermediaries are among the most important factors for successful marketing and promotion of tourist destination. Facilities and specialties of travel professionals include national tourist offices, regional travel promotion organisation, and airlines including other carriers, tour wholesalers, tour operators, travel agents, travel clubs and convention and conference organisers. The various channels of communication used to inform and stimulate include tourist literature in the form of catalogues, brochures and folders, direct mail, advertising, public relations and publicity. The media campaigns are timed in such a way that these correspond with the selling effort supporting a destination. It is very important to ensure that these activities match the level of tourist development to be achieved.

The Time Factor

The main purpose of developmental planning is to move towards self-sustaining growth; that is, to create a cadre of trained manpower, to increase knowledge of natural resources and their effective utilisation and to create institutions for enterprising investment. All this takes time. The plan could be for 25 Years, 10 years, 7 years or 5 years duration. Many planners are of the view that the first development plan should be a 10-year plan, as it requires an assessment of long term perspective. Time is a fundamental factor in the preparation of the plan and in the identification of the objectives to be attained upon its termination. The medium term plan ranges between three and seven years with five years as the most popular choice. The short term plan is an annual plan. The annual plan is the controlling plan as it is the authorised document to check its possible achievements being matched by-available resources year by year. It is governed by medium or long term plan, which sets its direction. The annual plan is the operative document, while long-term or medium-term plans are merely a set of intentions. Thus the need for orienting the short-term plan budgets with the long-term or medium-term plan budgets is the core of planning process. Time factor is the main element in the planning including planning tourism in any nation. It is vital to the prospect of achieving the economic and social expansion which is linked with tourism.

Of late, tourism is receiving ever increasing attention from national governments and from international developmental agencies, it can generate the much needed foreign exchange for financing other sectors of the economy of a developing country and also for bridging the trade gap. In its broadest sense, tourism can do more to develop understanding among, people, generate employment and raise the living standards than any other economic force known. There is unlimited potential for tourism development. If properly conceived and executed such development will prove not only to be financially viable but will also prove to be of immense benefit to a country. It is perhaps much easier to have planned development in countries where there is a potential which is only just beginning to be realised. However even in these countries with a long-established and a highly developed tourist industry, some measure of planning is essential. Planning is essential for three main reasons: first most countries, to a lesser or greater degree have planned economies and if tourism development is to be part and parcel of national economic development, then this sector of economy also should be subjected to planning. Secondly, the success of tourism, development depends very largely upon appropriate facilities being available in the right place and at the right time and these can only be provided by adequate research into national tourist assets and markets. Research has a very important part to play in the future planning of tourism development. The natural and man made assets are conserved and protected to maintain tourist appeal, for lack of care and coordinated development may impair and even ruin those assets upon the very foundations of tourist industry.

8

Environmental Aspects of Tourism

> "Leonardo da Vinci was in the habit of paying the price demanded by the owners of captive birds, for the pleasure of setting them free."
> "All progress and growth is a matter of change but change must be growth within our social and government concepts if it should not destroy them."
>
> —*Herbert Hoover*

Today there is a growing concern throughout the world for the protection of the environment and the individuals quality of life. Man in his quest for economic development and enjoyment of the riches of the nature has been carrying out a large number of developmental activities in all fields including tourism.

In the field of tourism there has been a growing concern over the years regarding environmental protection and conservation. A growing concern for the protection of the environment and the individual's quality of life is being felt. It is within this context that the relationship between tourism and the environment has-been receiving a growing level of attention from both the public and private sector organisations in various countries in the world. For instance, during the last decade and a half various international bodies have cooperated in the preparation of a host of studies, plans, programmes and activities on tourism and environment. At every leading platform where tourism is discussed, environmental protection receives attention.

The International Union of Official Travel Organisations (IUOTO), the predecessor of World Tourism Organisation (WTO), was one of the first organisations to come to the defense of environmental protection as early as in the year 1950 having one of its main objectives as the study and development of natural tourist resources. In the year 1954, the study of environmental questions became institutionalised in the activities of IUOTO and the protection of tourist heritage was included on the agenda of each IUOTO Assembly.

The tourism boom which characterised the 1960s as a result of the introduction of jet travel was also responsible for the advancements in the development of statistical measurements and evaluation of tourism. More and more governments realising the importance of tourism to their country's economies started collecting and compiling the basic tourist statistics to determine the benefits and also to plan for future developments. Various surveys conducted showed that natural tourist resources were the primary factor that attracted the tourists even in the countries rich in cultural heritage. There was a large movement from urban areas to beaches, mountains and other natural resources for rest, recreation and amusement.

This impact of mass movement of tourists to various tourist destinations was, however, not healthy. There appeared an environmental threat both aesthetic and ecological from overcrowding of particularly attractive areas. The great increase in number of visitors to these areas resulted in rapid, unplanned construction of hotels and other dwellings for use of tourists and for migratory service employees. This unplanned growth threatened to destroy the very environment that was the tourist attraction in the first place.

Increased interest began to be generated in what was termed as 'ecological impact' of tourism. Awareness and also the recognition of 'ecological threat' led IUOTO to recommend to world governments that they implement a resolution adopted in 1960 by its Fifteenth General Assembly in the following terms:

> "The General Assembly, considering that nature in its most noble and unchanging aspects constitutes and will continue increasingly in the future to constitute one of the essential elements of the national or world tourist heritage:
>
> "*Believes* that the time has come for it to deal with the problems raised by the dangers threatening certain aspects of nature....
>
> "*Decides* consequently to recommend to all IUOTO member countries to exercise increased vigilance regarding the attacks made on their natural tourist resources."

Tourist Environmental Policy

A policy was set forth by IUOTO in a research paper entitled "Study on human environment" which was submitted in 1971 to the Twenty-Second General Assembly held at Ankara. (Turkey). The Tourist Environmental policy had the following characteristics :

(i) recognition that protection of the environment, which is at the very basis of the development of tourism, has often been neglected in physical planning policies. This entailed promoting an awareness that the real interests of tourism did not lie in the immediate profitability of plan but in a rational utilisation of tourist natural resources which, far from damaging them, would contribute to their development. Accordingly, it was seen as essential to base development policies on long term prospects and on the basic needs of tourists;

(ii) recognition that as tourism was largely international in nature offering the natural resources to individuals of another country for their cultural enrichment and well-being; the protection of the tourist capital was in the interest of everyone and must be dealt with at world level. Underlying this recommendation was an awareness that close international cooperation was necessary so that no region would be at a disadvantage as a result of having adopted high-quality environmental protection measures;

(iii) recognition of a lack of uniformity in the way in which environmental protection was handled at national level. In many cases there were no provisions to ensure that tourism interests were represented within bodies with responsibility for the environment and physical planning. It was therefore seen as necessary to establish or strengthen collaboration between all bodies dealing with the problems of nature protection. The need was also seen to set up a special body at national level responsible for;

(v) coordinating steps to protect nature, a proposal that was subsequently to be adopted by the United Nations Conference on the Human Environment at Stockholm;

Central to such a policy was seen to be the establishment of an inventory of natural tourist resources with a view to identifying in particular:

(i) protected areas or natural reserves where attempts at the very least should be made to conserve or re-establish the natural balance (national parks, forest reserves, and wildlife sancuaries etc.);

(ii) mixed natural areas in which the establishment of industry must be so planned as to safeguard the main tourist resources.

(iii) areas reserved primarily for tourism because of their natural attractions and from which industries would be excluded (beaches, mountain and hill resorts, etc.).

In areas where tourism development was to be permitted on a larger scale, planning measures were seen as essential if the growth of tourism itself were not to produce adverse environmental effects; the pollution of bathing water for instance. Legislation was seen as playing a key role in the implementation of the tourist environmental policy. It was needed not only in national parks or nature reserves but also in tourist areas in general so as to prevent anarchic construction of dwellings, dirty camping grounds or beaches, forest fires or the proliferation of advertising hoardings outside of towns.

Major Guidelines

The core feature of the new tourist environment policy was the guidelines for the development of new tourist resorts. These suggested that new developments should confirm to a definite plan drawn up by a multidisciplinary team of experts in legislation, tourism and ecology. According to these guidelines, if the conception of the plan was the responsibility of regional or local authorities, account should be taken of the developments in neighboring areas or localities so as to achieve coordination of measures necessary to protect natural surroundings. It was also considered desirable to establish suitable redeption capacity all the resort in order to plan the communication and transport infrastructure and the distribution of areas for building a recreational plant so avoiding traffic problems, air pollution and noise congestion, etc. Lastly, architecture and the general aspect of buildings and the situation of sports facilities or camping, sites should be so designed as to ensure harmony with natural surroundings and vegetation. In planning parks, forests or even the countryside, the competent authorities should also ensure that ecological principles were applied and prevent the destruction of trees, flora and fauna by determining the areas to be set aside for the construction of buildings and by creating paths and other means of access which were not harmful to the beauty of the sites.

The water pollution and beaches was recognised as a serious threat to main tourist areas and it was recommended that specific measures be taken to limit or prevent these effects.

UN Conference on Human Environment

The United Nations organised a conference in Stockholm on Human Environment which symbolised the growing importance that the people of the world attach to maintaining and improving the quality of Human life and to enrich the human environment. It is a fact that all over the world man has been using the natural resources without any thought of the future. It is the wrong use of these resources which causes problems. Now environmental pollution poses a serious threat to life on earth and this is true not only of the areas where there is a great concentration of industries, but also areas where there is a great concentration of tourists.

The disadvantages of haphazard and unplanned development of tourism are well illustrated by many areas in North America and Western Europe and also to a greater or lesser extent throughout large parts of Asia's tourism circuit. Yugoslavia's Adriatic coast and the Seychelles are other examples. Many of the world's finest resorts have become ugly. Russia's popular Black Sea resort, Sochi, has proclaimed itself the world's first 'no smoking city". New laws ban smoking in all restaurants, cinema theatres, public transportation, hospitals and health resorts and on the beaches.

In North America and Western Europe various beaches bear a mute testimony to the havoc that can be wrought by uncointrolled development of tourism. Destinations once noted for their particular character are reduced to unattractive showpieces as many countries endeavor to keep pace with the visitor inflow. Despite a measure of governmental control during the development, the great increase in number of visitors to these areas resulted in rapid, unplanned construction of hotels and dwellings for tourists and for migratory service employees. These expansions threatened to destroy the very environment that is the tourist attraction.

Tourism development has caused special ecological problems not encountered in other types of economic activity. The environmental resources 'exploited' for tourism attract tourists because of their outstanding beauty, recreational possibilities or educational and cultural interest The modern tourists most paradoxical traits is its capacity to destroy those attributes which attracted the visitor in the first place. The well known economic analyst and futurologist, Herman Kahn, described the rapidly expanding tourism as "...next only to Atomic Power in its potential for environmental destruction..." Mass tourism has brought in its wake certain ecological and environmental pollution problems. The environmental amenities which attract tourists have tended to be taken for granted. Preservation of their quality has only recently begun to concern tourism development planner. For tourism the quality of the environment is the basis for attracting visitors and needs to be conserved Tourism development can become a positive factor for improving the environment, if certain amount of intelligent basic planning is done.

In fact the quality of the tourism product depends upon a high quality natural environment. The interrelationship was pointed out by the International Union of Official Travel Organisations (IUOTO), predecessor of the World Tourism Organisation, as long ago as the 1950s. It was reiterated during the 1960s in the face of growing interest in environmental conservation. It has been noticed that major social benefits accrue to tourists themselves. But tourism also has valuable spillover benefits for tourist receiving countries. Notable among these is the contribution of tourism to the preservation of historic sites and cultural values. Careful cleaning and beautifying ancient monuments, clearing the areas around the monuments and improving them, for tourism purposes is a case in point.

Through tourism development, the environment is not degraded but in fact can be improved. So great has been the national and international demand for tourism and recreational facilities that governments have increasingly to face up to the choice between extending Public access and availability of sites, and conservation and Protection against over-development. Governments are increasingly aware that future growth of the industry will necessitate careful management and avoiding over development of regions of natural beauty.

9

Tourism and National Development

"Every good citizen makes his country's honour his own, and cherishes it not only as precious but as sacred. He is willing to risk his life in its defense and is conscious that the gains protection while he gives it."

—*Andrew Jackson*

Tourism emerged as a global phenomenon in the 1960's and the potential for tourism to generate economic development was widely endorsed by national governments, which looked at tourism to generate foreign exchange earnings, to create employment and to bring economic benefits to regions with limited options for alternative economic development. National tourism authorities were created to promote tourism and to maximise international arrivals. The success of these authorities and of Tourism Ministries was judged by the growth in international arrivals figures. As tourism expanded and its significant economic contributions were lauded, an awareness of its negative environmental and social impacts also increased. A more sceptical attitude to the economic benefits of tourism also emerged. The importance of environmental and social sustainability was more widely accepted, and emphasis has increasingly been placed on the generation of economic benefits at the local level.

The tourism industry can be viewed as "a great school for the modernisation of a people's values". The regional and international connections of the industry, and its international competitive nature, mean that tourism can be an important conduit for the introduction of modern management techniques and technologies. This can be a problem if the industry is reliant on imported technologies and labour brought in from abroad or from the metropolitan centres. On the other hand, it presents excellent opportunities for developing entrepreneurship, for staff training and progression and for the development of transferable skills.

Tourism development has generally been focused at the macro level: on international promotion, attracting inward investment and major hotel and resort developments, and on national and regional master planning. The primary concern has been with maximising foreign exchange earnings, in part to finance investment in technology and other imports for economic development and to finance debt.

Developing Countries and LDCs in International Tourism

International Tourist Arrivals

Since the 1950's developing countries have received increasing numbers of international tourists, largely from developed countries. International tourist arrivals have been growing significantly faster in developing countries than they have in the European Union (EU) or Organisation for Economic Cooperation and Development (OECD) countries. Developing countries had 292.6 million international arrivals in 2000, an increase since 1990 of nearly 95%. The sub-group of 49 LDCs had 5.1 million international arrivals in 2000, they achieved an increase of nearly 75% in the decade. This performance by developing countries compares very favourably with the growth of tourism to countries of the OECD and the EU, which achieved around 40% growth.

International Tourism Receipts

Over the last ten years there has been a higher rate of

growth in the absolute value of tourism expenditure as recorded in the national accounts in the developing countries than in the developed countries. The absolute earnings of developing countries grew by 133% between 1990 and 2000 and in the LDCs by 154%, this compares with 64% for OECD countries and 49% for EU countries.

TABLE 1: INTERNATIONAL TOURIST ARRIVALS IN THOUSANDS

Country Groups	*1990*	*2000*	*Increase*	*% increase*
OECD	338,200	471,164	132,964	39.3
EU	204,961	283,604	78,643	38.4
Other Countries	3,465	6,652	3,187	92.0
Developing Countries	150,563	292,660	142,097	94.4
Least Developed Countries (LDCs)	2,921	5,106	2.185	74.8
Other Developing Countries	13,755	25,562	11,807	85.8

Source: WTO

TABLE 2: ABSOLUTE VALUE (US$ MILLION) OF TOURISM EXPENDITURE BY COUNTRY GROUP

Country Groups	*1990*	*2000*	*Increase*	*% increase*
OECD	201,082	330,464	129,382	64.3
EU	119,998	179,041	59,043	49.2
Other Countries	1,366	2,388	1,022	74.
Developing Countries	59,645	138,937	79,292	132.9
Least Developed Countries (LDCs)	1,021	2,594	1,573	154.1
Other Developing Countries	11,045	17,041	5,996	54.3

Source: WTO

Figures relate to the credit component of the Travel item of the Balance of Payments of the corresponding countries of reference. This item is traditionally referred to as Tourism.

It is remarkable to note that the developing countries and particularly the LDCs secured a larger increase in the income per international arrival between 1990 and 2000 than did the OECD or the EU. The LDCs secured an increase of 45% between 1990 and 2000 and the developing countries nearly 20%, this compares with 18% for OECD countries and 7.8% for the EU.

TABLE 3: AVERAGE VALUE PER INTERNATIONAL ARRIVAL OF TOURISM EXPENDITURE BY COUNTRY GROUP

Country Groups	*1990*	*2000*	*Increase*	*% increase*
OECD	595	701	107	18.0
EU	585	631	46	7.8
Other Countries	394	359	-35	-8.9
Developing Countries	396	475	79	19.8
Least Developed Countries (LDCs)	350	508	158	45.3
Other Developing Countries	803	667	-136	-17.0

Source: WTO

Figures relate to the credit component of the Travel item of the Balance of Payments of the corresponding countries of reference. This item is traditionally referred to as Tourism.

The average value has been calculated by dividing absolute value taken for the travel item in the Balance of Payments by the international arrival figure.

Data from the Balance of Payments can be used to calculate the importance of tourism (the Travel item in the Balance of Payments) as a proportion of international trade in services. For the OECD and EU country groups tourism constitutes around 28% of trade in services in 2000, this significantly less than the 43% recorded for developing countries and 70% for LDCs. For the OECD and EU country groups the credit travel item of the Balance of Payments, taken to equate to tourism receipts, amounts to around 6% of total Goods and Services in 2000. In the developing countries group it averages 6.5% and in the LDCs 15.3%.

In 2000 tourism ranked third among the major merchandise export sectors for both developing countries and LDCs.

TABLE 4: VALUE IN US$ MILLION OF MAJOR MERCHANDISE EXPORTS BY COUNTRY GROUP

	Developing Country	*R*	*LDCs*	*R*
Manufactures	900,649	1	720	2
Food	120,262	2	334	4
Tourism	113,902	3	335	3
Fuels	73,624	4	2316	1
Ores & metals	41,585	5	111	5
Agriculture	25,167	6	68	6

Source: WTO

Remarkably, in the developing countries the export value of tourism grew by 154% in developing countries second only to the growth in the manufacturing sector. In the LDCs tourism grew 47%, behind manufactures and fuel but ahead of food, which showed decline.

TABLE 5: GROWTH BETWEEN 1990 AND 2000 IN TOP 4 EXPORT SECTORS FOR DEVELOPING COUNTRIES AND LDCS

Tourism and Merchanduse Exports	*Developing Country*	*R*	*LDCs*	*R*
Manufactures	208%	1	217%	2
Food	58%	2	-71%	4
Tourism	154%	3	47%	3
Fuels	16%	4	1444%	1

International Tourism in the LDCs

The category of Least Developed Country was first used by the United Nations in 1971 to encourage the international community to recognise these countries as structurally disadvantaged and facing the risk of being overcome by those disadvantages. Since 1971 only Botswana has graduated from LDC status, and tourism played a very significant role in that process with the annual number of international tourism arrivals increasing by more than half a million visitors between 1985 and 1998. Cape Verde, Maldives, Samoa and Vanuatu have all been considered for graduation since 1994 and in all four of them tourism has been the single most important factor explaining the socio-economic progress which would form the basis of their graduation. As Pierre Encontre of UNCTAD concludes, "international tourism has been one of the very few economic sectors able to place some poor countries on a better development path" and to enable them to reduce their marginalization from the global economy.

In the Maldives, annual visitor arrivals tripled between 1985 and 1998, in the same period the proportion of tourism exports to GNP increased from 75% to 89%, making the Maldives the LDC most dependent on international tourism, followed by Samoa and Vanuatu, both with over 20%. International arrivals to other LDCs grew fast between 1995 and 1998 Angola and Chad experienced more than 75% growth (albeit from low base lines), Cape Verde, The Gambia, Lao, Mali and Zambia all enjoyed growth above 20%. Sudan, Sierra Leone, Sao Tome, Kiribati, Ethiopia, Eritrea, the Central African Republic and Burundi, however, all saw reductions in international visitor arrivals.

If petroleum industry exports are discounted (and they are significant only in Angola, Yemen and Equatorial Guinea) tourism is the primary source of foreign exchange earnings in the 49 LDCs. The combined tourism export receipts of all LDCs in 1998 accounted for 16.2% of their non-oil export receipts. This is 39% more than cotton and 82% more than textiles, their second and third most significant non-oil exports. In more than one third of LDCs tourism ranks among the top three sources of foreign exchange earnings, and it is the most important source of foreign exchange earnings in seven of them.

Tourism can contribute to development and the reduction of poverty in a number of ways. Economic benefits are generally the most important element, but there can be social, environmental and cultural benefits and costs. Tourism

TABLE 6: INTERNATIONAL TOURISM RECEIPTS AS % OF GDP, 2000

LDC	*% of GDP*
Maldives	57.7
Vanuatu	27.4
Samoa	17.0
Tanzania	8.2
Comoros	7.4
Cambodia	7.2
Lao P. Dem. R.	6.7
Eritrea	5.9
Kiribati	4.6
Senegal	3.2
Zambia	3.1
Mali	3.1
Madagascar	3.1
Nepal	3.0
Lesotho	2.7
Bhutan	2.1
Sierra Leone	1.9
Malawi	1.6
Rwanda	1.3
Haiti	1.3
Ethiopia	1.1
Yemen	0.9
Togo	0.4
Guinia	0.4
Sudan	0.3
Angola	0.2
Burundi	0.1
Bangladesh	0.1

Tourism as % of GDP data from the World Development Indicator database. World Bank.

contributes to poverty reduction by providing employment and diversified livelihood opportunities. This in turn provides additional income or contributes to a reduction in vulnerability of the poor by increasing the range of economic opportunities available to individuals and households. Tourism also contributes to poverty alleviation through direct taxation and the generation of taxable economic growth; taxes can then be used to alleviate poverty through education, health and infrastructure development. It should not be forgotten that some tourism facilities also improve the recreational and leisure opportunities available for the poor themselves at the local level.

TABLE 8: CHANGE IN REVENUE FROM INTERNATIONAL ARRIVALS IN CURRENT US$ VALUES

LDC	*% of GDP*
Lao P. Dem. R.	3700
Tanzania	1037
Comoros	650
Bhutan	400
Myanmar	367
Bangladesh	355
Yemen	280
Maldives	261
Madagscar	198
Ethiopia	172
Nepal	161
Rwanda	140
Zambia	122
Kiribati	100
Samoa	100
Malawi	69
Mali	51
Vanuatu	49
Sudan	43
Lesotho	41
Angola	39
HJaiti	17
Senegal	-16
Sierra Leone	-37
Guinea	-60
Burundi	-75
Togo	-91
Eq. Guinea	-100

Tourism as % of GDP data from the World Development Indicator database. World Bank.

Tourism, Taxation and Poverty Alleviation

Tax revenue from tourism is an important economic benefit at national and local level. Taxes can provide the financial resources for development of infrastructure, some types of attractions and other public facilities and services, and tourism marketing and training required for developing tourism, as well as to help finance poverty alleviation programmes by governments. In addition, tourism-related tax revenues can, and do, help to finance general community improvements and services used by all residents.

WTO's 1998 report on tourism taxation emphasizes that taxation policies in a country must be carefully evaluated in an integrated manner to ensure that tourism-related taxes are giving the necessary substantial revenues; but taxes should not be so high for the country's international competitive position to be adversely affected and produce a loss of tourist markets. A balance must be achieved between, on the one hand, a level of taxation that maintains a competitive position for the country and reasonable profits for the industry and, on the other hand, receiving adequate revenues to support investment in and maintenance of the tourism sector, and to contribute towards general community welfare.

Tourism and Poverty Reduction

Tourism is not very different from other productive sectors, but it has four potential advantages for pro-poor growth:

— It has higher potential for linkage with other local enterprises because customers come to the destination;

— It is relatively labour intensive and employs a high proportion of women;

— It has potential in poor countries and areas with few other competitive exports;

— Tourism products can be built on natural resources and culture, which are assets, that some of the poor have.

Many disadvantages of tourism such as leakage and volatility of revenue are common to other economic sectors. But tourism may involve greater trade-offs with local livelihoods through more competition for natural resources, particularly in coastal areas.

Tourism as a Development Strategy for Developing Countries and LDCs

The WTO is convinced that tourism has considerable potential for growth in many developing countries and LDCs where it is a significant economic sector and growing; and that it has advantages when compared with other economic sectors.

Disadvantages of Tourism as a Development Strategy

— Foreign private interests drive tourism and it is difficult to maximise local economic benefits due to the high level of foreign ownership, which means that there are high levels of leakage and few local linkages.

There is no body of evidence to confirm that the leakages associated with tourism are typically greater than for other comparable export sectors, nor of any evidence that the supposed levels of foreign ownership are any higher than for comparable sectors. It is clear that the many small enterprises and individual traders sustain themselves around hotels and other tourism facilities and that these SMMEs are not foreign owned. There is often confusion about levels of foreign ownership, local ownership is often masked by franchise agreements and management contracts. WTO is studying this issue in collaboration with UNCTAD as part of its poverty elimination research.

— Tourism can impose substantial non-economic costs on the poor through loss of access to resources (particularly beaches), displacement from agricultural land and social and cultural disruption and exploitation.

Many forms of development bring with them disadvantages of this kind, negative impacts that need to be managed. The economic and non-economic negative impacts need to be determined and the issues addressed. It is for this reason that the WTO supports a holistic livelihoods approach to assessing the impacts of tourism—positive and negative—on the poor. The issues of environmental management and planning at local level are real, and not unique to tourism; they need to be addressed through the good governance agenda.

— Tourism is vulnerable to changes in economic conditions in the originating markets, which cause major swings in levels of economic activity in tourism in the destinations, and international visitor arrivals are also vulnerable to civil unrest, crime, political instability and natural disasters in destinations.

It is not clear that the volatility of export markets for tourism is significantly greater than for other commodities. Tourism has the advantage noted above that it is not subject to tariff or other non-tariff barriers and that the destination has some control over civil unrest, crime and political instability.

— Tourism requires highly sophisticated marketing

International tourism marketing is expensive, although there are more efficient and less costly forms of marketing, which are not always deployed. Attendance at international trade fairs is expensive but these marketing costs are carried at national level. The individual traders and SMMEs should not be marketing there—their market is the international and domestic tourists in the destination where they live and the hotels, resorts and inbound operators who are in contact with the tourists. Individual handicraft producers rarely export directly, they sell through wholesalers into international markets.

Tourism to many developing countries and many LDCs has been growing strongly in modern times and there are strong reasons to think that these trends will continue. There is a market opportunity in tourism for many, but not all, developing countries. Many developing countries have comparative advantage in tourism—or at least tourism constitutes one of their better opportunities for development. The disadvantages, which are often identified in relation to international tourism in developing countries, are more apparent than real when tourism is compared with other sectors. WTO has long advocated that tourism is considered alongside other industries as a development option and that where tourism presents the best opportunity for local economic development and antipoverty strategies, development banks and bilateral and multilateral development agencies should back it with determination.

10

Tourism Planning in India

> "A vision without a task is a dream;
> A task without vision is drudgery;
> A vision and a task is the hope of world."

India adopted a policy of development through planning in 1952 when the first five-year plan for development of Indian economy was drafted by the newly established Planning Commission. Although tourism activity had started in a modest way in the early fifties of the 20th century in India, the Planning Commission did not take note of it till the Second Five Year Plan (1957-62). A modest provision of Rs. 336 lakhs was made in the plan for development of tourist infrastructure for a five-year period within central and state sectors. In the fifties, there was little awareness in the country of the economic or social significance of tourism. Development had to begin with the provision of basic infrastructure, especially at important places of tourist interest where there were little or no facilities. The plan was divided into three parts. Part-I schemes dealt with the development of accommodation at places of international tourist interest, where foreign tourists could be attracted. The expenditure on such projects was incurred totally by the central government. Part-II schemes included development of tourist facilities at places of interest of domestic tourists, which could also interest overseas visitors. On such projects, the central government met half the expenditure and the states met the rest. Part-III scheme included projects which were primarily of domestic interest and were financed by the state governments. A number of tourist bungalows were constructed all over the country under the Part-I scheme, now named 'Travelers Lodges', and some of them are still managed by the Indian Tourism Development Corporation (ITDC). Most accommodations built under Part-I scheme were, transferred to the States.

During the Third Five Year Plan (1962-67) this practice was continued, resulting in a network of tourist facilities in areas where none existed before. Bodh Gaya, Khajuraho, Bhubaneswar, Konark, Mahabalipuram, Sanchi, Tiruchirapalli, Kanchipuram, Madurai and several other places were provided basic facilities acceptable to foreign tourists. The Fourth Five Year Plan (1967-74) had a chequered story. Since there were not enough funds for a continuous plan, separate annual plans were prepared and executed. Under the new arrangement, the Central Department of Tourism completely took over the planning and development of facilities suitable for overseas tourists while the state governments were given assistance to develop facilities for domestic tourists. State governments were at liberty to shape their plans the way they liked NO matching, subsidies, of fifty per cent were given by the center. It was a good decision as the states started developing their own plans independently of central help though central guidance through the Department of Tourism and the Planning Commission was available. In the annual plans, in addition to the development of infrastructure, tourism promotion overseas, especially the production of tourist literature for overseas markets, became part of the plan. The new arrangement enabled the Central Department of Tourism to expand its tourist promotion overseas by making available adequate quantity of better quality and variety of literature in a number of foreign languages.

According to a survey carried out by the Indian Institute of Public Opinion for the Department of Tourism, the share of destinational traffic to India in 1962 was only 43.2 per cent. It rose to 52.2 per cent in 1964-65 and 73.3 per cent in

1972-73. Destination traffic at present is estimated to be over 75 per cent. Another change noticed in the pattern of traffic was the predominance of the younger age group among international tourists visiting India. The largest number of tourists visiting India was in the age group of 31-50 years followed closely by 17-30 years. Occupation-wise, the largest group consisted of professionals, educationists and students, followed by businessmen and those who professed no business presumably retired or dependent housewives. The primary reason for a change in pattern of traffic to India was the introduction of reduced fares on international air sectors. The approach to planning and development of tourism had, therefore, to undergo a change too. India was getting more destinational tourists who could be persuaded to stay longer. A whole new field of recreational activities had to be developed in the country. It was decided in the mid-sixties to meet the requirements of the new class of visitors. A programme drawn in the fourth plan and continued in the fifth plan started with impressive allocations, but every year, it had to be pruned due to constraint on resources.

In spite of all these difficulties, sixteen youth hostels of international standard were constructed and furnished in different parts of India to serve as catalytic models for the states to construct similar hostels elsewhere. Several forest lodges, tourist bungalows and two major resorts—the Kovalam Beach Resort and the Gulmarg Winter Sports Resort—were the results of the fourth and fifth plans, for destinational tourist traffic. The preamble to the fifth, five-year plan for tourism explained the role of the center and the state governments. The center would undertake projects which relate to the promotion of international tourism and the states were advised to confine their projects to serve the needs of domestic tourists or budget tourists from overseas. The objectives laid down for the Central Department of Tourism were the provision of accommodation and transport to match the anticipated growth in international tourism to develop new resorts and tours to spread the traffic to different regions of India.

Further, the sixth five-year plan envisaged very high targets of tourists —1.7 million by 1985 and 3.5 million by 1990—based on fifteen per cent annual growth of visitors to Indi. The targets, obviously, were highly exaggerated dreams which proved utopia.

For the first time in the sixth five-year plan, the Planning Commission recognised the importance of tourism in the following words: Tourism, both domestic and international, had rapidly won considerable recognition as an activity generating a number of social and economic benefits like promotion of national integration and international understanding, creation of employment opportunities, removal of regional imbalances, augmentation of foreign exchange earnings, thus redressing he balance of payments situation, etc. It is significant that many of these beneficial aspects of domestic and international tourism have special relevance to the socio-economic scene in India as emerging in the Sixth Plan period. Tourism, also tends to give support to local handicrafts and cultural activities, both in urban and rural areas. Expenditure by tourists has a multiplier effect and also generates considerable tax revenue for government, both in the Central and State sectors. It is also relevant that the various multi-faceted socio-economic benefits of tourism are achieved with a relatively low level of investment.

Having put forward the case for tourism convincingly the plan provided a meager outlay of Rs. 187 crores for the period 1980-85 under the central and state sectors. This worked out to 0.18 per cent of the total plan-one of the lowest allocations for any sector. Two interesting concepts were introduced in the sixth plan—the concept of travel circuits and tourist villages. Sixty-one travel circuits were identified with 441 centers to be developed in the decade of the eighties. No tourist villages have been identified even today.

The travel circuits approach aimed at spreading tourism geographically and to enable every state in India to offer something to the visitors. Although the objective was desirable, the concept led to spreading India's resources so thinly that there was no visible development at any place during the eighties. The diversification of tourist centers all over India had to be matched with consumer demand. The consumer-especially the foreign visitor-was not likely to change his preference simply because it was a political necessity in India. As for tourist i villages, the concept is laudable as it brings the visitors close to the Indian realities. But, again the plan remained on papers. At times, one wonders whether Indian planners read the previous plans when they write a new one.

The concept of Janata hotels, developed by the Janata government during the brief period they were in power, was given up in the new plan. The cost of building Janata hotels was not very different from better hotels. It was not possible therefore to offer low tariffs.

There were, however, provisions to expand in the sphere of supplementary accommodation like youth hostels, tourist bungalows, and tourist lodges, etc. Some expansion did take place in this area.

In the seventh five-year, plan (1985-90) tourism received significant notice. Tourism-related activities were given the status of an industry which implied that-such business activities would in future be entitled to the same incentives and concessions as were applicable to an export industry. The concept of a large number of circuits gave place to the emphasis on outdoor holiday tourism-developing and strengthening infrastructure at beach and mountain resorts along with the normal activities of cultural tourism. India hoped to attract more people coming for an outdoor holiday. Financial allocations for the Department of Tourism of the central government were enhanced from twenty-one crore rupees in the sixth plan to Rs. 120 crore in the seventh plan. Similarly, allocations for the states were increased three hundred per cent. The India Tourism Development Corporation (ITDC) was asked to fend for itself—its allocation in the seventh plan were only eight crore rupees against forty-two crores in the sixth plan. It was directed not to build any more luxury hotels and to confine its activities to building only three-star accommodation.

The Eighth Five Year Plan (1992-1997) underlines the fact that in states and 3 union territories had already declared tourism as an industry—four more states had declared hotels as an industry. The plan recommended that other states may also accord similar priority to tourism.

The thrust during the eighth five-year plan was through the private sector. State governments however' were expected to play a significant role in providing the essential infrastructure for tourism.

An important scheme included in this plan, was the involvement of the private sector by providing better incentives and equity support towards the project costs.

Another significant scheme for strengthening the tourism infrastructure was the 'Special Tourism Areas" scheme under which participation of central/state governments and private sector is envisaged.

Thrust in this plan was also on various activities concerned with adventure sports and adventure tourism, including mountains and beach tourism.

Further, the government has announced a number of measures in the areas of industrial, policy, trade policy exchange rate management, fiscal policy, financial sector reforms, and overall macro-economic management. The initiative taken by the government allows direct foreign investment up to 51 per cent in high priority industries and, hotels and tourism related industries are part of the list Industrial Licensing has been abolished in most industries and hotels and tourism are among those freed from licensing. Non-resident Indians NRTs have been given a special package of incentives to participate in tourism projects.

The total allocation for the Eighth Plan for tourism was Rs. 990 crore of which Rs. 385 crore was earmarked for development of tourism infrastructure, Rs. 315 crore for marketing and publicity, Rs. 100 crore for Tourism Development Fund and Rs. 60 crore for manpower development through Hotel and Tourism Training Institutes. The plan also envisaged the establishment of an Institute of Water Sports in Goa at a cost of rupees 5 crore. An Institute of Mountaineering and Skiing had a provision of Rs. 4 crore. Domestic tourism, hitherto ignored received attention of the central government with an allocation of Rs. 73 crore for its promotion. The Tourism Department Fund, a new scheme, envisaged the construction of tourist accommodation of all types and other tourism-related projects like establishment of golf courses, amusement parks, recreational and adventure sports activities with the help of the state governments.

The Ninth Plan (1997-2002) for tourism was ambitious which envisaged an expenditure of Rs. 1000 crores on tourism development over the five-year period. Like the previous Plan, the 9th Plan expected the Government to act as a facilitator using the synergy of the private sector for developmental using tax concessions and other facilities as baits. It also envisaged the strengthening of India's tourist organisation and expansion of human resource development training facilities.

An Assessment

Despite tall ambition, India's efforts at planning can not be regarded impressive. Planning is also concerned with future implications of current decisions. In all Nine Five

Year Plans, the targets set were too high and the resources available were too little. Now, the Tenth Plan is ahead on.

India's first Director General Tourism the late S.N. Chib was invited by the United Nations to plan Sri Lanka tourism which he did extremely well. Later, he was hired by the Bahamas to do that country's tourist planning and promotion. A few of India's tourist officers have been deputed to other countries to advise them on how to plan their tourism.

The resources were thinly distributed over a number of projects that resulted in delays and cost escalations. Apart from the political pressure from the central minister for his state, each state minister felt that his state was, the victim of central discrimination. Each one was convinced that his state ' needed central attention the most. In order to please all Mates, the center attempted to satisfy them by giving a Tourist Bungalow here and a Forest Lodge there and a Youth Hostel in the third place, even though the state had no saieable tourist attractions. The decision to locate, a Travelers' Lodge or Youth Hostel was taken on considerations other thin merit. Out of fifteen travelers' lodges built during the three plans, only four were profitable. The Department of Tourism is still subsidising India Tourism Development Corporation (ITDC) for the losses incurred on these lodges.

No tourist place in India has been developed which can be cited as a good example of successful total planning. All projects have been victims of delays with little monitoring of their actual progress.

The building of youth hostels all over the country was a good decision. But the selection of sites was not based on objective surveys. Most of these hostels are located far away from the downtown area. The management pattern evolved had dual control-both of the state and the central government. The occupancy ratio was low and all youth hostels are incurring losses in spite of increasing popularity of travel. Their existence can be justified only on the basis of social justice. The forest lodges constructed in the central sector are also economically not viable and have still to be subsidized.

The two destinational projects—Kovalam and Gulmarg though laudable in their conception are far from being profitable. The accommodation built at Kovalam in the public sector has an annual average occupancy of less than 50 per cent.

The Gulmarg winter sports project was ambitiously conceived, but resources could not be found to put up a good 100 room hotel and a two-thousand-meter-long aerial ropeway with ancillary facilities to make this project economically viable. On hindsight, the delays were providential.

As a result of the limited resources being spread over vast areas, the national objectives in tourism development were seldom achieved. A plethora of demands are received by the central government from the states for mounting sound and light spectacles, 'floodlighting of monuments, resort development, construction of aerodromes, air-linking of centers, etc. As a result, the available resources are spread thinly-preferring quantity to quality. The scarce funds were spent in providing air inks and extending tourist facilities in the constituencies of ministers.

The Sixth Five Year Plan (1980-85) proposed the development of 61 travel circuits with 441 tourist centers, with little money to achieve results. The arrivals target were set at 3.5 million-up from 800,000—another impossibility considering the available international and domestic air capacity. No attempt was made to liberalise the entry of more international airlines to increase the capacity for the required growth in arrivals. The domestic air capacity was insufficient even to meet the demand at the 1980 levels. No expansion of Indian Airlines was on the cards to meet the target of 3-5 million arrivals. As the government changed, the circuits were forgotten. India crossed 2 million, mark in arrivals only in 1995. A sad commentary on Indian planning. Had India concentrated on ten circuits instead of 41 during the plan period, some visible development would have been on the ground in very short span of time.

Training is another area where planning was not very effective. There was expansion in Hotel Management Institutes but the quality of training suffered due to poorly trained teachers. Trainers and instructors were seldom sent on Refresher Courses. The hotel industry has undergone complete transformation with the introduction of high-tech information and reservation systems. But, Indian institutes have not been able to catch up with the new systems.

Now, the Indian Institute of Travel and Tourism Management (IITTM) has also changed course depending on the state to which the minister-in-charge belonged. A foreign expert recommended its location in Bangalore as the then minister was from Karnataka. After the minister quit, it was located in Delhi, but it was relocated at Gwalior as the incumbent minister was from Madhya Pradesh. Some senior faculty members opted out leaving the institute in the lurch.

The best part of the Indian planning has been the loans disbursement to the hotel sector followed by other government incentives thrown in. The hotel industry has received tremendous boost with the availability of loans and incentives. Presently, India appears to have an adequate supply of rooms to meet the current demand except in metro cities and more rooms are in the pipeline to meet the increased demand in future.

Planning for tourism development started some 60 years ago when the effects of unregulated development became evident in countries like Spain and France. The World Bank, the World Tourism Organisation and the United Nations have shown concern over the degradation of environments, and the impact of tourism on heritage and culture of host destinations through unplanned tourism. The governments have since stepped in to introduce regulations concerning land-use, zoning, density of population, environments, design, architecture, traffic circulation, etc., to make tourism good for local residents as well as visitors. Every destination has a carrying capacity and attempts are made through planning to ensure that no overcrowding Is caused resulting in resentment among the local population. To achieve the best results, tourism planning seeks to match supply with demand.

Remarkably, Governments play an important role in tourism planning as private sector, which is motivated by profit alone, cannot be allowed to use the land according to their whims.

At the national level, the tourism planning process passes through the following stages:

- — Establishment of goals based in research;
- — Market and resource analysis;
- — Conceptual planning and approval thereof;
- — Master planning;
- — Staged implementation of the programmes; and
- — Evaluation, direction and monitoring to ensure quality.

No doubt, India was one of the late starters in tourism field. Tourism became part of the Indian planning only in the second five-year plan (1957-62), Initially, tourism was a very minor part of the total plan. Various plans enabled the Government of India to put up tourism infrastructure at tourist centers where none existed. Government also undertook some major projects like development of a ski resort at Gulmarg and a beach resort at Kovalam in Kerala. In the eight five-year plan, (-1993-97), tourism was recognised as a significant factor in bridging the balance of payment gap; In the eighth plan, tourism development was virtually left to the private sector under new government guidelines. To encourage development in the tourism field, a number of economic and fiscal incentives have been offered to private entrepreneurs. Foreign equity has also been allowed up to 51 per cent and even higher in tourism-related projects including hotels.

But the NDA government has recklessly followed privatisation in tourism sector and the current UPA government.

11

Global Ecotourism

> "It is not the time a man spends in planning—it's the faith and confidence he puts in his planning that really counts."

Sustainable tourism, Nature-based tourism and Ecotourism. All three terms are neither synonymous nor mutually exclusive. All tourism comprises either mass tourism or alternative tourism. The former is characterised by large numbers of people seeking replication of their own culture in institutionalised setting with little cultural or environmental interaction in authentic settings. Alternative tourism, however, is usually taken to mean alternative forms of tourism which put emphasis on greater contact and understanding between hosts and guests as well as between tourists and the environment. One type of alternative tourism is natural area tourism which is tourism in natural settings.

Examples can include nature-based tourism, in which viewing nature is the primary objective, and 'adventure tourism,' in which the focus is on the activity, for example, white water rafting or scuba diving. Ecotourism is another subset of natural area and may combine elements of both nature-based tourism and adventure travel. The Ecotourism Society defines it as 'Ecotourism is responsible travel to natural areas which conserves the environment and improves the welfare of local people' (Western 1993). The Australian definition of ecotourism is 'Ecotourism is nature-based tourism that involves education and interpretation of the natural environment and is managed to be ecologically sustainable. The definition recognises that 'natural environment' includes cultural components and that 'ecologically sustainable' involves an appropriate return to the local community and long-term conservation of the resource (Australian Department of Tourism 1994). Ecotourism may be farther described as having a number of essential characteristics and emerging styles. These elements combine to shape ecotourism in its present form.

There are five key principles which are fundamental to ecotourism. They are that ecotourism is nature-based, ecologically sustainable, environmentally educative, locally beneficial and generates tourist satisfaction.

1. *Tourist Satisfaction.* Satisfaction of visitors with the ecotourism experience is essential to long term viability of the ecotourism industry. Included in this concept is the importance of visitor safety in regard to political stability. Information provided about ecotourism opportunities should accurately represent the opportunities offered at particular ecotourism destinations. The ecotourism experience should match or exceed the realistic expectations of the visitor.

2. *Nature-Based.* Ecotourism is based on the natural environment with a focus on its biological, physical and cultural features. Ecotourism occurs in and depends on, a natural setting and may include cultural elements where they occur in a natural setting. The conservation of the natural resource is essential to the planning, development, and management of ecotourism.

3. *Ecologically Sustainable.* The sustainability of natural resources has been recognised by the federal and state governments in Australia as a key guiding principle in the management of human activity. Ecotourism is ecologically sustainable tourism undertaken in a natural setting. The

challenge to ecotourism in any country or region is to develop its tourism capacity and the quality of its products without adversely affecting the environment that maintains and nurtures it. This involves ensuring that the type, location and level of ecotourism use does not cause harm to natural areas.

4. *Environmentally Educative.* The educative characteristic of ecotourism is a key element which distinguishes it from other forms of nature-based tourism. Environmental education and interpretation are important tools in creating an enjoyable and meaningful ecotourism experience. Ecotourism attracts people who wish to interact with the environment in order to develop their knowledge, awareness and appreciation of it. By extension, ecotourism should ideally lead to positive action for the environment by fostering enhanced conservation awareness. Ecotourism education can influence tourist community and industry behaviour and assist in the longer term sustainability of tourist activity in natural areas. Education can also be useful as a management tool for natural areas. Interpretation helps tourists see the big picture regarding the environment. It acknowledges the natural and cultural values of the area visited as well as other issues such as resource management.

5. *Locally Beneficial.* Local communities can become involved in ecotourism operations, and in the provision of knowledge, services, facilities and products. These benefits should outweigh the cost of ecotourism to the host community and environment. Ecotourism can also generate income for resource conservation management in addition to social and cultural benefits. The contribution may be financial with a part of the cost of the tour helping to subsidise a conservation project. Alternatively it could consist of practical help in the field with the tourists being involved in environmental data collection and/or analysis.

Emerging Styles of Ecotourism

In planning and management of ecotourism it is also important to be aware of a number of different styles of ecotourism. They may vary considerably in regard to a range of factors including:

— the types of natural settings they require
— the extent of direct contact and involvement with the natural environment
— the group sizes involved
— the use and extent of personal interaction with tour guides
— the reliance on mechanised means of transport and supporting infrastructure, and
— the type of visitor satisfaction and experience realised

In Australia the Queens land Ecotourism Plan identified three broad styles of ecotourism. They include *Frontier Ecotourism, Small Group Ecotourism* and *Popular Ecotourism.*

Frontier Ecotourism involves individuals or small groups of generally ten or less people who utilise non-motorised forms of transport (e.g. walking or canoeing) to visit relatively remote and lightly unnatural areas. Visitors are generally very self-reliant and have few demands for supporting service and infrastructure. There is a very special and unusual 'first-hand' experience that often requires high degree of challenge and some knowledge of outdoor survival skills. Examples include trekking rafting and kayaking.

Popular Ecotourism involves the transport of larger numbers of visitors to, through or across a country's best known and most popular natural attractions. It relies on high-capacity mechanised forms of transport such as buses or large boats. There are low requirements for self-reliance and the degree of challenge is generally low. There may be substantial requirements for supporting infrastructure and services (e.g. visitor centers, food and drink outlets, boardwalks and toilets. This style of ecotourism is available to all visitors irrespective of age or physical capability.

Many other tourist activities which are closely related to the ecotourism but are not within the strict definition of ecotourism. Examples of such activities include aquaria, botanical gardens, zoos which displays native fauna, and visitor centers and displays of native flora and fauna in locations which are remote from their natural setting. While all of these examples can have substantial educational and interpretive components and similar objectives to ecotourism, they do not occur in and depend on a natural setting and are therefore not exclusively the subject of ecotourism.

Ecotourism in India

In the last thirty years India has opened its doors to international visitors and is now fostering tourism largely to gain an increase in foreign earnings to help its economy. In 1996, 2.2 in international tourists visited the country, an increase of 12.6% on the previous year. However, India's tourism infrastructure is barely keeping pace with the industry increase and problems are evident in the accommodation, transport and personnel sectors. In addition India has real problems with environmental pollution and tourist pressures causing substantial damages to its natural treasures. The case of sustainable development has already been put before India (Roy, Tisdell & Sen 1995). The authors advocate the adoption of Gandhian planning with its emphasis on small-scale developments at the village level being in harmony with the natural environment. By extension this sustainable approach is exactly what is needed for Indian tourism developments in environmentally sensitive areas as advocated by Singh & Kaur (1985), Dowling (1990) and illustrated in the case of Tamil Nadu (Hyma and Wall 1979, Inbakaram and Kumaran 1995).

Another example is the Adventures Wilderness School in Rajajinagar, Bangalore. The school runs small group ecotours into the rainforest of the Western Ghats in which foreigners learn about the forest and its tribal villages (Cutter 1995). Other examples include the development of designated touring circuits which have been established by the Department of Tourism in Rajasthan, Himachal Pradesh and Kerala (*Know India Newsletter* 1996). Many of the circuits include a strong focus on wildlife and adventure travel and could be further infused with an ecotourism content. By extension, the National Tourism Awards which include the 'Best maintained tourism-friendly wildlife sanctuary' could be expanded to include a general Environmental Category to recognise ecotourism and nature-based-tours, attractions and accommodation. The future prospects of Indian tourism is now at a critical juncture. To address this problem it is suggested that India's flirtation with mass tourism may be better refocused and directed towards sustainable tourism. Strong elements in support of this approach include India's many natural and cultural attractions, its unique blend of natural and cultural environments, and its expertise in organised small group package tours. On adoption this approach should help India achieve its conservation and tourism goals in a planned and sustainable manner and learn from other Asian countries such as Thailand which already has a National Ecotourism Plan. Similarly, another key for India to achieve sustainable ecotourism development will be for it to become involved in the Indian Ocean Tourism Organisation (IOTO). The organisation comprises a regional travel industry body open to all nations whose principal land mass touches, or is surrounded by, the Indian Ocean. It includes the countries of south Asia, east Africa, Australia and the island nations of the Indian Ocean such as Maldives, Mauritius and Seychelles.

The prime motive of IOTO is to enhance regional cooperation and understanding through sustainable tourism. The approach of IOTO will be to complement and add value to the strategies and activities of public and private sector tourism organisations around the Indian Ocean positively positioning and marketing the Indian Ocean Region as a unique tourism destination area.

One more key aspect of ecotourism development in India is to foster sustainable development planning principles such as that advocated by the Environmentally Based Tourism Development Planning Model (Dowling 1993). This will assist the planning of regions so that a balance is maintained among the natural, social, cultural, and economic environments. Elements of this kind of approach have already been included in the regional tourism plan for Goa (World Tourism Organisation 1994).

Strategies

Tourist management in natural areas serves two main objectives - the reduction of adverse environmental impacts and the enhancement of tourist experiences. To be acceptable to tourists, management intervention should be low key and persuasive. Explanations and education through interpretation is the key to affecting tourist behaviour in ways considered to be environmentally and socially acceptable. Tourist management measures have been described as involving a spectrum of approaches from soft, to intermediate and hard (Jim 1989). Soft techniques are aimed at influencing user 'behavior, intermediate techniques focus on redistributing use and hard techniques are those which are regimented and aim at rationing use. Such a spectrum of tourist management approaches is offered for consideration and possible application at individual sites within a region.

Environmental Protection

The distinct natural environment and unique lifestyle of the region are what attracts visitors and these need to be protected for the benefit of both the local communities (tourism's hosts) as well as the visitors (tourists). Major areas which are identified as being important for environmental protection are called Significant Areas and are not included in the areas identified as having potential for ecotourism development. The development of tourism in natural settings brings with it an inherent responsibility to ensure that the resource is not degraded.

One form of tourism development policy in natural areas is to contain facilities and activities in specified areas in contrast to allowing dispersion of development and/or activities throughout a region. These Ecotourism Zones should be located where they do not pre-emptare as more suitable for other types of development or environmental preservation. The tourists either remain within the cluster or take day tours to attractions outside the areas. Clustering is superior to dispersal in terms of benefits to visitors and reduction of unacceptable impacts to the most community and environment.

The environmental argument for clustering is two edged. The argument in favor is that it can leave much of the environment (between clusters or nodes) in a relatively natural state and thus, by implication, enjoyable, renewable and cheap to maintain. The alternative, that of continuous strip development, is usually regarded as unsatisfactory for both environmental and practical reasons. Another strategy used to reduce the negative environmental impacts of nature based tourism is to separate out land use zones according to the EBT Approach.

The monitoring of impacts is important with the need to adapt and fine-tune management strategies in response of feedback on progress and preferences.

The major challenge for a region is to ensure that ecotourism demand does not exceed the resources available for its development. This demand resource match is crucial to the future well being of the whole regional ecotourism industry as it clearly separates key areas which should be set aside for protection from those which may be developed for ecotourism. A number of key issues exist in regard to supply.

They include providing a diversity of ecotourism opportunities throughout a region, determining appropriate types and levels of ecotourism activities and services, and managing natural areas effectively for ecotourism. Where there is a desire to develop an ecotourism product it is essential that this product comprises activities that are both environmentally and socially acceptable. One approach to identifying such activities is by The Compatible Activities Matrix, First the region's entire range of ecotourism activities is identified, inventoried and categorised according to whether they are based on land, water, land & water, or in the air. Next they are evaluated in terms of their environmental and social compatibility. An environmentally compatible tourism activity is one whose impacts on the biophysical environment are either minor, negligible, nil or positive. A socially compatible ecotourism activity is one which is generally accepted as being able to co-exist both spatially and temporally with another ecotourism activity, for example, canoeing and rafting.

The development of ecotourism in the region will also comprise the identification of development of existing and potential touring routes which link gateway areas with destination zones. The touring system includes the attractions, transport, services, and information functions for those who utilise tour of several locations. Attractions are most closely associated with the touring route and they arjususally visited only once on a tour.

Marketing

Marketing and promotion element of the strategy fosters the identification of target markets and the development of efficient and effective distribution system for the delivery of the product. It aims to raise region profile in this target market so it can compete effectively with other ecotourism markets within country and/or surrounding region. Difficulties exist in marketing a sector which currently comprises many small operators with a diverse range of products and a lack of uniformity or agreed standards for operation or products.

However with proper management and marketing, the potential could exist for a region to become an ecotourism destination. The challenges involved in marketing an ecotourism product include: identifying and promotional opportunities for diversity and the special attractions of a region's natural areas in a way which ecologically sustainable; redressing any lack of knowledge about ecotourism market demand visitor motivations, expectations and needs.

Infrastructure Building

The main infrastructure requirements must be sustained for the effective delivery of an ecotourism pressential components of this arm of an ecotourism strategy include the stimulation of appropriate accommodation suitable for the ecotourism market, increase in access through the provision of development of airports, railways and roads, as well as other infrastructure development.

Factually, the provision of infrastructure should support but not determine the development ecotourism opportunities. Where possible ecotourism should make use of established infrastructure. The provision of infrastructure should be the minimum that is necessary to be consistent with desired style of an ecosystem and facilitate the delivery of quality ecotourism products. Ecotourism also has a role to play in the application of environmentally sensitive or 'alternative' technologies to real world situations.

Infact, the tourism industry must have a clearly identifiable vision for its future if it is to achieve a high degree of integrity in the market place. To achieve this it is essential that there is a clearly identifiable and consistent standard of quality that is accessible to the consumer. The tourism industry has a prime responsibility for maintaining high levels of quality in service and content, particularly through the provision of training, accreditation and literature. The tourism industry has been becoming increasingly aware of the need for environmental guidelines to protect its long-term interests.

This has often led to the adoption of guidelines on environmental issues. This recognition of environmental responsibilities needs to continue to be emphasised and implemented on a practical level. Industry should therefore provide the development initiatives and the venture capital to meet the primary infrastructure needs of ecotourism developments. It could also develop and adopt an Ecotourism Code of Ethics to provide self-regulation of the industry and meet recogniseds.

Training and accreditation are two methods of establishing standards and providing a competitive edge in the marketing of the ecotourism product. A number of training schemes are available in Australia such as the Inbound Tourism Operators Association (ITOA), Guide Training Scheme and the recently released National Ecotourism Accreditation Program (DIST & TCA 1996). Training needs include environmental education, interpretation and environmental management. There is also a need for managers of natural areas to develop skills in tourism operations and management.

Other challenges include ensuring operators are equipped with skills needed to provide high quality ecotourism experiences and the minimisation of any potential adverse impacts of their operations.

They must also have sufficient knowledge and understanding of operator needs and the ecotourism industry in general. A number of possible approaches to meet the requirements of training include:

(a) identify and address training needs for ecotourism operators, guides and natural area managers
(b) develop training programs for tourism operators to enable them to communicate messages appropriately, be aware of the means to minimise adverse impacts of tourism, and provide opportunities for active involvement in environmental protection and management
(c) provide training for natural area managers jointly with tourism operators to promote a better understanding of each party's interests and concerns, include skills in communication in the training of operators and natural area managers, develop Codes of Practice for ecotourism operators, guides and tourists,
(d) raise awareness of the value of and the need for interpretation
(e) use incentive to encourage training,
(f) require that appropriate training be a pre-requisite for accreditation.

Ecotourism at the community level must be developed within the context of sustainable regionational and even international tourism development. At the regional and national levels, develop policies and programmes, laws and regulations, and marketing, all influence tourism develop The three main principles of sustainable development which can also be applied to region ecotourism development are:

— Ecological sustainability ensures that development is compatible with the maintenance essential ecological processes, biological diversity and biological resources
— Social and cultural sustainability ensures that de-

velopment increases people's control overlies, is compatible with the culture and values of people affected by it, and maintains strengthens community identity, and

— Economic sustainability ensures that development is economically efficient and that resources managed so that they can support future generations.

The growth in ecotourism, or the ecological perspective for tourist visits, appears to be related to:

— the general increase in community environmental awareness
— media exposure of natural Australia; and
— the cost of city-based tourism as well as the degree of satisfaction gained from non-recreation activities.

Despite the quality of the natural attraction, growth of visitation will slow unless a range of facilities is provided. It can be interpreted that without a range of facilities services, only the adventurous tourist will be attracted. However, with facilities, the market broadened considerably and visitor rates grow rapidly with associated economic benefits to community.

Ecotourism can also act as an exemplar for other forms of environmentally responsible tourist promoting best practice in planning, design, management and operation. Any regional ecotourism development strategy should capture this vision by incorporating the following key elements:

— ecotourism is dependent on the natural environment,
— environmental protection and conservation are prerequisites for the development of an ecotourism industry, ecotourism is part of the tourism industry;

— ecotourism can be an environmental exemplar for other forms of tourism, and

— ecotourism enhances awareness and appreciation of the natural environment

However, ecotourism is not to be seen as an economic panacea for the problems of underdevelopment and there are a number of issues facing the future of ecotourism which include:

(a) changing consumption patterns;

(b) education of the industry and public;

(c) making ecotourism profitable;

(d) achieving sustainable development ;

(e) effectively and ethically marketing and promoting ecotourism and

(f) protecting indigenous cultures.

It is a well established fact that not all places have tourism potential and not all communities want to go down the tourism development track. Therefore their needs to be some thorough investigative studies carried out before assuming that ecotourism will indeed provide economic, social and environmental benefits for a business, community or region. The key to capitalising on the potential benefits offered through regional ecotourism development is to maximise the opportunities and minimise the adverse impacts through environmentally sustainable development planning as outlined in the Environmentally Based Tourism Development Planning Framework (Dowling 1993), If this is carried out then a sound base will have been established for regional ecotourism to develop and flourish in harmony with the natural and cultural environments.

Carrying Capacity

Tourism resources available in the various countries

consist the same time of space, facilities, and values. These are resources whose use cannot be left uncontrolled without running the risk of their deterioration, or even their destruction. The satisfaction of tourism requirements must not be prejudicial to the social and economic interests of the population in tourists areas, to the environment or above all to natural resources, which are the fundamental attraction of tourism and historical and cultural sites. All tourism resources are part of the heritage of mankind. National Communities and the entire international community must take the necessary steps to ensure their preservation. (Manila declaration on world tourism 1980). Recognition of the growing problem of tourist saturation and of the importance of controlling tourist resources has led in recent years to increasing interest in the concept a Tourist Carrying Capacity and its measurement. The Carrying Capacity of an area is the maximum level of development and the number of people who can use a site without generating an unacceptable alteration in the physical environment and adverse effect on the society, economy and culture an without leading to an unacceptable decline in the quality of experience gained by visitors by staying within the Carry Capacity limits the resources for tourism are maintained for continuous future use.

Capacity and Saturation

Capacity and saturation problems arise in three tourist Spaces:

> The tourist generating zone—saturation caused by failure to stagger departures (owing to climate, employment conditions, school holidays etc.) of concentration of demand of particular times on certain types, of tourism (sun/sea/sand, winter ski, cultural).

The transit zone-saturation of the means of transport (air, sea or land) from the generating zone to the destination zone. The receiving or destination zone—saturation to a level which damages the overall environment of the destination (in physical, social or economic terms) and or destroys the tourist image and leads to visitor dissatisfaction.

Criteria Controlling Optimum Capacity

Criteria controlling capacity thresholds can be divided into two broad categories, those affecting the indigenous environment and those affecting the tourist image/product.

The Indigenous Environment. Those criteria affecting the existing physical economic or socio-cultural environment will generally control the saturation level in sensitive areas (e.g. areas of ecological or cultural values) These criteria includes

Physical

— the acceptable level of visual impact

— the point at which ecological damage occurs

— the need for, conservation of wildlife and marine life

Economic

— the volume of tourism providing optimum economic benefits

— the level of employment suited to the local community

Social/Cultural

— the volume of tourism that can be absorbed without detriment to the social/cultural life of the community

— the levels of tourism that will help maintain monuments and cultural traditions without detrimental effects.

Resource Availability

— the availability of public utilities e.g. water

— the availability of transport facilities
— the availability of other essential facilities such as hospitals and adequately trained tourism personnel

Tourism Image/Product

In areas where the environment is less sensitive the volume of tourists is likely to be controlled (both maximum and minimum) by the required tourism image/product.

The main criterion should be to satisfy both visitors and local residents. Evaluation of tourists needs should be carried out directly with market demand analysis in the originating zones. The criteria will include

Physical

— The climatic characteristics combined with freedom from pollution
— The attractiveness of the landscape or townscape
— The quality of accommodation and attraction

Economic

— the cost of the holiday

Social/Cultural

— the intrinsic interest of the indigenous community and its culture
— the quality of local crafts and gastronomic attractions.

Resource availability

— the standards of transport, infrastructure and tourist services.

Need to Evaluate Capacity/Saturation

The specific need to evaluate capacity and saturation thresholds is two fold, first to enable governments to plan ahead in order to avoid future saturation problems and secondly to overcome the disadvantages where saturation already exists or is near approaching. Fundamental to saturation is seasonality. No tourist areas have reached saturation throughout the year and in many cases stress and structural imbalance only occur for a short peak period. These peak periods lead to large unproductive investments used only for short periods which disrupt the environment and bring economic and social disbenefits. Concentration in time results in too many buildings, lose of green areas, overstraining of infrastructure, overcrowded space and facilities. Existing tourism plant can accommodate increased volumes with proper, distribution and staggering of use. Seasonality in therefore an overriding consideration in the concept of carrying capacity and saturation. Apart form seasonality the criteria of carrying capacity vary with context and in particular between developed and developing tourism areas. Developing tourism areas-countries regions or locations where tourism has not developed to any degree but which have potential. In these cases long, medium and short term development plans need to be prepared by government or public/private development agencies. Developed tourism areas — countries regions or locations where tourism has reached or is expected to reach overcapacity and saturation. In these cases remedial action and management policies are needed.

Capacity Measurement

Carrying capacity and saturation of tourism areas is a reality, not just a concept. There is a definite need establish acceptable levels both for use in initial planning and in cases where saturation exits. The measurement of capacity/saturation criteria can be quantified in time space and tourist function rates.

Time. The time period will vary with the scale and type of tourism consideration and may be.

Peak Capacity. The maximum number of persons at any

one time. Calculation for this period use is usually taken as about two-third of the actual peak which can occur for short periods.

Daily/Weekly. The maximum number of person that can be accommodated in a day/ week i.e. the peak capacity and the turnover during the period considered.

Yearly Capacity. The number of person who can be accommodated bearing in mind seasonality owing to climate demand pattern variations.

Space. The space criteria can be expressed in units of area or length by means of the following co-efficient:

$$= \frac{1}{\text{Required area (or length) per user}}$$

The practice, both research and planning use many different techniques and methods which often make comparisons and the consolidation of data into useful standards. Different techniques commonly used include. Unit measures: absolute e.g., accommodation, transport and utility capacities.

Density Zones: the number of persons who can be accommodated per hectare for different activities and varying locational situations e.g., 1,000 persons per hectare for beaches.

Capacity: no of persons /unit/ area X total area

Equipment artic: The area/unit of equipment per number of persons, e.g., 1 restaurant per 2000 tourists

Tourist Function Rates

Tourist function rates enable the tourist capacity and use to be related to the resident population, transport capacity, kilometric density, seasonality economic benefits and other factors as required. For example the tourists function rate can be defined as the ratio of tourist bed places to the permanent population of an area.

$$\text{Tourist function rate} = \frac{\text{bed places} \times 100}{\text{Population of locality}}$$

Such function rates allow comparison of the tourist density in one location with another, and with the development of a body of knowledge and experience could be capacity levels.

Threshold Analysis

The concept of thresholds relates to critical levels which are either needed to support certain facilities or beyond which new factor come into play. The economic viability of a tourist attraction may depend on certain minimum volume of visitors for example.

The threshold capacity is number of visitors required for economic viability or the maximum number of visitors that can be provided with water without having to develop a totally new water source.

$$\text{Threshold Capacity} = \frac{\text{Available water supply}}{\text{Consumption per day/person}}$$

Non-measurable Criteria

Many criteria are difficult to measure and some are virtually nonmeasurable, for example ecological and cultural impacts or the psychological effects on visitors. Techniques for overall assessment of the effect of development include cost-benefit analysis and impact studies.

Cost Benefit Analysis

Cost benefit analysis is a technique which attempts to set out and evaluate the social cost and benefits of projects to decide whether or not they should be undertaken. Cost benefit analysis is invaluable in ascertaining in financial and economic terms the costs and benefits to the tourist and the local community.

Impact Studies

The use of impact studies is seen by some as an alternative to the carrying capacity concept. The idea of environmental impact studies is to examine development proposals for the purpose of identifying the future environmental effects, and modifying the proposals to avoid any detrimental effects many be indicated by the study.

Standards

(1) *Common Standards.* Accommodation and tourist facilities, considerable quantified data exists on standard requirement for accommodation and facilities at the development level-hotel, holiday village, villa and apartment floor areas and sizes by category, catering, shop entertainment and swimming facilities provisions per person per category. Overall tourism resort areas can vary between low densities of twenty beds/hectare to over hundred beds/hectare. In cities densities may depend on the tourist product and image desired. Infrastructure: quantified information on transport needs and the demand for utility services (water, electricity, sewage, telecommunications) per, head is available as well as on the support population needs.

(2) *Special Standards.* Special standards are those relating to the particular tourist attraction and specific tourist product, which derives from the basic environment e.g., mountain ski, Coastal beach The approach to tourism carrying capacity standards should be based on these and the principles of:

— Preserving areas of unique scientific (e.g. nature reserves) historic (e.g. archaeological sites and cultural value (e.g. sensitive ethnic areas) in their entirety if they might be damaged by tourism, even though this prevent their use for tourism.

— Ensuring that in area developed for tourism there is no irreversible loss or damage to the Heritage.

— Preventing non-essential tourism activities where they are likely to damage the environment and could be equally well provided elsewhere.

Carrying capacity analysis is an essential technique in the planning for sustained tourism development. This technique is now being widely applied in tourism and recreational planning to systematically determine the upper limits of developments and tourists use of an area without degrading it and also helps establish the optimum use of tourism resources.

12

Economic Importance of Tourism

Of all the development activities, mountaineering and trekking have the potential to usher in an all-round development in hillly region. As we know that tourism involves expenditure and resources use to achieve multiple ends, returns become important. Returns can be economic, social, cultural, political, psychological and ecological. To achieve them, ends and means count a lot. The returns, positive or negative, which are not related to the objectives, can be deemed as unintended consequences. Tourism has been largely conceived of in economic terms. Therefore, the economics of mountaineering and trekking is very important, when we talk about mountain tourism.

Mountaineering and trekking requires lots of money from the pockets of tourists, the government and private operators. Adventure tourism has to go to such areas, which are difficult in approach. Tourist attractions in Garhwal are not only located in remote corners but also are difficult in approach. Simultaneously clothing, equipment and food for such activities are varied and costly. Hence acquiring such things is difficult and expensive for the domestic tourist if not for the foreign tourist. On the other hand tour operators also face great difficulties in arranging such things. First because, they are expensive, second they are rarely available in India. Economics is the game of demand and supply. Simplest thing to earn profit is to increase supply when demand is increasing, but in adventure tourism demand for mountains, treks and infrastructure is great in Himalayas, whereas the supply of goods and services to cater to the tourist demand is very scanty. Supply side i.e. transport, roads, accommodation and road-side amenities are either very weak or at its initial stage. However, they are coming up, though at a slower speed.

Besides this it is well known that hilly region, due to its difficult topography, deficient mineral resources and fragile eco-system, is not suitable for any manufacturing industry. Hence its mountains, rivers, forests, glaciers, peaks, pastures and tarns can be the only source of economic development (through mountain tourism) of underdeveloped region. Davis gave four reasons for the encouragement of tourist industry in developing countries.

(a) Tourism is relatively labour-intensive and compares favourably with other economic activity as a generator of employment.
(b) In many developing countries, the demand prospects for international tourism are considerably brighter than they are for traditional exports.
(c) Tourism can often generate economic growth in countries or regions "that however much they offer to tourists, have little or nothing in the way of resources to offer to anyone else. The sector can thus help to instigate disequilibria.
(d) Tourism can speed up the development process because the gestation period of most tourist investment projects is relatively short.

Most of these are existing in developing countries of the world. Therefore tourism development might be defined specially as the provision or enhancement of facilities and services to meet the need of the tourists. If tourism is to become successful and a self-perpetuating industry, it needs to be planned and managed as a renewable resource industry, based on local capacities and community decision-making. Right decision at right time is most essential. Right decision about the funds (big businessmen, government and banks) is of foremost importance. Finally, tourism development must combine planning e.g. existing potentials, goals, infrastructure, facilities and developmental strategy with marketing and management. All these things are of paramount importance in such sensitive business. Planning is concerned with anticipating and regulating change in a system, to promote orderly development, so that the social, economic and environmental benefits of the development process could be acheived.

Very soon tourist destinations started facing environmental problems. Primary concern of tourism business was economic gains. The existence of tourism potential, however, need not necessarily lead to a flourishing tourist industry. Therefore the objective of every potential holding area is not only to maintain it but also to provide it to the tourist with care.

Therefore 'what' (potentials), 'how' (planning) and to whom' (tourist) are to be decided first before we embark on launching tourism in the area as an industry and later on they are the factors on which rests the entire dynamics of tourist economy. The potential of this industry is spread everywhere on earth from easy plains, rivers, forests, sea-shores, sky to mountaintops. There is also a branch of economy that avoids central places and the agglomeration of industry. This is tourism.

Tourism is drawn to the periphery of settlement districts as it searches for a position on the highest mountains in the most lonely woods, along the remotest beaches. Tourism industry, hence deals with identification of potentials, planning for their betterment, developmental strategy, marketing and management, without one the other remains useless. Without the intervention of the tourism industry, the tourists would necessarily tend to neglect the tourism assets, however valuable these may be. The tourism industry is a vital link between the tourism assets and the tourism market. Since the tourism industry provides the vital tourism growth, but inefficient and inadequate tourism industry retards such growth, whereas a strong and efficient tourism sector promotes and accelerates the growth of the region. The need of leisure and pilgrim tourist differs from those of business tourists. And even within each of these market segments, the requirements vary in accordance with the income pattern, as well as sex, age and other characteristics of the tourists therein. While the tourism industry is, thus an essential prerequisite for the growth of tourism, its importance, however, is essentially dependent on a country or a region. Taking the case of Bermuda, situated hundreds of miles from a landmass, was once small agricultural producer, but with the growth of population, tourism was an obvious choice to improve the island's economy. Now it is the major industry of the country.

Tourism and leisure industry in the world has an interesting history. Prior to the industrial revolution in Europe, the aristocracy had a virtual monopoly of leisure and tourism. Gradually with the passage of time on some workers did manage to arrange short holidays largely limited to Christmas and Easter. Holidaying for masses throughout the Victorian era was almost entirely confined to day excursions. Upto 1900 holiday was taken for granted as a luxury and until 1960 working week was about 45 hours, but later it was reduced to 40 hours a week. In USA, hundreds of firm's - now handle the week-end holidays. Reduction in working hours, increased disposable income, fast transport system and monotonous character of city life not only accelerated tourism but also diverted it towards remote countryside and nature. Weekly leisure time gave rise to the demand for essentially local leisure facilities, but the annual leisure pattern in the developed countries is of a different significance when it comes to determining how and where the disposable free time is spent. Four weeks paid holiday of 1980 has popularised holidaying abroad. Tourism, as we know it today, is a relatively new phenomenon, which generates new demands on land for use and enjoyment on a, scale not envisaged until recently. The struggle for the countryside, remote areas close to nature, in fact is becoming everywhere popular and more complex. The tourist, the farmer, the sportsman and the resident himself all claim title to its use. Each has his own activity for which he can make a good case. Each, if given the chance, would exclude one or all the others.

Hence the system of taking decisions must match the new complexity of tourist industry and the pressure from others. Reconciling development and conservation thus depends upon a skillfulsorting out of goals and values, both public and private.

The tourist demand and local uses can seldom clash, but can be checked by wise management and planning. It can reduce the conflict and ensure the full use and enjoyment of scarce resources in economic, social and aesthetic terms. To date, most tourism goals and planning have been oriented towards business interests and economic growth. The prime motive for tourism development and planning has been commercial and economic gain. The mere existence of tourism potential, however, need not necessarily lead to a flourishing tourist industry. It can be disastrous too. Therefore the planning, policy framing, administration and careful implementation is most essential.

In planning tourism to an area, one must not forget the aesthetics of the region, which determine the rate of development of tourism. In fact, it is extremely important that the natural beauty of potentially popular destinations be preserved and protected by sensible planning. Key tourism planning phases are:

(i) Assessment of tourist demand and supply;
(ii) Establishing objectives;
(iii) Territorial planning;
(iv) Basic infrastructure;
(v) Human resource planning;
(vi) Financial planning;
(vii) Administrative structure;
(viii) Marketing and promotion;
(ix) Monitoring progress; and
(x) Time factor.

Prior to the establishment of. tourism industry, if we look upon all above segments of planning, there will be no chance for haphazard development of the region or imbalance in the multiple resource use system. So the first thing is: what are the assets that can be developed into destination? What is the number of tourists, whether it is increasing or decreasing, what should be the objective? And to achieve. These objectives what should be the planning? How infrastructure should be developed, how finances can be allocated, and what will be the priority in investment, how local human resources can be utilised, what will be the administrative set up? How marketing will be looked after with an idea of promotion with specific time period? If this all is framed well in time and chalked out properly there is no question of failure or dark future of tourism.

The planning system must also be flexible in time and in scale. There is no absolute or all-time best use of resources. The pattern of demand changes over the years, therefore, flexibility in tourism planning is must. This flexibility should be adopted in different spheres of tourism planning. If tourist arrivals to a particular destination keep on increasing, the planners have to think about augmenting the facilities for increasing number of tourists, but this increase can be adjusted up to a certain extent i.e., up to the carrying capacity of the region.

The planners have to think about the ways and means of diversifying the crowd to other destinations rather than concentration of tourists at a particular place.

13

Tourism Under WTO Regime

GATS (General Agreement on Trade in Services) sets in place a system that will lead to the gradual elimination of some barriers to tourism growth, such as restrictions on hiring of foreign personnel, establishment of management operations and opening of franchise companies. This report explains how that will happen.

The guiding philosophy of GATS is that the easier it is for companies to compete and do business, the more trading ensues and the more economies grow.

In order to do business as effectively as possible, companies need level playing fields so that they can have equal access to natural resources, expertise, technologies and investment, both within countries and across borders.

GATS objective is to liberalize trade in services by setting the same rules for both foreign and domestic trading partners, providing "most favoured nation" treatment for all GATS members, and by avoiding disruptive changes in policies affecting trade. GATS lays the foundations of a new multilateral trading system that will be implemented gradually over the upcoming years. Contrary to widespread belief, nothing will happen overnight.

GATS is a new international trade agreement signed by 125 nations in Marrakesh, Morocco, on 15 April, 1994. It sets global trading rules for service industries, such as telecommunications, financial services, transportation, business services and tourism. It provides procedures for governments to liberalize trade in services through negotiations.

GATS is administered by the Geneva-based World Trade Organisation. Formerly called GATT, the World Trade Organisation is also charged with supervising 14 other treaties on international commerce that resulted from the Uruguay Round of trade negotiations between 1986 and 1993. Some of the other agreements include the "new" GATT (General Agreement on Tariff's and Trade 1994) which covers trade in merchandise and TRIPS (Agreement on Trade Related Aspects of Intellectual Property Rights).

GATS signatory countries have submitted schedules of commitments that specifically spell out their national trading rules for each service sector. One hundred countries have submitted schedules of commitments on tourism services, more than any other services sector.

The World Trade Organisation will bring countries together to negotiate and balance their commitments on liberalisation in successive rounds of negotiations across all services sectors.

GATS recognizes that countries are at different stages in their development and services regulations. It provides special treatment for developing countries, particularly the least developed ones, with a view to increasing their participation in world trade.

GATS applies to measures affecting trade in services in three ways:

(i) Juridical: GATS is legally binding on the signatory countries.

(ii) Contractual: GATS signatory countries agree to specific rights and obligations which may be disputed, settled or enforced through established procedures.

(iii) Strategic: In their commercial policies, member countries are expected to be guided by GATS rules towards progressive liberalisation. This means gradually according market access, national treatment and most-favoured-nation (MFN) treatment to all members.

GATS is not a free trade agreement, but a tool leading to trade in services without discrimination or other non-tariff barriers. GATS does not mean immediate and full liberalisation, but a beginning of the liberalisation process.

GATS does not intervene in the economic policies and regulations of its member countries, such as taxes, incentives, interest rates, etc., unless such policies are applied unequally to domestic and foreign services suppliers.

GATS does not deal with frontier formalities which affect travellers, such as visas, passports, customs duties, exit taxes, or taxes on tourism services. Nor does it apply to foreign exchange allowances or restrictions affecting international travellers.

In tourism, restrictions affect companies in many ways, such as:

(i) their ability to move staff to a foreign country (intra-company transfers),
(ii) to create and operate branch offices abroad,
(iii) to effect currency payments and transfers,
(iv) to use trademarks, etc.

Even when meeting all of a country's requirements for doing business in that country, a foreign tourism enterprise—hotel, travel agency, restaurant, transport company—may still be prevented from conducting business it the national government claims there is not an "economic need" for that business.

GATS intends to do away with this cloudy trading environment by first:

(i) clearly defining the general obligations or rules for trading, such as: market access, national treatment and most-favoured-nation (MFN) status.

(ii) determining the modes of supply of services or types of service transactions to which such rules should apply.

(iii) asking countries to define their measures by making specific commitments that aw in line with the general obligations or rules.

(iv) while stating that the Agreement is for total coverage and applies to all services sectors, hence the tourism sector.

The Two Pillars of GATS

National treatment	*Market access*
Each government shall treat foreign services suppliers no less favourably than its own services and service suppliers.	Each government shall accord services and services suppliers of other governments treatment no less favourable than that agreed and recorded in its "schedule".

Most-Favoured Nation (MFN)

A government must not discriminate between services or service
suppliers of other members.

Modes of Supply of Services Under GATS

(i) cross-border (e.g: tour operation travel assistance)

(ii) consumption abroad (e.g: by international visitors)

(iii) commercial presence (e.g. establishing a branch office)

(iv) by natural persons (e.g. hotel manage, consultant tour guide)

In the future, countries that agree to GATS are supposed to allow foreign service suppliers full access to their domestic markets and thus be treated equally as domestic suppliers.

For tourism and travel-related businesses this will mean:

(i) Tour operators, hotel enterprises and other tourism- and travel-related companies from one country will be able to set up operations in other countries.

(ii) In the hotel sector, GATS will facilitate franchising, management contracts, technical service agreements, licensing and patents.

(iii) If national treatment is fully granted, foreign companies will be able to sell their services under the same terms and conditions as domestic companies and suppliers.

(iv) Such treatment will also make foreign companies eligible for a government's domestic incentives and benefits.

(v) They will be able to move staff to a foreign country and base thorn there without restrictions.

(vi) They will be allowed to effect international transfers and payments for current transactions without restrictions.

Commitments relating to market access and national treatment obligations and, in a different way, to most-favoured-nation treatment. Measures mean laws, regulations, rules, procedures, decisions, administrative action and guidelines, and practices. Commitments introduce such measures to the Agreement. It produces several effects:

(i) it allows the country to actually form part of the Agreement

(ii) it determines, the degree of openness of the country's market to foreign suppliers of the services in question

(iii) it makes commitments points of reference for post and future negotiations.

Theoretically, a country can enter GATS solely on the basis of just one service sector.

Depending on the possible commercial value and rationale of a commitment, it can be regarded as a concession, compensation, benefit or restriction on behalf of that government.

Four "levels" of commitments are foreseen in the schedules:

(i) full (no limitation— "none")

(ii) with limitations (citing an actual measure that binds or improves the existing restrictive regulatory situation)

(iii) no commitment ("unbound" for measures inconsistent with market access or national treatment); or simply explaining that "no commitment is technically possible".

Normally, commitments are related to specific services sectors, although there may also be horizontal commitments i.e. relating to all sectors at once.

Countries may also enter additional commitments in the form of undertakings which apply to domestic regulations such as qualifications, technical standards, licensing requirements and procedures.

Once fixed in GATS, commitments may be withdrawn or modified. After 1 January 1998, governments can withdraw or modify their commitments. If such amendments affect the benefits of members, compensation must be offered on a MFN basis.

GATS promotes multilateralism in international trade: a measure expressed by a commitment affects all GATS member countries, even if the commitment is a result of a bilateral negotiation.

Measures inconsistent with MFN treatment (which

originate because of members' bilateral and regional agreements concluded outside the GATS negotiations) must be published in Lists of Article II (MFN) Exemptions forming an integral part of the Agreement. It provides for machinery and negotiations by which measures corresponding to exemptions must be terminated. Normally, they should disappear as of 1 January 2005.

GATS provides for rules regarding recognition of the education or experience obtained, requirements met, or licenses or certifications granted in a particular country, for the purpose of authorisation, licensing or certification of services suppliers in another country.

Such recognition is not deemed as a commitment in the GATS sense, i.e. it does not spread to all members. It may be based on an agreement with the country concerned or may be accorded autonomously. The GATS principles for such recognition apply in the way that the country offering recognition to another country must afford adequate opportunity for other interested members to negotiate their accession to such agreements or to demonstrate their eligibility to recognition.

The transparency discipline of GATS requires each Member to publish promptly (at the latest by the time of their entry into force) all laws, regulations or administrative guidelines as well as international agreements which significantly affect trade in services covered by the member's specific commitments. Members must also respond promptly to all requests for specific information, particularly through enquiry points which should be established by the end of 1996.

This can be viewed at from the following points:

(i) economic importance of tourism services

(ii) the definition and coverage of tourism services

(iii) actual commitments on tourism

(iv) controversy over the meaning of consumption abroad

(v) the degree of actual liberalisation in the tourism sector

(vi) relationship between the main tourist generating countries and developing tourist receiving countries.

Economic Importance of Tourism

The value of internationally-traded tourism services can be related to the receipts from international tourism. According to WTO/OMT estimates, at the world level such receipts (excluding international fare receipts) in 1993 accounted for nearly thirty-two per cent of the total exports of commercial services, of which over thirty-five per cent were in developing countries.

Tourism is seen as the largest services sector and the largest item of international trade.

Coverage of Tourism Services

GATS deals with services supplied by natural persons (individual services suppliers) and juridical persons (formally established companies), also to natural or juridical persons, in other words, in the tourism context, to travellers and tourism-related enterprises whenever such transactions are carried out between national and foreign persons.

SUPPLY OF A SERVICE

Supply of a Service Includes the Production, Distribution, Marketing Sales and Delivery of a Service

For the purpose of identifying commitments, GATS conventionally singles out so-called tourism and travel related services (TTRS), along with other sectors corresponding to business; communication; construction; distribution; education; environment; finance; health; recreation, culture and sports; and transport. Within this classification TTRS sub-sectors are not further developed unlike in the majority of other sectors.

Tourism and Travel Related Services Under GATS Classification

travel agencies and tour operator services
hotel and restaurant (including catering)
tourist guide services
other (unspecified)

For tourism this classification can be considered "open-ended" or even incomplete since a number of important, distinct tourism-oriented services such as computer reservation systems (CRS), travel assistance, car rental, tourist health services, convention centres, and many others are scattered under various sectors or are not specified at all.

This situation was responsible for the non-uniform presentation of commitments, thus giving rise to a certain confusion: while some countries registered rent-a-car commitments under the item "other" of TTRS, others did it under road transport services; while some included "hotel management" under TTRS, others would rather identify it under business services; for some, "marina operations" was part of TTRS ("other"), for others of recreational, cultural and sporting services, etc.

Although an important and inseparable part of the tourism sector, tourist transport services, including passenger transportation by air, are all included under transport services. However, as regards air transport services, GATS applies temporarily only to measures affecting:

(i) the selling and marketing of air transport services
(ii) computer reservation system (CRS) services

and not:

(i) traffic rights, however granted, or

(ii) services directly related to the exercise of traffic rights.

Tourism Commitments

Commitments on tourism and travel related services ranked higher than for any other services sector. As many as 100 countries (including the European Union's twelve members in 1994) and dependent territories submitted commitments under this item out of the 107 countries and territories which entered their schedules in the Marrakesh Agreement. This figure is well above those for financial and business services which came next. There were four countries which submitted only TTRS commitments.

Thirty-seven countries presented commitments on computer reservation systems. They were entered under air transport services and TTRS ("other"). Two countries mentioned GRS in their lists of MFN exemptions. A careful reading of the Services Agreement suggests that when entering specific commitments regarding tourism, countries were rather cautious by actually fixing the existing regulatory situation governing at the time of the negotiations, or by fixing measures below the already existing market access opportunities.

Actual Liberalisation in Tourism

The tourism sector was considered relatively "easy" to negotiate in the core, front-line activities such as hotel and tour operations, although actual commitments revealed a number of limitations particularly in the area of national treatment and the presence of individual service suppliers. Nevertheless, it was not found necessary to open a separate track of negotiations on tourism, as was the case for financial services, telecommunications or maritime transport services, on which special annexes had to be drafted.

Underdeveloped or developing tourist destinations attract rather than discourage the main suppliers of tourism services for commercial presence combined with investment. If there had been market access restrictions, these could have been overcome without great problems by large companies.

Understanding Consumption Abroad

Consumption abroad, i.e. by international visitors, is the most important mode of delivery of tourism services. International tourism is a sector where consumers need to travel to a foreign destination in order to buy a service or product. Yet, the measures affecting such travel are not yet dealt with by GATS.

Consumption abroad should be understood as the freedom for one member's residents to purchase services in the territory of another member, once they are already there. In other words, the movement of consumers across international borders is not regarded as pertaining to consumption abroad under the present GATS text.

Limitations of consumption abroad occur when this freedom is curtailed in whatever way (thus, e.g. diminishing the sales of tourism companies) or when the supply of a service by foreign-based companies to internal consumers is obstructed in the national territory. Limitations to this mode of supply of tourism services can be identified by analysing what is meant by "supply of a service", being the production, distribution, marketing, sales and delivery of a service.

Tourism and Developing Countries

GATS Art. IV advocates increasing participation of developing countries. This objective is of special relevance to tourism in which there exist considerable imbalances between developed and developing countries with regard to tourism receipts and tourism-accrued economic benefits.

Vertical integration and the concentration of distribution channels which are managed from within the developed tourist generating countries can be held responsible for such effects as:

(i) retention of economic receipts from tourism within the distribution channels

(ii) low remuneration of destination services (domestic accommodation, attractions, local guides, etc.)

(iii) imports (leakages) from destination countries which are needed to maintain tourism facilities in service order.

The developing countries must strengthen their domestic services capacity, efficiency and competitiveness, improve their access to and share in distribution channels and information networks, as well as receive market access in modes of supply of export interest to them. Under GATS all such improvements can be negotiated by means of commitments. Members, especially developed countries, must establish, by 31 December 1996, contact points to facilitate the attainment by developing countries of these goals.

GATS intends to bring order to the conditions of trade in services. From the perspective of a single country the price to pay will be less flexibility but the advantages seem important. Abiding by GATS creates a predictable trading environment and thus contributes to increased confidence of potential investors in the recipient market. The exercise of all freedom in trade policy measures is not feasible either. It undermines the sustainability of trade in general, including for those who now exercise their dominant position in this area.

On the other hand, GATS does not clash with traditional incentives: grants, tax holidays, work permits, etc. which are so important to attract tourism investments, but which are designed for brief periods. Some countries, particularly the developing ones, due to their weak negotiating capacity, may also have found it difficult to extract durable, equitable benefits from investor countries by simply using incentives. In the case of GATS measures, equitable compensation is sought and should be offered.

Fixing incentives as GATS commitments is risky. The result could be the distortion of the competitive conditions between different sectors or too high a price to pay by offering new concessions should the incentive-type commitment be withdrawn. It is therefore advisable not to bind incentives as commitments, but to retain flexibility in this area. On the other hand, when incentives are offered and not fixed as commitments, they should still be available to all eligible companies, national and foreign, in order to go by the national treatment obligation.

Not always, the right to personnel mobility, for example, will not apply to measures affecting persons seeking access to the local employment market, nor to measures regarding citizenship, residence or employment on a permanent basis.

The right to effect international payments may be subject to foreign exchange controls and restrictions to safeguard the balance of payments; however such measures, should they occur, will require notification and consultations.

If governmental agencies purchase services for governmental purposes (e.g. contracting a state reception), the GATS principles of most-favoured-nation treatment, market access and national treatment, will not apply.

Members of the Agreement will also be free to adopt restrictive measures in order to protect public morals, privacy of individuals, and the environment, to maintain public order, prevent deceptive and fraudulent practices, and for safety and security in general. This requirement may apply differently to domestic and foreign companies.

GATS will benefit tourism and travel in several ways. Since the overall objective of GATS and other accords of the Marrakesh Agreement is to spur trade and economic growth, there will be more demand for exhibitions, incentive and business travel, meetings and conventions. More trade in both goods and services will mean more movements of people and more business opportunities for the travel trade.

With disappearing trade restrictions for tourism companies, tourism will grow and increasingly focus on quality. The tourism sector will benefit not only by allowing major tour operators and hotel chains to expand their reach worldwide, but also by opening up competition to small-medium scale companies. So far, they have been overshadowed by big companies and monopolies, and not strong enough to overcome the existing trade barriers. Under GATS, a monopoly situation will be dealt with by the GATS rules on monopolies and exclusive service suppliers.

Liberalisation in all other than TTRS sectors (business services, communication, construction, finance ...) will help tourism companies to do their job better: quicker and at lower cost. Other Marrakesh accords will also help. GATT 1994 reduced barriers to the importation of tourism activity related merchandise, and TRIPS will sort out problems with trademarks and service marks of which tourism services abound. For example, requirements that foreign marks be used in conjunction with local marks would, as a general rule, be prohibited.

The following example shows how GATS will benefit the tourism industry, national economy and employment.

Global Distribution System Through CRS

A developing country may restrict the establishment of CRS, because it is perceived as putting its national airline at a disadvantage.

Under GATS, Country A where a CRS is based will be able to approach Country B where it is restricted and ask that the restrictions (e.g. to commercial presence) be lifted. Country B will then decide what market liberalising measure it wants in return from Country A or from other countries in which CRSs are based and which may equally be interested in accessing its market. In addition to fair access terms, the compensating measures sought by Country B could be in the tourism sector or in another sector. Countries involved will then negotiate.

If the talks succeed in lifting the limitations and allowing the CRS into the new market, this market opening will be available to CRSs from all countries and the following advantages could result:

(i) *Investment:* The CRS that is seeking to establish itself in Country B will have to invest in Country B. This will have a positive result on the latter's balance of payments and economy.

(ii) *Access:* Country B will receive fair access terms in the CRS for its tourism services suppliers.

(iii) *Training and employment:* Local staff will have to be trained and employed because bringing in a full expatriate staff may be prohibitively expensive. This will attract know-how and technology and create new jobs.

(iv) *Payments:* Local telecommunications costs have to be paid, thus increasing country's revenues.

(v) *Taxes:* Payment of local taxes boosts revenues for national treasuries.

(vi) *Prices:* Declining prices for consumers and increasing commissions for travel agents can result because of the new competition.

(vii) *Benefits in other services sectors:* the negotiated compensations vary and could include, for example, increased business services opportunities for professionals of Country B in all other GATS countries.

The potential recipients of CRSs are regarded as late coiners. National regulations are outdated or do not exist, and uncertainty still governs as regards the multilaterally agreed rules on CRS. Thus regulations can neither be cited as commitments nor used as a reference for hypothetical negotiations.

There is a high concentration of CRSs and the possibilities of building alternative networks are low. Barriers to new entrants are high. These include:

(i) difficulties in making effective use of the network.

(ii) in using networks, small air carriers and tour operators face prohibitive booking fees.

Once foreign-based networks are established, they may develop anti-competitive attitudes: CRSs, e.g., may present problems of bias in the priority accorded to different service suppliers.

The CRS commitments were received from a few groups of countries: the European Union's members (12), EFTA countries (6), a few other developed and European countries, as well as ten developing countries outside Europe. Only one country committed itself to grant market access and national treatment without limitations. The remaining countries included a number of limitations, e.g. EU and EFTA countries in respect of national treatment for cross-border supply and commercial presence, the developing countries in respect of both national treatment and market access, and almost all countries restricted the presence of natural persons. On the other hand, consumption abroad was not bound (not fixed as a commitment) by two countries only.

The absence of CRS-relaled lull or restricted commitments

in GATS does not prevent CRS from being effectively established in the new recipient markets. The difference is that the actual arrangements with CRS may not yet be reflected in GATS.

Taking into account the specificity of tourism services under GATS as already discussed, that depends on how much the developing countries will actually open their markets and how rapidly they will strengthen their industries and make them competitive internationally.

Though people in some developing countries reacted negatively to GATS at the early stages of negotiations, fearing a "foreign invasion", it must again be emphasised that liberalisation measures will not be implemented overnight. Liberalisation by GATS is a long-term process of consultations and negotiations to be carried out at five-year intervals, usually between groups of countries which have been identified as principal suppliers and recipients of a specific service.

As pointed out in the example concerning GRS, GATS will help strengthen the ability of developing countries to compete by attaching conditions to their market opening commitments and requesting the transfer of technology and expertise.

Also, the least-developed countries were given an additional year to negotiate and present their first package of commitments.

Moreover, developing countries will be the main ones to use the safeguard provisions of GATS, such as protecting the balance of payments. Compared with the present situation, the advantage of GATS will be that all the relevant measures are adopted in a transparent way, in a multilateral framework and as a result of consultations.

Developing countries can seek the freedom to deploy not only their key personnel, but also regular personnel in the main tourist generating countries. They can also request the presence in these countries of their individual services suppliers: GRS experts, chefs, hotel managers and developers, and many others, without the requirement of commercial presence. Such permission must be fixed in the schedules of commitments.

There is plenty of work to do. GATS opens the tourism market to business opportunities and pressure from all countries which will eventually form the World Trade Organisation (already today the bulk of transactions related to international tourism is effected among World Trade Organisation countries). GATS challenges the traditional tourism policies carried out at national, bilateral or regional levels. So far, they have been usually targeted at tourism infrastructure and plant, and the facilitation of travel flows, but not to trade issues.

National Tourism Policies

Without neglecting these objectives national tourism policies should now shift to address commercial aspects, better capitalize on comparative advantages (tourism resources) and move towards creating a competitive trading environment for national companies by fostering their efficiency and the ability to supply quality products and exploit all the modes specified in the Agreement and the elements of supply of a service (distribution, marketing, etc.).

GATS calls for more tourism staff training (inclusive of tourism policy-makers and negotiators in the GATS context) to respond to international demand, the enhancement of investment incentives, a new generation of international tourism agreements (e.g. regarding tourism promotion abroad), efficient help to small-medium scale tourism companies to identify and consolidate their market position vis-a-vis large tourism projects, the adequacy of tourism products which can be traded internationally, harmonisation between national tourism policies and those regarding international transport, a new regulatory framework for tourism (e.g. for GRS, consumer protection, taxes).

Tourism Industry Organisations

Since GATS, after all, is all about helping to improve market conditions for the private sector to do business, tourism industry organisations must take an interest in, and be admitted to, decision-making regarding the implementation of this agreement. This can be done on both national and international levels. Tourism companies must be aware of what is negotiated on their behalf by governments, and how to defend their interests, particularly using GATS dispute settlement procedures. The tourism industry should also be able to view their individual interests in a broader context of all services sectors.

National Tourism Administrations

National Tourism Administrations and Tourist Boards may wish to re-define their field of competence and action to take stock of the commercial aspects of tourism and work with national trade representatives, chambers of commerce, transport organisations and bodies representing other services sectors.

Given the results of the Uruguay Round, governments should increase their awareness of the importance and specificity of tourism services and provide for measures allowing tourism industry representatives, legislators and tourism-related public bodies and officials to share responsibility for decisions concerning the operation and development of GATS, particularly in future rounds of negotiations.

In order to take a better stock of the content and volume of the tourism sector, for the purpose of future negotiations, it would be advisable to develop a new, all-inclusive and dynamic classification of tourism and travel related services, whenever work on services classification is resumed. This possibility happily coincides with the current activities of the World Tourism Organisation geared to implement satellite accounts for tourism and the Standard International Classification of Tourism Activities (SICTA), recently adopted by the United Nations Statistical Commission. SICTA identifies tourism and travel related activities by the percentage of sales going to tourist consumption and the share of each activity in tourist expenditure.

World Tourism Organisation

The World Tourism Organisation plans to cooperate with the World Trade Organisation and other international bodies concerned with economic development and integration such as UNCTAD and OECD, as well as regional and tourism industry organisations with a view to:

(i) monitoring the GATS implementation process in respect of tourism policies of its member States.

(ii) organising tourism policy forums and expert groups.

(iii) assisting countries in negotiating their tourism and travel related commitments in conformity with their tourism development plans and policies.

(iv) fostering the creation of statistical tools to measure the economic importance of tourism.

(v) developing the concepts of liberalisation of trade in tourism services for regional or sub-regional economic integration projects.

Partly no and partly yes. Countries are free to engage in such projects. If a country however, is a party to GATS, it must assume the corresponding consequences derived from GATS principles. A country may simultaneously engage in regional integration projects if:

(i) they provide for substantial sectoral coverage (most services sectors must be included, no mode of supply of services is a priori excluded); and

(ii) the regional agreement in question aims at the absence or elimination of substantially all discrimination.

The countries which are already parties to the agreements of this kind should provide to WTO/OMC's Council for Trade in Services all relevant information on the implementation of the agreements, and receive from the Council its recommendations concerning such agreements.

An example of a regional agreement using GATS principles is the North American Free Trade Agreement (NAFTA). Its principles apply automatically to tourism along with other services sectors, except for those sectors (not tourism) which are singled out in the annexes to the general NAFTA agreement.

GATS should not be considered a panacea for solving all the problems of tourism development, but forming part of the Agreement can help countries give a more adequate response to the needs of the tourism megamarket of the future. It will discipline their tourism policies and encourage them to seek equitable advantages from tourism development.

14

The Tourism Industry: New Horizons

The World Tourism Organisation (WTO) estimates that by the year 2020 there will be 1.6 billion international tourist arrivals worldwide, spending over USS2 trillion. This means that globally, arrivals will continue to grow at an average of 4.3% and spending at 6.7% per year, This surpasses the maximum probable expansion in the world's wealth estimated at a 3 % increase per year (WTO, 1988a). Regardless of whether these estimates are realistic or not, it is obvious that tourism, growing at an exorbitant rate, has yet to reach its full potential. Travel and tourism is also one of the world's fastest growing economic activities.

According to the World Travel and Tourism Council (WTTC), tourism is 'expected to contribute 10.8% to the global gross domestic product in 2000 (US$3.6 trillion), rising to 11.6% or US$6.6 trillion by 2010 (World Travel and Tourism Council 2000) They also estimate that capital investment for tourism will reach US$701 billion or 9.4% of total investment in 2000 and reach US$l 4 trillion or 10.6% of total by, 2010 (WTTC, 2000). The WTTC also estimates that travel and tourism-related jobs in 2000 will reach 192 million, accounting for over 8% of global employment. Over-59 million new jobs will be created over the next 10 years (WTTC, 2000).

According to the WTO (1998b, 1999) between 1989 and 1998, international tourism arrivals grew at an average annual rate of 10% and international tourism receipts (excluding transport) at 9% Annual percentage increases declined significantly in all markets during the 1990-1995 period due to the Gulf War and a poor global economy. When comparing 1997 with 1998, market increases occurred in all major outbound markets with the exception of the East Asia/Pacific region, primarily due to the Asian economic crisis of 1997. International arrivals are projected to increase from 673 million in 2000 to 1.05 billion in 2010, and 1.6 billion in 2020. These forecasts are based on annual, growth rates of 4.2% to the end of the 1990s and between 4 and 5% during first decade of the 21st century.

Regional Breakdown

Given the information above, it is difficult not to believe, barring a huge disaster, that tourism will demonstrate continued growth throughout the world. Tourism destinations, however, are likely to change. According to the WTO, Europe will continue to be the largest receiving region well into 2020 but will decline from 59% of the market share to 49%. East Asia and the Pacific region will pass the Americas, as the second largest receiving region. Africa, the Middle Eastland South Asia are projected to increase at a slower rate of 5%, 4% and 1%, respectively, by 2020 (WTO, 1998).

Specialty Market Forces

Travel motivations are major push factors in determining what kind of tourism people will seek. Overall the tourism market is becoming increasingly segmented with many new tourism alternatives. 'The new consumers want to be involved - to discover new experiences, to interact with the community, and to learn about and appreciate the destination at more than a superficial level' (Jones, 1998). In response to this trend, destinations are increasingly targeting their tourism product at specific markets or 'specialty travel markets'.

Ecotourism

Increasingly, parks, nature reserves and natural settings

are becoming popular tourist destinations. The development of environmentally sensitive hotels and resorts responds to the fast growing ecotourism markets and the general public's awareness of environmental preservation and sustainability. Sustainability is to improve the quality of life today without destroying it for future generations.

Cultural and Heritage Tourism

Culture and history are the most popular of tourist activities. Experiencing different customs and lifestyles, learning about historical Cultures, visiting historic sites, folklore and theatre characterizes this type of tourism.

Health Tourism

Natural hot springs, weight reduction.

Adventure Tourism

Adventure Tourism can range from high to soft adventure and, in that order, includes activities such as mountain climbing, scuba-diving or walking along perk trails.

Sports Tourism

Tennis, golfing, World Cup football, Olympic events.

Cruise Ship

81% sail from North American ports. US$18 billion in 1997, 205 ships. 8.5% growth since 1990 in North America, Europe growing rapidly.

In 1997, WTO Secretary General Francesco Franigialli confirmed that even as tourism in general continues to grow dramatically, the area of greatest expansion is that of specialty travel. Specifically, he stated that 'trends show a higher than average increase in new types of tourism including ecotourism and all nature-related forms of tourism, which today account for approximately 20% of total international travel' (WTO,

1998c). This is not to say that traditional tourism, such as mass tourism to amusement parks or beaches will cease to exist. The fact remains that' there will always be a market for traditional tourism; however, consumer preferences are expanding to alternative forms of vacationing, often as an 'add-on' to more 'traditional' tourism activities.

According to the Adventure Travel Society, 'Special interest travel is now the fastest growing segment of the travel market. It has grown 12% annually over the past 5 years. The last decade brought increased levels of physical fitness and a growing respect and concern for the environment' (Adventure Travel Society, 1998). It has been largely acknowledged that tourists are looking for more out of their vacation, just as people's tastes vary, so does their willingness to experiment, whether that is by trekking through an Amazon jungle, taking a class about Australian aboriginal culture or observing sea turtle in Costa Rica.

Ecotourism and Nature-based Tourism

Trends indicate that the growth of ecotourism coupled with the larger market segment of nature tourism far surpasses that of tourism in general. While the lack of clear differentiation between ecotourism and other forms of nature tourism makes tracking ecotourism development difficult, it is obvious that travel to natural areas is increasing at a tremendous rate. In 1996, the WTO predicted that there would-be an 86% increase in tourism receipts, of which the majority would come from 'active, adventurous, nature and culture-related travel' (Honey, 1999). In economic terms, the WTO announced in 1997 that 'ecotourism is worth US$20 million a year' at the World Ecotour Conference. Although this amount pales in comparison to tourism's estimated US$3.6 trillion contribution to the global gross domestic product, it still represents a substantial portion of total tourism receipts (WTO, 1998c). Some examples (mainly in North America) of the magnitude of ecotourism or nature tourism follow. At the same time, travelers seem to be willing to pay for an 'eco' experience. In a recent study, Travel Industries of America (TIA) found that 83% of all American travelers are inclined to support "green" companies and are willing to spend, on average 6.2 % more in travel services and products provided by environmentally responsible travel suppliers' (TIA, 2000). Another study of North American travel consumers in 1994 showed that 77% had already taken a vacation involving activities related to nature, outdoor adventure, or learning about another culture in the countryside or wilderness. Of the 23% remaining who had not, all but one respondent stated that they were interested in doing so.

Ecotourism is often 'clumped' together with other forms of nature tourism making it difficult to grasp its real magnitude and growth rate. In the absence of some of the traditional measurement tools often used to calculate general tourism expansion, those wishing to measure ecotourism growth must employ other indicators, which do provide insight into the current and future magnitude of the sub-industry. The following indicators include growth in ecotourism education, international recognition and regional support, international funding opportunities, and growth in tourism eco-certification and eco-labeling programmes. Each of these indicators provides a glimpse beyond the traditional statistical analysis, into the current position of ecotourism and its expected future growth.

Visitation to nature tourism destinations is on the increase worldwide. More and more destinations are trying to 'jump' on the nature tourism 'band wagon'. Many destinations are experiencing an increased number of visitors looking to include eco-activities in their vacation. Demand for destinations that include natural elements such as national parks and local parks, forests, waterways and others continue to increase. According to a 1998 Travel Poll by TIA, 'National parks are one of America's biggest attractions. Nearly 30 million US adults (20% of travelers or 15% of all US adults) took a trip of

100 miles or more, one-way, to visit a national park during 1997-1998. Residents of the Rocky Mountain region of the US were the most likely to visit a national park with 37% saying they included a park visit while traveling (during 1997-1998) (TIA, 2000). Although not all of the activities undertaken at these parks can be considered ecotourism, according to TIA 'a large share of these travelers 70%) participated in outdoor activities while visiting the national parks. Among these outdoors activities, hiking (53%) were the most popular, followed by camping (33%) and fishing (19%) (TIA, 2000). TIA also found that 'one-half of US adults, or 98 million people, have taken an adventure trip in the past 5 years. This includes 31 million adults who engaged in hard adventure activities like white-water rafting, scuba-diving and mountain biking. Adventure travelers are more likely to be young, single and employed compared to all US adults' (TIA, 2000).

Visit to natural areas increases, including ecotourism visitation, so does the demand for travel professionals to accommodate these tourists.

Over the last few years there has also been an increase in tourism professionals, such as travel agents, tour operators, tour guides, etc., that focus either on the ecotourism or at least, the nature tourism markets. Today, it is not difficult to find a tour operator that specializes in an 'eco-niche' such as bird watching or hiking, among others. At the same time, travel industry organisations have also developed around this trend. Some of these groups include Partners in Responsible Tourism (PIRT).

Ecotourism Education

Tourism, in general, is a relatively new field of study. Only in the last sixty years or so, has tourism studies gain (recognition as a social science. Twenty-five years ago, the George Washington University was one of the first colleges in the world to offer a graduate level degree in tourism administration. Today, there are many institutions around the world offering everything from undergraduate and graduate degrees to tourism certificate, diploma programmes. In addition to general tourism education, training in specific to specialty tourism such as ecotourism is also expanding. In 1999, the Ecotourism Society put together a sample list of universities in the US, Canada and the UK that offer programmes or courses in ecotourism. In these three countries alone, there are over 25 institutions of higher learning involved in ecotourism training (Ecotourism Society, 1999) Of course, ecotourism training is not limited to these few countries. Ecotourism specific education is gaining recognition throughout the world in both developed and developing countries. The Commonwealth Department of Tourism in Australia also offers a list of programmes in Australia besides many more parts of the world.

The UN also declared 1999 to be the 'Year of Sustainable Tourism, Small Island States and the Ocean'. The choice of ecotourism specifically only 3 years later, is not on a great success for industry, but it also signifies the gradually accepted distinction between sustainable tourism and ecotourism on the international development level. Regionally, many governments have adopted either ecotourism strategies within their national tourism plan or implemented ecotourism specific development projects. The Vietnamese government planned to adopt a 'National Ecotourism Strategy' in 1999, designed to highlight ecotourism as a national development priority. The government of Nepal implemented a 5-year Manaslu Ecotourism Project, designed to build infrastructure, help local communities benefit from tourism and at the same time help to conserve the environment (Shrestha, 1997).

In the US, the Environmental Protection Agency has begun a tourism industry-wide discussion on sustainable tourism development. The intention of this project is to create a working dialogue aimed at promoting sustainable tourism development and management by identifying what impediments and opportunities for sustainability the tourism industry are currently faced with.According to the WTO, Brazil launched a US$200 million program to develop ecological tourism in the Amazon' in 1997. The programme was funded by the Inter American Development Bank, with a focus on private sector investment in Amazon ecotourism, and the expansion and improvement of conditions for ecotourism within this area (WTO, 1998c).

UN's Council for Sustainable Development, there are a great number of smaller strategies taking place on a national or regional level to stimulate tourism at the micro-enterprise level and promote business linkages intended upon developing alternative tourism, such as ecotourism, that is planned from the beginning with the local community and the sustainability of the industry, as the prime benefactors. Some of the strategies that are already being implemented include the following (DFID,1999):

(a) The Fiji Tourism Development Plan has begun a programme of removal of red tape and regulations that suppress the informal sector.

(b) Enhanced community participation in areas where tourism is being used as a tool for economic development, such as the north coast of Honduras.

(b) Some South African national and provincial parks have facilitated access to markets 'for' local entrepreneurs 'by providing opportunities' to initiate suitable lodging outside the park or small business endeavors or advertising inside the park. The South African government asks potential investors to submit their plans for boosting local development when they bid for a tourism lease.

At the same time, strategies currently being employed

throughout the world at the non governmental level include the following (DFID, 1999):

(a) Provide credit and non-financial services for micro-enterprise.
(b) Understand tourism businesses so they are well positioned so that all stakeholders are satisfied.
(c) Build the capacity of poor people to assess tourism options.
(d) Facilitate communication and negotiation between the tourism industry and local people.

Some examples of the initiatives being taken by business to enhance linkages include (DFID, 1999):

(a) out-source contracting (e.g. laundry, transportation, food service, water sports concessions)
(b) support local enterprise
(c) encourage tourists to visit local sellers
(d) develop partnerships with communities
(e) enhance partnerships with donors,
(f) NGOs and governments.

International Funding or AID

One of the strongest indicators that ecotourism, and more generally, sustainable tourism, are gaining worldwide recognition, is the increasing amount of funding available for these endeavors. Official development financing or aid is usually mobilised through multilateral (representative of several governments) institutions, bilateral (one government) agencies, or regional development banks. Many of these institutions have begun to incorporate sustainable tourism development into larger regional or national sustainable development projects. Some of the organisations that have accepted sustainable tourism as a viable economic device for development include the World Bank, UN, USAID, and the

European Union. In the past, tourism has received 'mixed reviews' from various development organisations, largely due to the bad reputation the industry has acquired from poorly planned, non-sustainable tourism development. This problem occurs when tourisms is developed without stakeholder participation and planning. Often, tourism projects that are deemed 'economically beneficial' are not necessarily socially or environmentally beneficial, nor do the economic benefits fall to those most closely affected by the development. While it is true that this type of non-sustainable tourism development still occurs throughout the world, the popularisation of alternative tourism development such as ecotourism or cultural heritage tourism, is once again allowing tourism to be accepted as an economic tool for sustainable development (International Institute of Tourism Studies, 1999).

Recently, the World Bank Group, which includes the International Finance Corporation (IFQ and the Multilateral Investment Guarantee Agency (MIGA), has begun to formally reintroduce sustainable tourism as a tool for economic, social and environmental development. It is important to note that the IFC never stopped funding tourism projects, as did the World Bank, although ecotourism does not account for a large portion of their agenda (Honey, 1999). The IFC has devoted a special unit to general tourism development, which has invested over US$600 million in loans and equity investments for general tourism develop merit projects (Honey, 1999). MIGA only began its involvement with ecotourism in 1994 with the Rain Forest Aerial Tram in Costa Rica (Honey, 1999). Below is a list of some examples of World Bank projects that include ecotourism development:

(a) Lesotho-Maloti-Drakensberg- Transfrontier Conservation and Development Area Project
(b) Uganda-Protected Areas Management and Sustainable Use Project

(c) Madagascar-Second Environment Program Support Project
(d) Panama Atlantic Biological Corridor
(e) Costa Rica Development of Ecomarkets
(f) Georgia-Integrated Black Sea Environmental Project
(g) Indonesia-Maluku Conservation & Natural Resources Management Project.

The UN has also become involved with tourism projects through the United Nations Development Program (UNDP), which is the world's largest multilateral source for development cooperation (UNDP, 1999) and the Global Environment Facility (GEF). GEF was established as a joint international effort to help solve global environmental problems; The GEF Trust Fund was established by a World Bank resolution as a joint programme between the United Nations Development Program, UNEP and the World Bank (UNDP, 1999). In 1992, UNDP launched the GEF Small Grants Program (GEF/SGP). The GEF/SGP provides grants of up to US$50,000 and other support to community-based groups (CBOs) and non-governmental organisations (NGOs) for activities that address local problems related to the GEF areas of concern. Since its inception, the GEF/SGP has funded over 750 projects in Africa, North America and the Middle East, Asia and the Pacific, Europe and Latin America and the Caribbean. Today, the programme is operational in 46 countries (Christopher Holtz, Washington 1999, personal communication). We are reproducing a few tourism projects from their small-grants portfolio:

(a) *Dominican Republic:* Sustainable Ecotourism and Environmental Education in the Surrounding of Los Haitises National Park. Project dates: September 1997-September 1998
(b) *Belize:* Red Band Scarlet Macaw Conservation and Tourism Development Project. Project dates: June 1997-May 1998

(c) *Chile:* Training and Capacity Building in Tourism

9d) *Zimbabwe:* Unizingwane Ecotourism Project. Project dates: October 1997-October 1998.

(e) *Dominican Republic:* Ecotouristic Promotion with Gender Participation on Ecological Transept Los Calabozos-La-Guazara in High Watershed Yaque del Norte River. Project dates: September 1997-February 1998

(f) *Costa Rica:* Community-Based Ecotourism for Conservation of the Marine Turtle and Marine Resources in Gandoca. Project dates: February 1997-February 1998

(g) *Brazil:* Training Program for Income Generation and Environmental Education for Communities near the Chapada dos Veadeiros National Park. Project dates: September 1997-February 1998

The two groups discussed above, the World Bank and the UN, are arguably the largest international funding organisations on Earth. However, there are a number of national or governmental aid organisations such as USAID in the US, JICA in Japan, FID in the UK and many others. Each of these programmes also provides developmental funding to other countries around the world, including the funding of sustainable tourism projects.

Generally, the tourism industry is dependent on the environment for its sustainability and makes extensive use of the natural and cultural resources in its area of operation. The industry's prosperity is thus somewhat dependent on the conservation and responsible use of the environment. Several organisations including government organisations, not-for-profit industry organisations and NGO's have addressed the issue pertaining to environmental conservation and best practices within the tourism industry by introducing eco-labeling and green certification schemes. Each certification programme defines criteria and standards that enhance efficiency and reduce overuse and wastage. Each scheme is unique in that the certification period varies and may range from 1 to 3 years. Evaluation methods also vary from scheme to scheme. Although there is abundant information on the criteria required to participate in these schemes, there is a shortage of information on the evaluation mechanisms and duration period of each scheme.

In its early stage of development, ecotourism was regarded as a completely new concept. However, today, as we can see from the indicators highlighted here, the areas of both ecotourism and nature tourism has become a significant portion of the tourism industry in general. Growing environmental awareness worldwide, paired with advances in transportation and communication, will only help to foster future ecotourism growth. The markets for these types of sustainable tourism are likely to expand as more people in the world achieve the financial resources needed to travel. In addition, ecotourism development will continue to expand and increasing importance as more communities around the world begins to accept it as an essential strategy for able development plan. Thirty years ago, the term 'ecotourism' did not exist. Strong leadership, solid foundations and idealistic principles have brought ecotourism to where it is today.

We need to recommit to the promise of ecotourism so that the future generations can enjoy sustainable tourism experiences which produce sound economic, social and environmental outcomes. In 2000, ecotourism was practiced on every one of the Earth's continents. There is no doubt that the industry made tremendous strides in the last part of the 20th century. However, there is still much to be done. 'Green cloaking', mismanaged or poorly planned projects and lack of education, are just some of the obstacles 'real' ecotourism must overcome in order to continue to serve its purpose.

APPENDIX

CHRONOLOGY OF TRAVEL TRADE

1670: The 'grand tour' concept was developed especially for educational purpose.

1730: Health experts suggested that sea-water is found to be useful to 'cure' many diseases. The result was that many resorts around the English coast were established to attract visitors seeking 'to cure' themselves both by drinking seawater and by immersing themselves in it.

1815: Steamboat services were introduced from London to Gravesend. One effect of this development was the construction in all major resorts of a pier to accommodate the vessels on their arrival.

1820: The European cultural centres were opened to British travellers.

1830: The rail link was introduced between Liverpool and Manchester.

1838: Peninsular and oriental steam (P and O) company introduced steamship services to India and Far East.

1840: Sir Rowland Hill introduced excursion trains.

1841: A fortunate day came in the history of travel trade when Thomas Cook, as secretary of the South Midland Temperance Association, organised a trip by a train for 570 members of his association to a distance of 22 miles. He brought railway tickets in bulk to sell them back to people. The experiment was successful and everybody was exultant. Mr. Cook had done this job on a no profit basis. But, incidentally, it gave him a new idea and he turned it into a tour business.

1845: Four years later, he set up a 'World's First Travel Agency' to organise excursions. Due to this innovative approach Mr. Cook is known as the Father of Travel Agency Business. He co-ordinated railway and steamship excursions throughout England, Scotland and Europe. However, the railways only gave him 5 per cent commission which was not enough to meet his overheads, so he decided to diversify this business into tour operation.

1850: Thomas Bennett introduced first FIT for VIP's.

1855: Mr. Cook started operating package tours. He conducted the world's first international tour from England to the Paris. This was an 'inclusive tour'. In this way he developed the concept of 'inclusive tour.' In the next year he developed the concept of the 'Grand Tour' by organising a grand tour to the European continent.

1856: Coined the concept 'Grand Tour' for tourists.

It was a sheer coincidence that in the same year 1841, Henry Wells started his freight business in USA. Thomas Cook's company is still by the name Thomas Cook and Sons while Henry Well's company is known as American Express Company.

1870: In order to eliminate payment in cash, Mr. Cook introduced two systems:

— Traveller Cheque
— Hotel Vouchers

While American Express introduced

— Credit Cards
— Traveller Cheques

1878: Mr. Cook brought the first British Group of tourists to India by the P and O steamship company. The group landed in Mumbai, travelled to Agra by train to see Taj Mahal and also visited Kashmir Valley.

1880: Thomas Cook and Sons, established offices in Mumbai and Calcutta and formed the 'Eastern Princes Department'. In 1887, this department arranged the visit of Indian Princess to Queen Victoria's Jublee Celebration.

Select Bibliography

Ashworth, G.J. and A.G.J. Dietvorst (eds.), (1995), *Tourism and Spatial Transformations,* Wallingford, Oxford, CAB International.

Barke, M.J., Towner, and M.T. Newton, eds. (1996), *Tourism in Spain*. Wallingford, Oxford: CAB International.

Berger D.J., (1996), The challenge of integrating Maasai tradition with tourism, in M.F. Price (ed.) *People and Tourism in Fragile Environment*. John Wiley & Sons, Chichester, 175-198.

Bhauguan, H.H., (1972), *Public Sector Undertakings,* Vol. 4, No. 1, Feb., 1972.

Bhushan, Y.K., (1964), *Business Organisation and Management,* Sultan Chand and Sons, New Delhi.

Boissevien, Jeremy, (ed.), (1996), *Coping with Tourists: European Reactions to Mass Tourism.* Oxford Bergham Books.

Boniface, B.G. and Cooper, C.P., (1994), *The Geography of Travel and Tourism,* 2nd edn, Butterworth-Heinemann, Oxford.

Boo, E., (1990), *Ecotourism the Potentials and Pitfalls.* Vol. 2-Country Case Studies World Wildlife Fund. Washington, DC.

Bramwell, B., (1998), Selecting policy instruments for sustainable tourism. In: Theobald, W.F. (ed.) *Global Tourism: the Second Decade,* 2nd edn. Butterworth-Heinemann, Oxford, UK, pp. 361-379.

Briguglio, L. Butler, I.W., Harrison, D. and I cal Hilho, W. (eds.), (1996), *Sustainable Tourism in Islands and Small States. Vol. II: Case Studies, Cassell,* London.

Burchett, C., (1993), A profile of Aboriginal and Tories Strait Islander tourism—its history and future prospectus, in *Indigenous Australian and Tourism: A Focus on Northern Australia,* AGPS, Canberra, 20-25.

Burkart, A.J. and S. Medlik, (1974), *Tourism: Past, Present and Future,* Heinemann, London.

Burns, Peter, (1995), *Tourism: A New Perspective.* Englewood Cliffs, NJ: Prentice-Hall.

Burns, Peter, (1999), 'Paradoxes in planning: tourism elitism or brutalism?' *Annals of Tourism Research* 26 (2): 329-348.

Butler, R.W., (1993b), Tourism: an evolutionary process, in G. Nelson, R.W. Butler and G. Wall (eds) *Tourism and Sustainable Development. Monitoring: Planning, Managing,* University of Waterloo. Heritage Resources Centre, Waterloo, 27-44.

Buxton N., (1997), The Esk Valley Line Partnership, paper to conference on 'Community-Rail Partnerships'. Hudderfield, 8 April 1997.

Buzzworm, (1993), *Earth Journal 1993: Environmental and Almananc and Resource Directory.* Boulder, CO: Buzzwomi Books.

Christaller, W., (1996), *Central Places in Southern Germany,* trans. C.W. Baskin, Prentice-Hall, Eaglewood Cliffs. NJ.

Christian Aid, (1995), *Abuse of Innocence: Tourism and Child Prostitution in the Third World.* London: Christian Aid.

Clark, J.R., (1991), 'Carrying capacity and tourism in coastal and marine areas' *Parks* 2(3), pp 13-17.

Cohen, E., (1987), "Alternative Tourism : A Critique", *Tourism Recreation Research,* 12(2).

Cole, D.N. Petersen, M.E. and Lucas, R.C., (1987), *Managing Wilderness Recreation Use: Common Problems and Potential Solutions,* USDA Forest Service General Technical Report INT-230 Intermountain Forest and Range Experiment Station, Utah.

Colvin, J.G., (1994), Capirona: a model of indigenous ecotourism, *Journal of Sustainable Tourism*, 2(3), 174-177.

Common, M., (1995), *Sustainability and Policy: Limits to Economics.* Sydney- Cambridge University Press.

Commonwealth Department of Tourism (1994), *National Ecotourism Strategy.* Canberra-Australian Government Publishing Service.

Cook, S., (1996b), Draft matrix of limits of acceptable change indicators. Curry County Commissioners, Gold Beach, Oregon.

Cooper, Christopher P., (1994), *Tourism and Hospitality Education.* Guildford, University of Surrey.

Cornwall County Council, (1996), *Transport Polices and Programme: 1997-98 Submission.* Cornwall Country Council, Truto.

Cosgrove; L. and Jackson. R., (1972), *The Geography of Recreation and Leisure,* Hutchinson London.

Costanza, R., (1989), What is ecological economics? *Ecological Economics* 1 (1) 1-7.

Cox, Aidan and John Healey, with Paul Hoebink and Timo Voipio (eds.). (2000), *European Development Cooperation and the Poor.* London, MacMillan.

Craik, J., (1995), Are there cultural limits to tourism? *Journal of Sustainable Tourism* 3(2) 87-98.

Cris, Cooper, (1993), Tourism: Principles and Practice, London.

Croall, J., (1995), *Preserve or Destroy. Tourism and the Environment.* Calouste Gulbenkian Foundation, London.

Crowe, P.L., (1969), The tragedy of the commons revisited, *Science* 166, 1103-1107.

Cullimane, S.L., Cullinane, K.P.B., Fewings, J. and Southwell, J., (1996), Rural traffic management: the Burrator Reservoir experiment, *Transport Policy* 3(4), 213-224.

Davies E., (1987), Planning in the New Zealand National Parks. *New Zealand Geographer* 43(2), 73-78.

Davison, R., Vogel, D., Gricar, J., Harris, R. and Sorrentmo, M., (2003), Electronic Commerce on the New Silk Road: Rejuvenating a Historical Trade Network, The European Conference on Information Systems June 19-21 Naples, Italy.

Devon and Cornwall Rail Partnership, (1996) *Annual Report 1995-1996*. Devon and Cornwall Rail Partnership, Plymouth.

Dex, S., (1985), *The Sexual Division of Labour*, Wheatsheaf Books, Brighton.

Dicken. P., (1994), Global-local tensions: firms and states in the global space economy *Economic Geography* 70(2), 101-128.

Dickens, P., (1996), *Reconstructing Nature: Alienation, Emancipation and the Division of Labour*, Routledge, London.

Dieke, Peter U.C., (1994), 'The political economy of tourism in The Gambia.' *Review of African Political Economy* 62: 611-627.

Dorst, J. (1977), *Before Nature Dies*, Collins, London.

Dovers, S. and Handmer, J.W., (1993), Contradictions in sustainability, *Environmental Conservation* 20, 217-222.

Drake, S., (1991), Local participation in ecotourism projects, in T. Whelan (ed.) *Nature Tourism Managing for the Environment*, Island Press, Washington, 132-163.

Dredge, D. and Moore, S., (1992), A methodology for integration of tourism in town planning, *Journal of Tourism* 3(1), 8-21.

Driml, S.M., (1991), Research needs for rainforest economics. In N. Goudberg, M. Bonell with D. Benzaken (eds) *Tropical Rainforest Research in Australia*. Townsville: Institute of Tropical Rainforest Studies.

Drummond, L. and Marsden, T.K., (1995), Regulating sustainable development, *Global Environmental Change*, 5(1) 55-63.

Duffy, Rosaleen, (2000), 'Shadow players: ecotourism development, corruption and stale politics in Belize *Third World Quarterly* 21 (3): 549-565.

Dunford, M., (1990), Theories of regulation, *Society and Space* 8, 297-321.

Durning, (1994), Alan Thein. *Guardians of the Land: Indigenous Peoples and the Health of the Earth.* Washington, DC: World Watch Institute.

Dyer, R., (1995), *Cury County Receives $225,000 Grant,* News Release (June), Siskiyou National Forest, Grants Pass.

Ecumenical Coalition on Third World Tourism (ECTWT), (1992), *Caught in Modern Slavery.* Bangkok: ECTWT.

Eight Northern Indian Pueblos Council, (1996), *8 Northern Indian Pueblos 1996 Visitors Guide,* Eight Northern Indian Pueblos Council, New Mexico.

Eisenberg, G., (1989), Learning vacations. In: *Peterson's Guide,* 6th edn. Peterson Publishers, Princeton, New Jersey, p. ix.

Ekins, P., (1993a), 'Limits to growth' and 'sustainable development' grappling with ecological realities, *Ecological Economics* 8: 269-88.

Erbes, R., (1973), International tourism and the economy of developing countries. Paris: Organisation for Economic Cooperation and Development.

Escobar, A., (1995), *Encountering Development: The Making and Unmaking of the Third World,* Princeton University Press, Princeton, NJ.

Euroter, 82, rue Francois Rolland, F 94130 Nogent-sur-Marne, France (321) 4514-6421, fax (331) 439-49144. Publishes principles for developing green tourism in European villages.

Everett, Bob, (1996), "Solar Thermal Energy". In *Renewable Energy: Power for a Sustainable Future.* Ed. Godfrey Boyle. Toronto: The Open University,

Fennell, D.A. and Eagles, P.F., (1990), Ecotourism in Costa Rica: a conceptual frame work, *Journal of Park and Recreation Administration*. 8(1), 23-34.

Forbes, B., (1993), *Tourism Development Plan, 1993-1998*, Brooking-Harbor Chamber of Commerce, Brookings.

Foresta, R.A., (1984), *America's National Parks and Their Keepers*, Resources for the Future, Washington.

Forsberg, P., Harvey, B. and Kelsay, D., (1996), *Curry County: Public Resources from Private Initiative*, Egret Communications, Port Orford, Oregon.

Forster, D.P. and Jozan, P., (1990), Health in Eastern Europe, *The Lancet*, 335,453-460.

Foster, I.D., (1994), *Introduction to Travel and Tourism*, Macmillan, New York.

France, L., (ed.) (1997), *The Earthscan Reader in Sustainable Tourism*, Earthscan Publications, London.

French, H. Vanishing Borders, (2000), Protecting the Planet in the Age of Globalisation Washington, Worldwatch Institute.

French, H., (1990), *Green Revolutions: Environmental Reconstruction in Eastern Europe and the Soviet Union*. Worldwatch Institute, Washington DC.

Frenmont, P. (1983), *How to Open and Run a Money Making Travel Agency*, John Wiley and Sons, New York.

Friendship Press, (1995), *Having an Excellent Adventure: A Handbook for Responsible Travel—A Guide or Planners and Travelers*. Cincinnati: Friendship Press.

Frissell, S.S. and Stankey, G.H., (1972), Wildernes environmental quality: search for social and ecological harmony. Paper presented at Annual Meeting Society of American Foresters, 4 October, Hot Springs.

Frohlich, M., (1993), Is there a Tourist Culture ? in *Cultural Tourism : International Scientific Symposium*. ICOMOS 10th General Assembly, Sri Lanka, ed. Prematilleka, P.L., 66-69.

Frommer, Arthur. *Arthur Frommer's New World of Travel: A Guide to Alternative Vacations in the Americas and Throughout the World.* New York: Prentice Hall, updated annually.

Ganga, Gobind, (1994), *Ecotourism in Guyana: Implications for Sustainable Development.* Georgetown: University of Guyana.

Gascon, C., (1994), *Discover the Lower North Shore: Guide and Directory,* Coaster's Association, St. Paul's River.

Gilbert, D.C., (1989), "Tourism Marketing: Its emergency and establishment, in Cooper C., (Ed.), *Progress in Tourism Recreation and Hospitality Management,* Vol. I, London.

Glacken, C., (1967), *Traces on the Rhodian Shore, Nature and Culture in Western Thought from Ancient Times to the End of the Enghteenth Century,* University of California Press, Berkeley.

Globe 90, (1990), *Tourism Stream: An Action Strategy for Sustainable Development* Environment Canada, Vancouver.

Godwin, N., (1987), *A Complete Guide to Travel Agency,* Albanj, Delmer.

Goe, Y.C., Kevin, B., Dexter, J.L.C., and James, M., (1990), *Professional Travel Agency Management,* Prentice Hall, London.

Golembski, G., (1990), Tourism in the economy of shortage. *Annals of Tourism Research.* 17, 55-68.

Gollin, Jim, and Ron Mader, (1997), *Honduras: Adventures in Nature,* Santa Fe: John Muir Publications.

Gomoiu, M.T., (1991), *Status of the Danube Delta Biosphere Reserve Planning and Management Report 1991 A.* DDBRA, Tulcea.

Gonsalves, Paul, (1987), *Alternative Tourism: An Operations Mannual for Third World Groups.* Bangalore: Equations.

Goodall, B. (1992), Environmental auditing for tourism, in C. Cooper and A.J. Lockwood (eds) *Progress in Tourism and Hospitality Management,* Wiley, Chichester, 60-74.

Graefe, A.R. Kuss, F.R. and Vske, J.J., (1900), *Visitor Impact Management,* 2 vols., National Parks and Conservation Association, Washington.

Graham, Scott., (1992), *Handle with Care: A Guide to Responsible Travel in Developing Counties.* Chicago: Noble Press.

Grance, O., (1981), External influence and internal change in the development of geography, in D.R. Stoddart (ed.) *Geography, Ideology and Social Concern,* Blackwell, Oxford, 17-36.

Graphic Arts, *Culture Shock!series* Portland, OR: Graphic Arts Center Publishing, various years.

Gray, Matthew, (1998), 'Economic reform, privatisation and tourism in Egypt.' *Middle Eastern Studies* 34 (2): 91-112.

Great Barrier Reef Marine Park Authority, (1993), *Annual Report* 1992-1993. Townsville. Great Barrier Reef Marine Park Authority.

Greenpeace, (1992), *Impacts of Tourism Development in Pacific Islands.* San Francisco: Greenpeace Pacific Campaign.

Gregory A., (1983), *The Travel Agent: Dealer in Dreams,* 4th Ed., The Prentice Hall, London.

Grekin, J. and Milne, S., (1996), Toward sustainable tourism development the case of Pond lnlet. NWT, in R.W. Butler and T. Hinch (eds.) *Tourism and Native Peoples,* Toutledge, London 76-106.

Hanmer, Lucia, John Healey, and Felix Naschold. (2000), *Will Growth Halve Global Poverty By 2015?* ODI Poverty Briefing 8 (July. London: ODI).

Harrison, L.C.; and Husbands, W., (1996), *Practicing Responsible Tourism: International Case Studies in Tourism. Planning. Policy and Development.* John Wiley & Sons, Inc.

Hart, A.J., (1992), Planning for tourism in Christchurch in comparative study, unpublished MA thesis, Department of Geography, University of Canterbury, New Zealand.

Hill, C., (1990), The paradox of tourism in Costa Rica, *Cultural Survival Quarterly* 14(1) 14-19.

Hinch, T.D. and Butler, R.W., (1996), Indigenous tourism a common ground for discussion in R. Butler and T. Hinch (eds). *Tourism and Indigenous Peoples,* International Thomson Business Press. London, 3-19.

Hinrichsen, D. and Enyedi, G., (eds), (1990), *State of the Hungarian Environment,* Statistical Publishing House, Budapest.

HMGN: (1994), Ministry of Tourism and Civil Aviation Department of Tourism, *Nepal Tourism Statistics 1993,* Rising Sun Printers, Kathmandu.

Hoffman, M.S. (ed.), (1991), *The World Almanac and Book of Facts 1992,* Pharos Books, New York.

Holing, Dwight, (1991), *Earthtrips: A Guide to Nature Travel on a Fragile Planet.* Los Angeles: Conservation International and Living Planet Press.

Honey, M., (1994), Paying the price of ecotourism, *Americas* 46(6), 40-47.

Honour, H., (1975), *The New Golden Land: European Images of America from the Discoverers to the Present Times,* Pantheon Books, New York.

Honour, H., (1981), *Romanticism,* Penguin Press, Harmondsworth.

Hooks, bell, (1992), *Black Looks. Race and Representation,* Boston: South End Press.

Hunter, C.J., (1995), On the need to re-conceptualise sustainable tourism development. *Journal of Sustainable Tourism* 3 (3), 155-65.

Iwersen-Sioltsidis, Susanne, and Albrecht Iwersen, (1996), 'Tourism and developing countries.' *Intereconomics* 31 (6): 301-306.

Jafari, J., (1989), Soft Tourism, *Tourism Management,* 9(1) : 82-84.

Jefferson, Allan, and Leonard Lickorish, (1991), *Marketing Tourism: A Practical Guide.* Essex: Longman Group.

Jemo, I., (1996), *Experiences in the Postwar Reconstruction of the Historical Core of Dubrovnik.* Paper prepared for International Conference on Settlement Revitalisation in Postwar Reconstruction, Zagreb, April 26-27.

Jenner, P. and Smith, C., (1992), *The Tourism Industry and the Environment,* E.I.U. Publications. London.

John Muir Publications PO, Box 613, Santa Fe, NM 87504; (505) 982-4078. "Adventures in Nature" travel guide series.

Johnston, C.R., (ed.), (1990), Breaking out of the tourist trap. *Cultural Survival Quarterly* 14(1 & 2).

Jones, G., (1991), Le Development touiristique de la zone Vicux-fort/Blanc-Sablon en Basse-Cote-Nord du Golfe St Laurent, unpublished Master's thesis. Universite du Quebec a Rimousski, Rimounski, Quebec.

Jones, S.B., (1933), Mining tourist towns in the Canadian Rockies, *Economic Geography* 9, 368-378.

Kincaid, Jamaica, (1988), *A Small Place,* New York: PLUME/ Penguin Books,

King Mahendra Trust for Nature Conservation (KMTNC) (1994a), Annapurna Conservation *Area Project: Conservation for Development,* (KMTNC), Kathmandu.

Lemons, J. and Brown, D.A., (1995), *Sustainable Development, Science, Ethics and Public Policy,* Kluwer Academic Publishers, London.

Lew, A.A and van Otten, G.A., (eds), (1998), *Tourism and Gaming on American Indian Lands,* Cognizant Communications Corporations, New York.

Lowyck, E., Van Langenhove, L. and Bollaert, L., (1992), Typologies of tourist roles, in P.Johnson and T.Barry (eds), *Choice and Demand in Tourism,* Mansell, London. 13-32.

Lozawa, Tomoya, (1980), Trekking in the Himalayas, Yama-Kei, Publishers, Tokyo.

Lujan, C.C., (1993), A sociological view of tourism in an American Indian community maintaining cultural integrity at Taos Pueblo, *American Indian Culture and Research Journal* 17(3), 101-120.

Lumsden, L. (1992), The Peak District National Park: The Upper Derwent, *Marketing for Tourism: Case Study Assignments*, Macmillan, London.

Lundberg, D.E., Stavenga, M.H. & Krishnamoorthy, M., (1995), *Tourism Economics.* New York: John Wiley & Sons, Inc.

Mak, A., (1981), The Montagnais. In *The Lower North Shore.* Ministere des Affaires Culturelles du Quebec, Quebec, 86-99.

Mallari, A.A. and Enote, J.A., (1996), Maintaining control: culture and tourism in the Pueblo of Zuni, New Mexico, in M.F. Price (ed.) *People and Tourism in Fragile Environments*, John Wiley & Sons, Chichester, 19-31.

Mander, Jerry, and Edward Goldsmith, (eds.), (1996) *The Case Against the Global Economy.* San Francisco: Sierra Club Books.

Mathieson, A and Wall, G., (1982), *Tourism: Economic, Physical and Social Impacts*, Longman, Harlow.

Matley, I.M., (1976), *The Geography of International Tourism*, Resource Paper 76-1, Association of American Geographers, Washington.

Matthews, W.H., (1975), Objective and subjective judgement in environmental impact analysis, *Environment Conservation* 2, 121-131.

Maxwell, Simon, (1999), *The Meaning And Measurement Of Poverty.* ODI Poverty Briefing 3 (February). London, ODI.

McLaren, D., (1998), *Rethinking Tourism and Ecotravel.* Kumarian Press, West Hartford, Connecticut.

Meadows, D.H., Meadows, D.L. Randers, J. and Behrens, W.W., (1972), *Limits to Growth*, Universal Books, New York.

Medlik, R., (1988), 'What is Tourism? Teaching Tourism into the 1990s. Published in the Proceedings of International Conference. *Tourism Educators,* July, 1988, University of Surry, Guildford, U.K.

Mercer, D.C., (1970), The geography of leisure: a contemporary growth point, *Geography* 55(3), 261-273.

Partners for Livable Places, (1981), *Tourism and Communities: Process, Problems, and Solutions,* Washington, DC: Partners for Livable Places.

Pattullo, Polly, (1996), *Last Resorts: The Cost of Tourism in the Caribbean.* London: Cassell.

Patty, A., (1999), Australian sex tourists find their laws back home don't take a vacation. *The World Paper* January-February, p. 16.

Pearce, D.G., (1992), *Tourism Organisations,* Longman, Harlow.

Pennington, M., (1999), Talks pause with dissidents holding Myanmar Embassy. *Kansas City Star* 2 October, p. A17.

Peppet, D., (1984), *The Roots of Modern Environmentalism* Croom Helm, London.

Perkins, H., Devlin, P., Simmons, D. and Batty, R., (1993), Recreation and tourism, in A.Memon and H. Perkins (eds) *Environmental Planning in New Zealand,* Dunmore Press, Palmerston North, 169-192.

Pigram, J., (1990), Sustainable tourism: Policy considerations. *Journal of Tourism Studies.*

Pilarski, Michael, (1997), *Friends of Trees Guide to Hawaii.* Bellingham, WA: Friends of the Trees.

Poon, Auliana, (1993), *Tourism, Technology and Competitive Strategies.* Wallingford, Oxford: CAB International.

Potter, R.B.; Lloyd-Evans, S., (1997/98), "Sun, fun & a rum deal: perspectives on development in the Commonwealth Caribbean" *Focus,* v. 44, no. 4, pp. 19-26.

Potvin, J.R., (1991), *Indicators of Ecologically Sustainable Development, Synthesized Workshop Proceedings,* Canadian Environmental Advisory Council, Ottawa.

Powell, J.M., (1976), *Conservation and Resource Managements in Australia* 1788-1914, *Guardian. Improvers and Profit: An Introductory Strategy,* Oxford University Press, Melbourne.

Poynter, J.M., (1993), *Tour design, marketing and management,* Prentice Hall, New York.

Rao, T.V. and Pereira, (1986), *Recent Experiences in Human Resource Development,* Oxford Publications, New Delhi.

Redclift, M. and Benton, T., (1994), *Social Theory and the Global Environment,* Routledge, London.

Redclift, M., (1987), Sustainable Development and the market a framework for analysis *Futures* 20(6), 638.

Reed, D., (1990), *The European Bank for Reconstruction and Development: an Environmental Opportunity,* World Wide Fund for Nature, Washington.

Richter, L.K., (1988), Indonesian tourism: the good, the bad and the ugly. *Contours* 14(1), 29-30.

Rieffel, Rober, (1978), Nepal Namaste, Sahayogi Prakashan, Kathmandu.

Robert and Charles, (1990), Tourism principles, practice, and philosophies, John Wiley and Sons Inc., New York.

Roberts, J., (1996), Green Consumers in the 1990s; Profile and Implications for Advertising, *Journal of Business Research,* 36, 217-231.

Robinson, H., (1976), *A Geography of Tourism,* London, Macdonald and Evans, London.

Robinson, H., (1976), *A Geography of Tourism,* MacDonald and Evans, London.

Index

U

B

W

Y

Z